NOT LIKE
HOME

MCGILL-QUEEN'S TRANSATLANTIC STUDIES
Series editors: Alan Dobson, Robert Hendershot, and Steve Marsh

The McGill-Queen's Transatlantic Studies series, in partnership with the
Transatlantic Studies Association, provides a focal point for scholarship
examining and interrogating the rich cultural, political, social, and economic
connections between nations, organizations, and networks that border the
Atlantic Ocean. The series combines traditional disciplinary studies with
innovative interdisciplinary work, stimulating debate about and engagement
with a field of transatlantic studies broadly defined to capture a breadth and
richness of scholarship. Books in the series focus on but are not limited to
the twentieth and twenty-first centuries, normally falling within the subfields
of history, economics, politics and international relations, literature, and
cultural studies.

NOT LIKE HOME

American Visitors

to Britain

in the 1950s

MICHAEL JOHN LAW

McGill-Queen's University Press

Montreal & Kingston • London • Chicago

© McGill-Queen's University Press 2019

ISBN 978-0-7735-5883-0 (cloth)
ISBN 978-0-7735-5884-7 (paper)
ISBN 978-0-7735-5955-4 (ePDF)
ISBN 978-0-7735-5956-1 (ePUB)

Legal deposit third quarter 2019
Bibliothèque nationale du Québec

Printed in Canada on acid-free paper that is 100% ancient forest free
(100% post-consumer recycled), processed chlorine free

Funded by the   Financé par le
Government   gouvernement   Canada   Canada Council   Conseil des arts
of Canada   du Canada   for the Arts   du Canada

We acknowledge the support of the Canada Council for the Arts.

Nous remercions le Conseil des arts du Canada de son soutien.

Library and Archives Canada Cataloguing in Publication

Title: Not like home : American visitors to Britain in the 1950s / Michael John Law.
Names: Law, Michael John, author.
Description: Series statement: McGill-Queen's transatlantic studies ; 1 | Includes
    bibliographical references and index.
Identifiers: Canadiana (print) 20190106042 | Canadiana (ebook) 20190110384 |
    ISBN 9780773558847 (softcover) | ISBN 9780773558830 (hardcover) | ISBN
    9780773559554 (PDF) | ISBN 9780773559561 (EPUB)
Subjects: LCSH: United States—Relations—Great Britain. | LCSH: Great Britain—
    Relations—United States. | LCSH: Great Britain—Foreign public opinion, Ameri-
    can—History—20th century. | LCSH: Public opinion—United States. | LCSH:
    United States—Foreign public opinion, British—History—20th century. | LCSH:
    Public opinion—Great Britain. | LCSH: Travelers—Great Britain—20th century. |
    LCSH: Tourists—Great Britain—History—20th century. | LCSH: Tourism—Great
    Britain—History—20th century.
Classification: LCC E183.8.G7 L39 2019 | DDC 327.730941—dc23

Thanks to Lizzie, for her encouragement and gifts from the eBay archive

Contents

Tables and Figures

Tables

Figures

Abbreviations

BBC	British Broadcasting Corporation
BOAC	British Overseas Airlines Corporation
BTA	British Travel Association
BTHA	British Travel and Holidays Association
BTHB	British Travel and Holidays Board
GDP	Gross Domestic Product
IATA	International Air Transport Association
M-O	Mass-Observation
NATO	North Atlantic Treaty Organization
OCLC	Online Computer Library Center
PX	Post Exchange
RMS	Royal Mail Ship
SS	Steam Ship
TWA	Trans World Airlines
USAAF	United States Army Air Force
USAF	United States Air Force
WASP	White Anglo-Saxon Protestant

NOT LIKE
HOME

❖

CHAPTER ONE

Introduction: Americans and Britons

Late on Monday night on 5 April 1954, Juanita Stott and her neighbour India Ramsey drove from their small clapboard homes in Chapel Hill, North Carolina, to Seaboard Station in Raleigh to wait for the "Silver Meteor" train service to New York. Stott was forty-eight years old, single, a Methodist, who worked as a registrar at the nearby North Carolina State College. The train was due at 1:25 a.m. but was running late on the slow journey from Miami. This was the start of an adventure, a vacation in Europe, an event of significance. Stott's friends marked it as such. Despite the late hour, Bill Sandine, the president of her Sunday School, and Everette McDonald, another member of her church, were there to see her off. They had brought her two precious rolls of thirty-six-exposure colour film for her camera as a farewell present.[1]

❖ ❖ ❖

Not Like Home examines the experiences of Americans visiting Britain in the 1950s to show how direct contact influenced the relationships between them and the British and their attitudes toward each other's country. Studying the role of visitors to Britain provides three main insights: first, it gives a view of the country and its people through the eyes of outsiders, many seeing Europe for the first time; second, it explains the characteristics and practices of American visitors and compares them to their prejudiced caricatures in British newspapers and magazines; third, it considers the differences between British attitudes toward the United States and Americans themselves.

The history of Americans visiting Britain is as old as the United States, but they first arrived in numbers in the 1840s, encouraged by the introduction of regular Atlantic steamship services that could do the crossing in as little as ten days.[2] In the years before the American Civil War, as many as thirty thousand Americans visited Europe each year.[3] Their behaviour drew criticism from their hosts, prompting prejudices that continue to the present day. They were accused of rushing around, seeing everything too quickly without understanding it, and of being in Europe only so that they could boast about it to their friends on their return.[4] Before the First World War, many American visitors were of the elite, rich and stylish, evidenced most pointedly by their attendance at events on the London social calendar and in the marriage of American heiresses to impoverished British aristocrats.[5] Between the wars, the visitors were, increasingly, well-off middle-class Americans, keen to share in Europe's heritage.[6] They were sped on their way by transatlantic liners, which in the 1930s provided a glamorous combination of speed, style, and luxury. The number of visitors travelling in each direction was small in absolute terms, with an average of about eighty thousand Americans visiting Britain each year and less than half that figure going in the opposite direction.[7] During the Second World War, huge numbers of American soldiers served in Britain, an unusual and unpleasant experience, to which historical studies have given a great deal of coverage.

In peacetime, the 1950s stand out as the decade when working-class and lower-middle-class Americans (of which the majority were women) came to Britain en masse for the first time. The contrasts between the two countries were striking: Britain now financially and politically burdened by its declining empire and struggling to survive; the United States becoming richer and more powerful each year. The United States had attained world leadership by 1940, and the 1950s was the peacetime decade when its consequences were first played out. Histories of a single decade can be too narrow, overstate the case, or miss connections to earlier and later periods, but nevertheless, for this topic, the 1950s is reasonably self-contained. It was in 1950 that American tourism kicked off again, marking one end of the period chosen for this book. By the end of the 1950s, more and more Americans were visiting a prospering Britain. This decade of transition was succeeded in the 1960s by Britain becoming newly fashionable in American eyes.[8]

The dominating effect of American cultural imports in the 1950s was such that visits to Britain by American movie and pop stars were signal events. The arrivals of Bill Haley at Waterloo Station, Johnny Ray at the

London Palladium, and Marilyn Monroe at Pinewood Studios were occasions on which remote and glamorous American figures materialized to be seen and screamed at. Further down the celebrity scale were musicians such as Eddie Cochran and Big Bill Broonzy or a whole raft of American B-list movie stars. These popular figures might loom large in a consideration of Americans in Britain in the 1950s, but this book ignores them, because their experiences of Britain were highly mediated by their own celebrity. In truth, they were a physical manifestation of and extension to the Americanization of Britain brought about by the importation of cultural products such as sheet music, records, and movies.

In contrast, this book concentrates its attention on uncelebrated American visitors to Britain, using the memoirs of, for example, teachers, schoolchildren, older students, housewives, and retirees.[9] There are some exceptions to this principle, for instance, the writer and broadcaster Emily Kimbrough. She is included to provide a contrast between the wealthy, privileged Americans who thought themselves to be travellers in search of an authentic Britain and the visitors who knew they were tourists. The book also uses material from accounts written by American residents in Britain who became tourists in their summer vacations.

Americans and the United States in the 1950s

The 1950s in the United States is often characterized as undergoing a baby boom, a period when members of the armed forces returned from war, married, set up home, and started a family. Increasingly, these homes were in suburbia. Suburban living on low-cost builders' developments offered a house with its own back yard and, for white Americans, a refuge from increasing African-American occupation of the old inner cities. Suburbia, where all the houses look the same, can be accidentally conflated with a more general societal conformity, but in the United States in the 1950s conformance to the norms of home, church, and advancement at work was so dominant that occasional exceptions (beat poets, teenage bike gangs) took on undue prominence.[10] American men were tasked with getting on in life; regular promotions and making more money enhanced a man's social standing. Middle-class women expected to go to college, get a degree, then make a beautiful home for their families. Even liberal

presidential candidate Adlai Stevenson believed women graduates' purpose in life was to "influence man and boy in the humble role of housewife."[11] Working-class women were often obliged to combine this role with
full or part-time employment. Home and the acquisition of material
goods to fill it were central to life in the 1950s, an idea that the overwhelming popularity of television reinforced, increasing domesticity.

   A buildup of savings during the Second World War, released into
the economy at the onset of peace, was spent on housing, automobiles,
domestic consumer goods, and travel, prompting American economic
growth in the 1950s. Business owners, politicians, and union leaders all
thought that increased consumption was the best means of increasing factory production and wealth. Importation of consumer goods was to be a
problem later on, but in the 1950s, Americans expected to buy goods made
in American factories. Increased production led to rising wages for workers who could then join the cycle of home ownership, suburbanization,
acquisition of household appliances, and increased leisure. The cycle was
primed by widely available access to instalment credit, which expanded
from the long-term financing of house purchases to automobiles and large
household appliances.[12] This "virtuous" circle of consumption, production, and borrowing carried on, with just an occasional pause, throughout
the decade. One of the important aspects of consumption, particularly for
those who lived in suburbia, was its use as a demonstration of success and
financial achievement.[13] A new car on the drive or a remodelled house
was material evidence of a family's progress. As the country prospered,
employers also rewarded their staff with longer vacations. How ordinary
people spent their leisure time now contributed to their social status.

   Increased time away from work made possible the choice of new
types of leisure. Sociologist Margaret Mead recognized that this wasn't
just about wealth: "After the war, there came, understandably, a desire
to recoup these quantitatively perceived losses, to get some joy out of
life."[14] Financially successful families from White Anglo-Saxon Protes-
tant (wasp) backgrounds could join country clubs. Golf was a popular
hobby that also offered social status. Buying a boat and taking it to the
lake connected a popular leisure activity with the purchase of a luxury
good – so much the better for impressing the neighbours.

   Travel also thrived in the decade.[15] In 1957, sociologist James Bossemeyer wrote, "Today, Americans are the most mobile people the world

has ever known."[16] In a 1960 survey of Americans, when asked what they would most enjoy doing in their free time, 90 per cent said they wanted to travel. Most of that travel was within the United States, with vacations taken in new cars on new highways to Florida or California or perhaps to the lakes and mountains. Some 10 per cent of vacation spending was on trips abroad, with Europe, specifically France and Britain, as the favourite destinations.[17] During the 1950s, spending on foreign travel almost doubled in real terms over the course of the decade.[18] These trips provided a new form of distinction for those American families who already had a nice home and an automobile or two, and had also been to Disneyland.[19] Going to Europe offered a prized and unusual reward, which was the sophistication brought about by seeing history and heritage at first hand, and, equally important, by photographing it on a new camera using Kodachrome film, so that the neighbours could see your experiences in a slide show.

Britons and Britain in the 1950s

Historian David Kynaston splits 1950s Britain into three periods. The first few years of the decade saw Britain wrestling with the consequences of austerity required to resurrect an economy almost ruined by the costs of war. The Festival of Britain in 1951 and the coronation of Queen Elizabeth II in 1953 then signalled the second period, a return to "normal" life not experienced since the late 1930s.[20] Kynaston defines this middle period as being dominated by family life, in which Britain had its own baby boom and a further growth in suburbanization through the development of new towns. These years showed Britain at its most conventional, with a desperate need to attain some form of stability. Historian Nick Thomas has aptly described the 1950s as having "become synonymous with growing prosperity and 'having it so good,' shared values, respect for authority, social cohesion, community, consensus, meat and two veg suburbanism and, above all, happy families."[21] Radios and newly acquired television sets encouraged a life centred on the home. Fashions and behaviour stuck to conventional norms: men in their various occupations, women returning to the kitchen on marriage. However, Britain's traditional class structures were starting to break down. The wealth of aristocratic families continued its interwar decline, so that many stately homes became tourist attractions for visiting Americans. Working-class families benefited from a recovering economy and better social care, with some joining an expanding middle class.[22] The final period of the decade, from 1957 onwards, connected to the increasing prosperity of the 1960s. Unemployment was low, real wages were rising, and Britons began to imitate Americans in acquiring cars, televisions, and fitted kitchens, spending more time and money on leisure as the working week shortened.[23] Working-class voices began to be heard in pop music, in literature, and on stage and in film, presaging further development in the 1960s.

Politically, Britain was under Conservative control for most of the decade, but the move away from socialism did not repeal many of the numerous changes the Labour governments of 1945 and 1950 had introduced. As a result, the 1950s marked a period of continuity, in which the principles of universal social care and benevolent statism remained in place. Tellingly, the most prominent political topics of the decade involved Britain's relationship, in one way or another, with the United States.[24] The three most notable were: the Korean War in which Britain provided troops to fight alongside the United States; the continuing anxiety in Britain about the possibility of nuclear war; and the Suez debacle of 1956.[25] As is seen in Chapter 2, these political events had a strong influence on how Britons saw the United States and, to a much lesser extent, Americans.

In the 1950s, Britain was fascinated by the United States, evidenced by endless newspaper commentaries and letters to editors on American behaviour, politics, and social problems and a steady stream of opinion polls taken to sample British views on the topic. It could also be seen in a series of tart, sometimes spiteful, cartoons that appeared in British magazines and newspapers that portrayed visiting Americans as moneyed caricatures. This widely observed disdain of one former global giant for its successor reflected a cycle of behaviour noticeable in French views of Great Britain in the early nineteenth century and seen today in criticisms of Chinese tourists in Asia and Australasia.

Despite all this, movies and music imported from the United States were at a height of popularity.[26] American movies led the box office in Britain. American music, either from American stars or, more potently, from British singers using close impersonations of American accents, dominated the hit parade.[27] Nothing was more exciting for young and working-class audiences than to imagine leading an American way of life. This creeping Americanization was a problem for both those on the right, as it signalled a decline in British influence and national pride, and for those on the left, as it suggested that Britons were in thrall to an inauthentic capitalist society.[28]

Visitors to Britain

As the 1940s drew to a close, Britain's economy was in a deep crisis. Sterling's weakness in international markets required the Labour government to redirect its resources toward exports. Of strategic importance was the need to gain US dollar receipts, and in 1949 the pound was devalued to promote British exports and to make American imports prohibitively expensive.[29] At a stroke, vacations in Britain became 30 per cent cheaper for Americans; their tourist dollars, changed for pounds, had the same effect on the British economy as exporting cars. The tourist industry became one of the most important levers for improving Britain's financial position.[30] By the end of the 1950s, American visitors were contributing $165 million per annum to the British economy, making them second only to the car industry in dollar earnings.[31]

Action by the British government and its tourist authorities in the 1950s led to ever-increasing numbers of Americans visiting the country, a success achieved despite Britain's poor infrastructure and diffident customer service. Nevertheless, 2.25 million visitors came to Britain in these years (see Appendix 1).[32] As the decade progressed and access to paid vacations grew, these visitors increasingly came from wider sections of US society. The most important change was the participation of lower-middle-class and prospering working-class Americans, who were most likely to make a flying visit to Britain, seeing the most obvious sights. The introduction of jet airplanes in 1958, which reduced the time for crossing the Atlantic, contributed much to this phenomenon. In parallel, the United States Air Force (USAF), its personnel, and their families came to Britain, reoccupying its wartime airfields to deter the Soviet Union in what was a warm phase of a long Cold War. There was a steady rise in the deployment of officers and airmen, and a rapid increase in the numbers of wives and children, as the men married British women or brought existing families over to Britain.

The arrival of so many Americans into Britain in the 1950s allowed Britons to look beyond the clichéd representation of Americans in the British media to make up their own minds about them. People working in the service industries, living in tourist centres or near USAF bases, were most likely to be familiar with Americans and be influenced and have their expectations raised by them. In return, American visitors to Britain were able to see beyond schoolroom ideas of British tradition, to see the surprising realities of a country recovering from war and trying to build a new identity for itself.

Sources

The most important primary sources used in this book are the published memoirs and unpublished diaries of Americans visiting Britain in the 1950s. They were identified by using open search terms and catalogue indices in OCLC's "WorldCat" and "Archivegrid" websites, supplemented with searches in the Library of Congress and British Library catalogues and a bibliography of American autobiographies.[33] This search strategy revealed about ninety plausible sources. Some turned out to be of marginal interest or were miscatalogued, some were difficult to access. Thirty-five have been used in this book, and their details are set out in Appendix 2. Throughout this book these documents are referred to as "trip reports," a term which is used to embrace diaries, manuscript notes, oral accounts, and self-published, vanity-published, and mainstream books.

Some of this material was written by established authors working with large publishers. Their work has to be used carefully, as it was written to produce a particular reaction in the reader (often to suggest how sophisticated the writer is). Cultural historian Richard Pells uncharitably describes the examples he consulted as "amateur attempts at cultural anthropology, most of them distinguished by an inability to appreciate any country other than one's own."[34] Much more interesting and useful for this book's purpose are the self-published and vanity-press-published accounts, each of which, no matter how small the circulation, was deposited at the Library of Congress in Washington, DC. In the 1950s, the easiest way to get one's writing published was to use the services of a vanity press such as Vantage or Exposition, who would produce a small book run financed by the author.[35] These accounts were written mostly to impress relatives and neighbours but often unintentionally reveal much about the author, which is all to the good when one is attempting to assess their attitudes to Britain and the British. Unpublished diaries are even more helpful, because they were seldom written with the expectation that they would be read by anyone but their author. Some of these accounts contain little reflection and consist of a chronicle of observations and discoveries, a criticism with a long heritage, once made of Victorian travellers' accounts.[36] Most of the trip reports were published by vanity presses, with an even number of diaries and conventionally published books. One aspect of this search was surprising. Two-thirds of the trip reports were written by women, most of whom were college graduates. In the 1950s, female graduates could not always use their qualifications and intellect in the world of work, so found an outlet for it through their writing.[37]

As most of the accounts in this book are from women, it serves as a useful corrective to much writing in the period. However, the accounts are overwhelmingly from white, middle-class authors who had the necessary cultural capital to produce such works. Although some African Americans prospered in the 1950s, the overwhelming majority did not.[38] It is difficult to be completely sure, but it is hard to believe that African-American writers could record their thoughts on a trip to Britain without mentioning race, so it is safe to assume that the authors of the trip reports were white. Two were likely to be of Irish-Catholic descent, and their accounts are more skeptical about Britain than most.[39] At least one of the trip reporters was Jewish, but this is not explored in their memoirs. It is plausible that the proportions were an accurate reflection of the ethnic and religious backgrounds of those Americans travelling to Europe in the 1950s.

A second important source for this book was the newsletters of the *Bushy Tales* social-media website, which records the memories and opinions of American former teenage pupils at Central High, a USAF school based in London in the 1950s. The editor of *Bushy Tales* kindly agreed to host a short survey of its members, which was then followed up with correspondence with those who wished to discuss their experiences further. This data has the advantage of addressing a range of voices different to those in the trip reports. Without the constraints of adult life, these teenagers, who came from a variety of backgrounds, races, and religions, saw an unusual slice of British life. The recollections of the now-elderly students have had to be carefully interpreted, because of the dangers of response bias and nostalgia.

Statistical information on Americans visiting Britain in the 1950s has been pieced together from a variety of sources, a process not helped by the closure of the former British Tourist Authority library and the destruction of much of its contents. Detailed information on US passport applications and USAF deployments helped to fill the gaps. As leading tourism historian John Walton has noted: "The statistical base for establishing trends and comparisons in tourism flows and impacts has never been strong ... Operational definitions of tourist visits and stays have been unduly broad, and unable to differentiate between different modes of, and motives for, travel."[40] The analysis of visitor movements in this book reflects some of these concerns, but triangulation with other sources has provided comfort that the book's conclusions are appropriate.

This book is reliant on, but not rooted in, work on tourism history, demographics, military history, cultural history, the history of Anglo-American relations, and other cognate subjects. *Not Like Home* is the first monograph on this topic. In contrast, there have been two prominent books that have examined the American tourist experience in France, reflecting the predisposition of Americans to see Paris, which did not suffer aerial bombardment in the Second World War, as a romantic destination. Christopher Endy's *Cold War Holidays* (2004) explains how France used Marshall Aid and political support to build an attractive destination for American tourists. Harvey Levenstein's *We'll Always Have Paris: American Tourists in France since 1930* was published in the same year (irritating for both authors) and takes a broader approach. The causes of Americans' propensity to take vacations after the Second World War are well described in Susan Sessions Rugh's *Are We There Yet* (2008), although its focus is on domestic travel. As far as Americans in Britain in the 1950s are concerned, H.L. Malchow's important cultural history *Special Relations: The Americanization of Britain?* (2011) covers some of the ground of this book, concentrating its attention on the transmission of ideas between the United States and Britain. It is more focused on the 1960s than the 1950s.

Structure of the Book

Not Like Home sets out the preconceptions and realities of the encounters between Britons and American visitors in the 1950s. Chapter 2, "Archetypes and Representations," explains the long history of prejudice toward visiting Americans and shows that this reached something of a peak in the decade. It contrasts media representations of American tourists and servicemen and compares them to the more moderate views revealed by opinion polls and surveys. Chapter 3, "Demographics of American Visitors," is a detailed analysis of who visited Britain in the decade. It reveals that most tourists and USAF officers were urban and well-educated, contradicting the British prejudices that painted them as vulgar simpletons wearing cowboy hats. Chapter 4, "Selling Britain's Heritage and History,'" examines the largely successful attempts of the British tourist authorities, aided and abetted by American newspapers and magazines, to sell 1950s Britain to potential American tourists. The projection of history, a shared heritage, and natural beauty was at the core of the proposition, which led to some dissonance when the reality of poor, sometimes dirty, Britain was revealed to visitors. Chapter 5, "Crossing the Atlantic," considers, as the title suggests, the significance of the journey to Britain and the impact that cheaper, faster planes had on the types of American who could now make the trip. During the decade, long, luxurious voyages by liners were superseded by economy flights on Boeing 707s. Chapter 6, "Destinations and Travelling in Britain," looks at areas to which American tourists travelled. It identifies the well-worn paths to the Tower of London and Stratford-upon-Avon and shows how coach tours corralled visitors into seeing the same sights and recording the same thoughts in their accounts. Those who travelled independently by automobile, train, or even bicycle could gain a wider understanding of Britain and meet a greater variety of its citizens. Some were on a quest for a never-quite-attainable authenticity. Chapter 7, "Accommodating American Visitors," describes the terrible state of affairs in British hotels and restaurants in the 1950s, and the varying ways in which they did not meet American expectations. The chapter concludes with an assessment of the small number of American-styled hotels that developers built in the late 1950s to target tourists. Chapter 8, "Encountering the British – USAF Families," investigates how teenage students at the American Central High School in London experienced life in Britain.

Their youth and openness to new experiences allowed them to meet Britons of all types in a way that was not possible for tourists. Chapter 9, "Encountering the British – Trip Reporters," uncovers the responses of American tourists to Britain and its residents. It describes their encounters with British class and gender relations and reveals a surprising heterogeneity in British behaviour. Chapter 10, "Asymmetry and Ambiguity," concludes the book and synthesizes its arguments.

CHAPTER TWO

Archetypes and Representations

Britain has a long history of disdain toward its American cousins. It was fuelled in the nineteenth century by British visitors' shock at encountering the openness and equality of American society and their disappointment at the standards of accommodation, food, and table manners.[1] As American economic and political power grew, prejudices were reinforced by jealousy and fear.[2] In parallel, American cultural imports began their long process of destabilizing British traditions, which wrought further anguish.[3] One American visitor in the 1950s summarized British prejudices: "I'm not very proud of the pictures some English have of a typical American – gum chewing, Coca-Cola drinking, fast and luxury loving with a generous touch of criminal and wild west – and how about civil liberties and such?"[4]

By the early 1950s, Britain was struggling with austerity and the loss of its authority. The United States was moving in the opposite direction, increasingly wealthy and a world power. As Drew Middleton, the Anglophile *New York Times* correspondent in London, later recalled, "in the forties the United States to some extent had shared the leadership of the West with Britain. In the fifties, we took over."[5] This change in global influence prompted British anti-Americanism; resentment, wounded pride, and jealousy replaced the spirit of the wartime alliance.[6]

There were two separate but interrelated stances toward (a) the United States and (b) Americans. Political differences between Britain and the United States excited prejudices against American citizens, leading Britons to conflate state arrogance with individual behaviour. Bad conduct by individual Americans in Britain fuelled resentment toward their country; one drunk USAF airman could reinforce already-sensitive feelings about Britain's role as a nuclear landing strip. At the start of the decade, an American writer summed up British attitudes: "They don't like

Americans in crowds – in the mass. As individuals they more often as not find us charming."[7]

Hostility toward the United States was promoted by political actions, such as the United States' funding of Britain through the Marshall Plan and other large-scale loans from 1948 to 1951.[8] These actions eased Britain's impoverishment somewhat but came with conditions, such as the requirement that sterling be freely traded, leading to the Labour government devaluing the pound in 1949.[9] This made imports more expensive and exporting for dollars more attractive, although uncompetitive, inefficient industrial practices restricted the opportunities for British businesses.[10] Britain's diversion of resources to the export markets and continued domestic austerity made life hard in the first years after the war, and some Britons, incited by British politicians and newspapers, irrationally resented the United States as a result.[11]

This book is not the place for a full examination of Britain's history in the 1950s, which was complex and contradictory. Suffice to say that Britain's ambitions to maintain its influence over its imperial interests did not sit well with the new role of the United States as a global superpower competing with the Soviet Union and China.

At the beginning of the 1950s, a gulf in philosophy informed transatlantic political relationships.[12] The rise of McCarthyism drove those on the left in Britain (Bevanites, many students) to see the United States as a country near to becoming a fascist state. Even after the return of the Conservatives in late 1951, serious arguments arose. There was much debate during the Korean War and afterwards on how to resist communist infiltration in Southeast Asia, coming to a head in 1954 with an unresolved dispute between Secretary of State John Foster Dulles and Foreign Minister Sir Anthony Eden.[13] The Middle East was a continuing problem, with difficulties arising over Israel, Iran, Iraq, and spectacularly, in 1956, over the Suez Crisis, in which the United States took an independent stance, making it finally clear that it was not prepared to support British imperial objectives and that its own global interests would prevail if it had to make a choice.[14] Toward the end of the decade, Britons were alarmed over the storage of atomic and thermonuclear weapons at American air bases aimed at the Soviet Union, a cause that led to the formation in 1957 of the Campaign for Nuclear Disarmament.[15] These disputes, among many others, would have been enough to stoke antipathy between

Table 2.1

Gallup poll on the role of the United States in world affairs

	Topic	Approval	Disapproval
1951	In general	40%	35%
1954	In general	37%	40%
1957	Atomic warheads in Britain	18%	63%
1958	Good at making friends	22%	48%

Source: Gallup (ed.), *The Gallup International Public Opinion Polls, Great Britain, 1937–1975.*

two nations, but the dissonance between nostalgia for the shared wartime experiences of the previous decade and the final transfer of authority from one great power to another amplified the differences between Britain and the United States.

Opinion polls conducted throughout the decade are an intriguing but problematic source for studying Britain's views on the United States. Lack of consistency in the questions asked and the special circumstances of the time make interpretation challenging. Gallup, an American company, was the most prominent pollster, and used representative sampling to gain a deeper insight into public opinion than was achieved by its rivals' cruder methods, which suffered from various types of response bias. However, it did not ask a consistent set of questions of its respondents over the period, so only a broad analysis of results is possible. One question asked for approval or disapproval of the role of the United States in world affairs.

Table 2.1 shows the responses to this question over the decade, which indicate a steady decline in British approval of the role of the United States. The 1957 low point reflected both Suez and the arrival of nuclear warheads. In November 1956, as the inquest over Suez was at its most heated, Gallup asked a slightly different question: who, outside the Commonwealth, was Britain's best friend? Forty-two per cent of the respondents nominated the United States; France came second with 23 per cent. This can be looked at two ways. First, that there was a continuing warmth toward the United States dating back to the recent world war. Alternatively, this can be read as a statement of Britain's political isolation.

It had so few friends that, despite Suez, the United States came top.[16] Another series of questions asked if respondents were happy for Britain to take its political lead from the United States. The consistent response throughout the decade was that only a quarter of the respondents were happy to see Britain follow the United States in world affairs.[17] This sense that Britain was still an important, independent player on the world stage influenced much anti-Americanism in the 1950s. The same sentiment is a strong force in British politics to this day.

At the end of the decade, British prime minister Harold Macmillan's courting of presidents Eisenhower and Kennedy, together with public admiration for the former's wartime leadership and the latter's glamour and youth, ensured that the United States became increasingly popular with the British public. The American government's own Research and Reference Service, which surely must have been inclined to present a positive impression, recorded that, after Eisenhower's visit to Britain in 1959, approval of the United States had reached over 70 per cent.[18]

Drew Middleton wrote about anti-Americanism in his book *The British*.[19] Looking back on the 1950s, Middleton identified three key reasons for the bad feeling between the two allies. These were: McCarthyism, tariff barriers that restricted British exports, and American foreign policy. His conclusions were supported by a reader's letter to the editor of the *Manchester Guardian* in late 1950, which identified possible causes of the problem:

1 The Communist witch-hunt hysteria, which would be amusing if it were not deplorable.
2 The sensation mania in the American press and radio.
3 The thirst in certain circles for the atomic bomb to be dropped on Russia or a satellite.[20]

As far as American foreign policy was concerned, Middleton noted two particular components, the behaviour of John Foster Dulles and the bellicose attitudes of the US military. As Middleton put it: "The British people live packed on a relatively small island. The estimate is that six hydrogen bombs dropped in Britain would be the knockout. Consequently, people don't like loose talk about nuclear bombing. They have the shrewd suspicion that they and not the talkers are going to be the first target."[21] Middleton might have added a fourth reason to explain 1950s anti-Americanism: the dislike felt by intellectuals and other commentators for Britain's consumption of imported American culture. These feelings weren't new; each successive American craze had drawn complaints since the arrival of ragtime, and were embraced by those on both sides of the political divide.[22]

Late in the decade, the English poet and writer Martin Green explained in an essay, "A Mirror for Anglo-Saxons," the components of intellectual anti-Americanism in Britain. Green typified Britain as a nation that was just recognizing that its world influence had passed elsewhere. Tellingly, he observed that Britain's attitudes in 1958 were also present in Greek society after power had passed to the Romans and in France after the fall of Napoleon. He quoted journalist A.J. Liebling, who noted that in Graham Greene's *The Quiet American* (1955), Greene accused his American of "what the English themselves have always been accused of by the French: a lack of taste in food and drink, complacent ignorance of other languages and culture … and a tiresome faith in official sources and practical action."[23] Martin Green described Britain's position as "the apotheosis of shabby gentility – the impoverished older branch living off its relationship to the reigning house and having to sneer at their vulgarity as it does so."[24] The 1950s surveys that examined Britain's views of Americans give his conclusion much support.

Surveys about Americans

During the decade, there was a continuous debate about anti-Americanism, but only a small amount can be seen in the recollections of former students at Central High, a London school for the dependents of USAF personnel (see Chapter 8), and only one instance was found in the accounts written by American visitors used in this book (see Chapter 9). Clearly, these sources, written by those who enjoyed their time in Britain, do not include the unpleasant experiences of people who, as a result, did not want to write about it.

There is some evidence to suggest that published discourse may have exaggerated anti-Americanism. In 1954, a correspondent for the highbrow American *Harper's Magazine* recorded that there was little hostility found in Americans' encounters with Britons: "Before we set out, we'd heard about a lot of anti-American feeling in England, and so we were on the watch for it. Well ... we encountered no single instance of hostility or even discourtesy, and there were plenty of instances of friendliness beyond the call of duty."[25] Clearly, this writer was not a subscriber to *Picture Post*, which, in 1952, had published without comment a letter from one of its readers:

> It has been said by the Americans that we act with a superiority to them and treat them like kids. In my opinion, we *are* superior to them. The vast majority of people in these islands do not wish to live the American way of life, which includes jiving, jitterbugging, bebop, the wearing of silly looking clothes and weird haircuts.[26]

Although the prejudices of Britons toward their American cousins in the period after the Second World War are familiar, it is possible to put meat on the bone by examining the results of surveys and public discourse, with sentiments changing as the decade progressed. All three of the surveys discussed below had limitations in their method and sampling, but their results are, at least, indicative of the mood of opinionated British people on this topic. The first survey was conducted by Mass-Observation in 1947, the second as part of research for BBC radio in 1952, and the third for a feature article in *Life* magazine in 1957. The first two surveys asked their respondents what they thought of Americans, a question that could as easily embrace a cultural idea as much as an experience of any actual people they had encountered. The last survey distinguished between tourists and other Americans, such as soldiers, diplomats, businessmen, and politicians.

Mass-Observation (M-O) was an organization founded in 1937 by Tom Harrisson, an anthropologist, and Charles Madge, an artist. M-O's approach, at first, combined social science and situationist art, which used observation, inquiry, and survey.[27] The British government sponsored M-O during the Second World War to measure civilian morale, and this role continued through the 1950s.[28] It surveyed its volunteer correspondents on their views on Americans and the United States during the war and again in 1947, its survey method not using a representative sample of British respondents, as would be later found in Gallup polls, but depend-

Table 2.2

Mass-Observation survey of most commonly reported characteristics of Americans, 1942–43

Most liked characteristics	Most disliked characteristics
Friendliness	Boastfulness
Openness/Frankness	Bumptiousness/Baloney
Generosity	Materialism
Energy/Efficiency/Vigour	Speed before thoroughness
Democraticness [*sic*]/Lack of snobbery	Language and Accent

Source: Mass-Observation, "File Report 2548," 2 (1947).

ing on a panel of opinionated people who had the time and inclination to respond. Putting these limitations to one side, M-O reported a steady decline in support for the United States from 1942 to 1947, with some vituperative attacks on American character traits to go with it. Its surveys in 1942 and 1943 recorded traits that Britons often associated with Americans in the following decade (see Table 2.2).

M-O asked one question of its respondents over several years: "How do you feel about Americans?" This did not actively distinguish between the United States and its citizens, so the increasing anti-Americanism that it recorded was influenced by the effects on the British economy of the Anglo-American loan, rather than just changing views about Americans themselves. The percentage who answered the question favourably sank from 58 per cent in 1945 to 21 per cent two years later.[29] This volatile change pointed toward the feelings of humiliation experienced by Britain in the early postwar years, which were in marked contrast to the fortunes of the United States.

Direct quotations from the 1947 survey provide colour to these broad figures:

"I haven't got much good to say about them. They're too sure of themselves, they always know better than anyone else, they don't know how to keep their mouths shut. I prefer people here by far" (male, 37).

"On the whole, the people are presumptuous and bumptious. The whole country is a little child that hasn't grown up" (female, 21). (This quotation shows the possibility of conflating the behaviour of the United States and American citizens.)

"Some of them are good, others are equally bad ... they seem to take a great pride in things which are fundamentally very superficial ... on the whole, I like Americans" (female, 38). (This quotation was written by a woman who seemed to have met various Americans and was able to see them as individuals rather than as avatars of their country's politics.)

One other important source to use for examining these sentiments is Fred Vanderschmidt's caustic book *What the English Think of Us*, which he wrote during the hardships of 1948, but is still relevant in interrogating attitudes of the early 1950s. His account records resentment toward the United States due to the conditions attached to Marshall Plan aid, American attitudes toward Britain's involvement in Israel, and the vast differences in personal wealth enjoyed by ordinary people in the two countries. In turn, Vanderschmidt accused Britons of jealousy, laziness, and hypocrisy in their criticism of American racism.[30] He quoted from an undated readers' survey on Britons' views on Americans (from about 1947) carried out by the *People*, a British newspaper with a large working-class circulation.[31] He pointed out that the majority of responses were positive. They sat under the headline "Yes! We Certainly Like Americans."[32] A typical favourable response from a reader in Harrow, Middlesex, read, "May I please inform you that I and my family like Americans immensely? They are the nicest 'foreigners' we have ever met."[33] The reader's apostrophizing of "foreigners" is revealing. Some Britons did not think of Americans as foreigners at all, but as cousins. Being "family," expectations of them were higher than for other nationalities.

The topic of what Americans were really like was in great currency in Britain in the years after the war. It was, for example, the subject of a BBC radio broadcast in 1947 by American philosopher R.B. Perry, who characterized Americans' key qualities as "buoyancy, resourcefulness, and self-reliance."[34] Perry's ideas were congruent with British popular opinion on Americans' better qualities. The BBC sponsored a useful survey of attitudes

Table 2.3

BBC radio survey of attitudes toward Americans, 1952

Positive opinions of Americans	% noted	Negative opinions of Americans	% noted
Friendly	28	Boastful/swaggering	45
Hard working	20	Hustling/overcompetitive	24
Generous	19	Materialistic	16
Go-ahead ambitious	14	Immature	15
Good company/ cheerful	14	Ostentatious	14

Note: Percentage of respondents who volunteered particular characteristics (each respondent wrote an average of three opinions, so the percentages do not total 100).
Source: Belson, *The Impact of Television*, Table 1 – "Opinions of Americans, as volunteered by Londoners." One observation of the United States as a world power has been omitted, so as to show only the comments on American citizens.

toward both the United States and Americans in 1952, for a market test on the attractiveness of proposed radio programs. These programs aimed at middle-class, middle-aged, metropolitan audiences, so it was this group that was sampled; the author of the survey was well aware of its limitations and warned his readers accordingly.[35] Its results demonstrate that strong opinions are often accompanied by ignorance of the topic in question. Respondents were tested on their knowledge of American society by being asked, for example, to name four American universities and to explain the significance of Woodrow Wilson's presidency. Few of them could manage a successful answer.[36]

The survey asked respondents to make a set of unprompted statements about Americans, which were then categorized and summarized. Their thoughts were congruent with the feelings of the M-O panel nine years earlier and are summarized in Table 2.3. The full results are set out in Appendix 3.

This survey revealed two key findings: first, that the number of negative comments outweighed the positives, supporting the M-O survey observations, and second, that views were consistent over time, despite the dramatic political events over the previous nine years, such as VE day, the

Berlin Airlift, the Anglo-American loan, and the Korean war. This shows the power of experience and prejudice. It is likely that the views moulded in the Second World War drove these opinions through to the early 1950s. The great majority of British encounters with real-life Americans before 1950 were with US military personnel. Prejudices formed by these meetings were supplemented with the ideas of Americanness purveyed by the Hollywood movie industry, as seen in British cinemas, a force that was at its peak level of influence in this period.

These results have much less congruence with the equally unrepresentative *People* survey. There is just a suggestion, albeit based on limited data, that working-class Britons viewed Americans more favourably than did middle-class Londoners. This idea has support from the study of working-class cultural preferences, which concluded that this group preferred American literature and movies to the more stilted British equivalents.[37] They also applied this sentiment to people. For example, American writer Stanley Wade Baron noted the rapt interest with which he was received on a trip to impoverished Stepney, a borough in London's East End.[38]

Five years after the BBC radio survey, *Life*, the leading American photojournalism magazine, conducted a survey of European attitudes toward Americans, carried out in countries frequented by Americans, such as Britain and France. The respondents ranged from "leading intellectuals and high government officials to hack drivers and errand boys."[39] *Life* carried out its British interviews a year on from the debacle of Suez, when anti-American sentiments had been rekindled (see Table 2.4). Feelings in Britain still ran high. A researcher on the project noted that when a "refined young woman neighbor" came to tea and picked up a copy of *Life*, she "dropped it with a shudder and said, 'Americans, ugh! Beastly people!'"[40]

Robert Coughlan, the author of this five-page survey, produced a balanced account of European views, which, by late 1957 (the date of publication), had been moderated by encounters with millions of American tourists, businessmen, students, and diplomats. In Britain and Germany, the large-scale presence of American servicemen and their families also influenced attitudes. Coughlan thought that although Americans were widely criticized, they still "succeeded in winning foreign hearts."[41] He also recorded the differing responses to various types of American visitor. Coughlan concluded that Europeans thought American tourists were cau-

Table 2.4

Life magazine, survey of European attitudes toward Americans, 1957

Favourable characteristics	Unfavourable characteristics
Generous	Arrogant
Courteous	Brash
Optimistic	Parochial
Exuberant	Immature
Charming	Noisy

Source: Coughlan, "How We Appear to Others," 150.

tious and circumspect, always imagining that they were about to be exploited by the next foreigner they met. The trip reports seen later in this book show that this fear wasn't entirely imaginary, and that unprincipled Britons and other Europeans took advantage of visitors. The survey's respondents thought Americans to be the favourite of all visitors to Europe, as they spent the most money and were well-behaved and were "not hard to please." This last idea does not sit easily with the responses of many American visitors on the subject of British trains, hotels, and restaurants (see Chapter 7). Finally, American tourists were thought ignorant of local cultures, a notion strengthened by their rushing from country to country and attraction to attraction.[42] This was consistent with long-held British elite views on lower-middle and working-class tourists and earlier generations of American visitors.[43]

One idea that the surveys did not include, but which appeared to different degrees in the trip reports, was that American men had become emasculated by their wives. This idea arose in the nineteenth century when travelling Britons were surprised by the (to them) unusual level of courtesy expressed by American men to their womenfolk.[44] Its incarnation in the 1950s was most likely the result of distorted gender portrayals in Hollywood movies and to a lesser extent in novels and television. Movies after the Second World War often emphasized conventional relationships, reflecting a conservatism in society during the decade. As Germaine Haney, an independent and unconventional traveller noted, "Everybody I met in England believed firmly that the American husband goes around with a ring in his nose."[45] Visiting writer Muriel Beadle also noticed this ill-informed British prejudice, which imagined that all "American men are Milquetoasts."[46] It is possible that British cinema audiences may again have misinterpreted the courtesy that American men displayed toward women in the 1950s, such as opening doors, removing hats, and walking on the outside of the sidewalk.[47]

Attitudes toward American Servicemen

American servicemen and women (mostly men) were a familiar sight in Britain in the latter years of the Second World War. The US Army and US Army Air Force (USAAF) personnel brought to the home front the realities of the differences in culture and economic power of the two countries. The America portrayed by Hollywood did not sit well with the actuality of thousands of unpolished, sometimes rowdy, conscripted young men, many miles from home.[48]

The end of the war saw the departure of this army, but in 1948 the withdrawal of the Soviet Union from the four-power Allied Control Council created a political crisis over the future of occupied Germany. In June of that year, the Soviet forces closed access routes in their sector to the capital, Berlin.[49] This move threatened the area of West Berlin that Allied troops controlled. On 17 July, the USAF arrived to support the Berlin Airlift that flew relief missions from British airbases.[50] As the 1950s progressed, the Cold War antagonism between NATO and the Soviet Union escalated, resulting in American nuclear bombers arriving in Britain.[51]

It is hard to recapture today the depressed feelings of Britons in the early 1950s, a period in which most people thought a third world war to be both likely and final.[52] Into this atmosphere arrived American officers, airmen, and their dependents. To their surprise, they weren't welcomed as saviours; in fact, some regarded them as an occupying force using Britain as a convenient and disposable forward base. In 1952, the magazine *Picture Post* pleaded for more understanding and reflected the general feeling of gloom: "Get to know them ... preferably in your or their own home. For it is deadly certain that we are going to have to live with these goddam Yanks – and very likely that many of us goddam Limeys will have to die with them.[53]

British communists, who were active in the early 1950s and content to toe the Stalinist line, led criticism of the USAF. Although they painted an extreme view of the US forces, the wider public shared many of their conclusions, albeit in a moderated form. A good example of communist sentiment toward the USAF was a 1953 polemic, *Get Out!*[54] That its East-Anglian author A.L. Morton led the way was understandable, because it was this part of England that was home to many USAF airbases. Morton pulled no punches:

> Here in East Anglia we have no less than five of these plague centres, and you cannot go into any of our main cities and towns ... without being sickened by the arrogant slouch that is the hallmark of the Yank soldier everywhere – in or out of uniform. Wherever they go, they spread corruption and moral degradation among our young people. They are above the law and treat British people and British ways of living with the open contempt of a master race.[55]

Get Out! emphasized the problems caused by badly behaved Americans, who would have suffered criminal charges if they had been British, but who were treated leniently by American military law. Morton held the USAF responsible for a rise in prostitution, venereal diseases, and corruption of the local youth by American culture – and other crimes.[56]

Picture Post, which was written for a mainstream audience of working-class and lower-middle-class readers, concurred with some of these opinions.[57] It agreed with Morton on the problems of off-duty American airmen, stating that "Americans drink, on the whole, rapidly and noisily. There are inevitably pub arguments." They also concurred that in many East Anglian towns "brothels, exclusively catering for Americans, are operating ... despite regular police raids." The magazine sympathetically rationalized the airmen's attraction for local girls: "Here are big-spending, interesting young men with luxurious cars, eager to show them a good time, free with their compliments, fascinating with their Hollywood accents. It is the movies come to life."[58] *Picture Post*, however, unlike the Ipswich branch of the Communist Party, took a balanced approach to the problem and praised American servicemen for leading a popular evangelical-Christian campaign and those airbase wives who had reached out into the local community.[59]

Critical Views of American Tourists

British views toward American tourists were complex and influenced by differences in culture, but also by political developments and disparities in standards of living. Attitudes waxed and waned during the decade and were affected by the type of tourist arriving in Britain, and their behaviour. Britons received Americans politely in public, but sometimes made fun of them in private. Jokes on this topic had long appeared in *Punch* magazine, which catered for middle-class readers, many of whom felt threatened by the growing ascendancy of the United States. One American resident in London provided good advice: "Always be what you are: an American. For one thing, the British will respect you more. If you find that some of them just don't like Americans, you may find, like me, they make an exception in your case."[60]

As the decade progressed, views of both visitors and natives moderated. The Suez crisis in 1956 had hardened British attitudes toward the United States, but the ill-feeling it generated was soon put aside.[61] Increasing prosperity in Britain and the arrival of less-wealthy American visitors also lowered the general level of envy. In 1957, the *New York Times* investigated this alteration in attitude, and asked three of their European correspondents, including Drew Middleton, to respond to the question "US tourists: Good or ill-will envoys?" Middleton wrote an optimistic account of relations in Britain. He concluded that there had been a change in the type of Americans who visited Britain. No longer were they the sort of people that in 1950 "demanded much that was impossible, they were noisy in their claims of American supremacy [and displayed] ostentatious and foolish spending." In contrast, the new visitor was more earnest, and more interested in Britain's unique and long history.[62] Author John Steinbeck called these "the great body of quiet, patient, courteous tourists who come yearly to Europe."[63] New York writer Robert Duffus admitted that some Americans were obnoxious, some of them weren't.[64] Czech writer and gourmand Joseph Wechsberg drew a similar conclusion: "the American abroad … alternately delights and exasperates the local population with the kindness of his heart and the loudness of his voice."[65]

Actual Appearance

In the 1950s, the uniform, global style of dress expected today was not present; the ubiquity of blue denim and polo shirts from the Gap was many years ahead, so American visitors looked different to the British, and, of course, they were wealthier than the locals. One of the most important distinctions was their love for expensive cameras and taking photographs of their trip, which was something the British magazines liked to make fun of. One *Punch* columnist drew attention to this predilection and was snobbish about both the tourists' lower-middle-class occupations and their provincial origins. That they could afford more than one expensive camera added to the writer's resentment:

> Vacationing carpet factors from Sarasota and St. Paul, behung and besotted with light-meters, genuflect for prizeworthy angle shots … [they] fumble ecstatically with lenses and filters. Mustn't miss this, no, not on their lives they mustn't. Then back they go, rescrewing gadgets, sweating a little and beaming achievement.[66]

American writer Stanley Wade Baron noticed this habit, which suggests that commenting on it wasn't just a feature of British prejudice and jealousy: "they carry complicated cameras on leather straps, and crouch for trick angles."[67] His compatriot Edith Patterson Meyer summed it up for the prospective tourist: "Most Americans would no more think of starting for Europe without a camera – or cameras – than without a coat."[68] Taking photos was more than a cartoon cliché. It is clear from their trip reports that American visitors did carry lots of cameras and obsessed about using them to record their attendance at key sites. One writer described her husband as "strung about with cameras and gadget bags in addition to his suitcases. I am carrying a camera, two small bags, and our coats … we must look very funny to the natives."[69] A minister from California went further, recording the sounds of his vacation on a miniature tape recorder, which was quite a common hobby at the time, its practitioners calling themselves "tape-worms."[70]

In 1953, Baron reported on how to identify an American. "There seem to be extraordinary numbers of Americans in London. They all wear seersucker jackets and mustard-coloured trousers; the girls well-groomed in bright cotton dresses, more suitable for Florida or the Bahamas."[71] The loudness of American visitors' clothing was often remarked on in Britain in the early part of the 1950s, but it reflected general standards of leisure dress in the United States, rather than something specifically associated with vacationers.[72] To this can be added a predilection for bright ties (men) and sunglasses (both genders).[73] Students adopted a different style. Baron described one male student as coming "straight out of the college campus: his hair is crewcut and he wears saddle shoes and a loud sports jacket."[74] Sporting students who wore sweatshirts adorned with the large letter of their alma mater were easy to identify.[75]

In 1954, American writer and broadcaster Emily Kimbrough described her English chauffeur's explanation of how to spot Americans on London's streets: "Sometimes it was by their hats ... or by their shoes. The obvious ways were the cameras they carried and the big pocket-books (handbags) the women had." Kimbrough spotted a couple on the sidewalk she thought were American, but her chauffeur disagreed: "Look at the way they are walking ... her so independent and him just ambling along anyway he fancies, paying her no mind. If it was Americans, he would have his hand under her elbow and [be] helping her up and down the kerb, steering her like, half carry their women they do."[76]

By 1956, fashions had changed somewhat, Rhona Churchill, writing in the *Daily Mail*, typified American men as wearing a "well creased grey suit and soft hat."[77] In that same year, the *New York Times* declared that American visitors were harder to spot in London:

> He is likely to look more British than the British, except that his jacket's sleeves cover his wrists and the shoulders are likely to fit him better. About the surest ways to identify a fellow American male is the square, monogrammed breast pocket handkerchief. As for the American female, she stands out in the theater lobbies in her sheath style dress and the design and quality of her shoes and her nylon hose.[78]

By this date, upmarket guidebooks and travel magazines explained to Americans how to disguise themselves in London by adopting local fashions. Edith Patterson Meyer set out the differences. "Clothes are more formal and conservative than in America. English women seem to dress a little less femininely than their American cousins, going in for tweedy fabrics, stout hose, and sensible shoes."[79] Of course, Meyer might have been going to a particular sort of party in London. Perhaps not, as she explained the differences between styles in the two countries:

> Recently an American friend arrived back in New York from England wearing a beautiful suit which seemed a trifle long and a bit baggy about the hips. An English friend was with me when I bought it, my friend explained, and she said, how well it fits – not vulgarly tight and short! I can't wait, my friend confided, to get it to an American tailor to be vulgarized.[80]

Upmarket American *Holiday* magazine recommended tweed jackets for men and women, dark business suits for men, and cotton dresses for women.[81] Despite all this advice, American tourists could still come in for criticism and commentary that was more typical of the late 1940s. For example, in 1957, the *Daily Mirror* commented on Americans in Paris, coupling it with a whiff of snobbery: "One million Messieurs and Mesdames shoved off, smartish, for the holiday, as thousands of Elmer K. Pappenheims and Cyrus G. Organbackers moved in – their wives nobly braving the sweltering heat in the customary mink uniform."[82]

Representations of American Appearances

If, as Martin Green proposed, it was inevitable that intellectual and privileged Britons should despise the characteristics of American culture they saw looming large in Britain, the idea also was shared by much wider sections of British society.[83] *Punch* ate up this type of thing, as did the more conservative *Daily Express,* which focused on less-wealthy readers. British films, novels, and radio shows also routinely lampooned American tourists and airmen.

Cartoons provide one of the most accessible and widely understandable forms of satire and have a long history in Britain as a source of humour at the expense of visiting Americans. An example from as early as 1906 shows an American mother with her jauntily dressed son and daughter, each holding a camera to capture their visit to London (see Figure 2.1). By 1935, a cartoon postcard identified American tourists by their appearance alone

Figure 2.1 "Life in London – American Visitors in Town,"
from a 1906 postcard.

(see Figure 2.2). The male figure is hatless, unusual in Britain in the 1930s. He smokes a cigar, also uncommon, as Britons preferred pipes and cigarettes. More pertinently, he smokes it outdoors, something that a Briton would not do.[84] His bow tie, loud overcoat, and spats are also key to his identity. The woman is less of a caricature, and her fur coat is the only sign of her wealth and vulgarity. The joke here is that the naive Americans have mistaken a local jail for the Tower of London.

Cartoons often conflated male tourists (which as Chapter 4 shows were typically from metropolitan backgrounds) with the cinematic version of a Texan oilman or rancher. This was, itself, a modification of that older

Figure 2.2 "Is this known as the 'Bloody Tower'?"
from a 1935 postcard.

symbol of American manhood, the cowboy. This connection in the public imagination dated back to the nineteenth century, when American fiction, followed by real-life cowboys, arrived in Europe to much acclaim.[85] Hollywood's continuous export of cowboy movies to Britain reinforced the idea of Americans as "western" archetypes. Russell Brockbank's 1951 cartoon for *Punch* of an American tourist with a ten-gallon hat (see Figure 2.3) is revealing in its details. The Britons shelter from the rain or run from it, the American man ignores it. While his oversize hat provides surprising protection from British weather (which is the joke here), the cartoon shows American strength and British weakness. The Texan visitor is

Figure 2.3 Cartoon by Brockbank #1. *Punch*, 30 May 1951.

oblivious to British conditions, an idea that reflected the attitude of the
United States toward Britain's political and economic position. The Texan
is well drawn. Present and correct are his camera, cigar, floral-print tie,
belt (not braces), and wire-rimmed spectacles.

In Figure 2.4, the cartoonist has included many of the same accessories:
a modest-sized hat, cigar, wire-rimmed spectacles, and tie. The tie is something else, its recursive fractal design signalling both self-absorption and
inauthenticity, the old world looking at the new and seeing materialism
and a machine-made blank where a person should be. This was an erudite
form of disdain in a genre of usually unsubtle material.

The archetypal male American tourist was present in British magazines
throughout the 1950s. In 1958 a small drawing in the *Listener* accompanied
an article by Alistair Cooke on "The American Abroad." Kindlier drawn
than its predecessors, its tourist had a smaller, soft-brimmed hat, but cigar,
specs, camera, and tie are included, with the addition of a guidebook in
his pocket.[86] At the beginning of the 1960s, this image was still present, seen
in a newspaper designed to appeal to American residents in Britain. This
cartoon, by an American, Bob Guccione (later the founder of a leading
1970s pornographic magazine, *Penthouse*), satirized the complacent British

Figure 2.4 Cartoon by T.P.
Punch, 4 November 1951.

readings of his compatriots. It shows the American to have "a thick chin for taking 'good-natured' anti-American cracks" and a pocket guidebook entitled "England in 24 hours," and correctly identified the camera he carries as an "old custom."[87]

British cartoonists used American women less frequently in their drawings than their male counterparts. Brockbank, a leading contributor on this subject, drew one cartoon showing a couple of tourists driving their enormous imported car (see Figure 6.3 on page 109). Brockbank rendered the husband as a cipher, just the top of his hat visible to the reader; such was the force of the American tourist trope that this little feature was enough to identify the whole. His wife, a nervous passenger, was identifiably American due to her "pixie" haircut, cat's-eye spectacles, dark-lipsticked, cupid's-bow lips and a leopard-print shirtwaist dress.[88] The size of the car can also be read as a metaphor for American power and modernity, and the obscuring of the male driver as a gesture to the idea that American men were subservient to their wives.

One leading cartoonist portraying Americans in Britain was (Ronald) Giles. From the late 1940s to the early 1990s, Giles was Britain's most well-known cartoonist, drawing over seven thousand cartoons for the *Daily* and the *Sunday Express*.[89] In the 1950s, he regularly featured Americans in his drawings, mostly of USAF personnel, capturing them in sloppy poses, smoking and with their caps on the backs of their heads. He also used Americans as a device to show the human aspect of America's international relations. For example, in 1959, a Coldstream Guard kicked a female American tourist for encroaching on him at the Changing of the Guard ceremony and was disciplined for his pains. Giles celebrated the event by drawing a supportive cartoon that shows a bowler-hatted ex-Guardsman clipping a female American tourist on the bottom with his umbrella. The caption reads "'And have one with me' said a senior officer who, while approving of the sentence passed on the Guardsman who kicked the mickey-taking tourist, felt deep down in his Coldstream heart, like me – that a score had been made for the Brigade." Giles's drawing (a detail of which is shown in Figure 2.5) reinforced, by then, elderly British stereotypical views. The father wears a western hat, sunglasses, a cigar, and several cameras. His little boy wears jeans and a T-shirt, and is shown climbing all over a guardsman; his little girl, perhaps five years old, wears a sun hat and sunglasses and smokes a cigarette. His elder daughter plays an archetypal American role of swooning teenager, dressed in very short shorts and a T-shirt, with her hair tied back with an Alice band. Giles's representation of the children references a British belief that American children were spoiled and badly behaved, an idea drawn from the movies. He draws the mother of this group in a grotesque style. Wearing a large straw hat and carrying a very large handbag, she points her movie camera right up the guardsman's nose. Her T-shirt and Capri pants hang loosely over her enormous frame, epitomizing one cliché of Americans abroad, with some misogyny thrown in.[90]

British movies of the 1950s often had screenplays that featured visiting Americans. This was due to the investment of Hollywood movie studios in the British film industry, the desire of British studios to attract American moviegoers by using a star they could recognize, and because

Figure 2.5 Cartoon by Giles. *Daily Express*, 5 August 1959.

American actors conveyed a modernity not easily imitated in Britain.[91] The movies came in a wide variety of styles, including horror, adventure, musicals, and romance. The following examples explain their various forms: *The Quatermass Xperiment* (1955) was a cinematic version of a British television series. In the movie, Quatermass, a dominant and irascible American scientist, faces the horrific consequences of the failure of his project to put men into space.[92] American actor Brian Donlevy played Quatermass, and his performance brought to life the political and economic dominance of the United States at a time when space monsters substituted for wider fears about atomic weapons and the Soviet Union in the public mind. For example, in an early scene, Lionel Jeffries, playing

Blake, a British civil servant, is dominated in conversation by Quatermass, who tells him "You can't stop it now." Blake replies, "You mean I can't stop you now," suggestive that Britain in decline couldn't compete with American individualism.[93]

Happy Go Lovely (1951) offered a more straightforward account of the impact of American visitors on British society. It featured American actress and dancer Vera-Ellen and her compatriot Caesar Romero. In the movie, both are involved in a stage musical at an Edinburgh theatre.[94] The flimsy romantic plot placed Vera-Ellen's transatlantic can-do attitude up against David Niven's stuffy British traditionalism. It was a terrible movie, but suggested that, in a time of much austerity, the United States could provide glamour sorely lacking in Britain. Four years later, *A Yank in Ermine* (1955), a movie on a similar theme, considered the impact of a young and simple American inheriting a British earldom.[95] American "B" movie actor Peter Thompson starred as its hero, Joe Turner, a USAF airman. Turner was accompanied by two cronies, one played by British character actor Jon Pertwee, who had a terrible American accent that added to the overall feeling of inauthenticity. Once again, American simplicity played out against the usual British stereotypes of blustering aristocrats and working-class ciphers. At a time of great tension between the two countries, the movie provided a conciliatory message to its audience. Joe's prospective father-in-law, a gruff-but-kindly type, explained Americans to his pretty daughter. "You mustn't hold it against the fellow, y'know. Their standards are different. Being successful is what counts with them."[96] At the end of the movie, with the star-crossed lovers united, Joe made a reconciliatory speech drawing on the idea that the two countries shared a common heritage. "We're the same kind of folks. We may do things a little differently back in the States, but we do exactly the same things, deep down we're the same at heart."[97]

Putting aside the commercial attractions of casting Americans in British films, these movies allowed British audiences to rationalize the changing relationships between the two countries. They placed Britain's new subservience to the United States into a personal context, which allowed moviegoers to feel that Britain was still relevant and closely connected to the emergent superpower.

Reginald Arkell's novel *Trumpets Over Merriford* aimed directly at the relationships between Britons and Americans. It was a much-read book, with three printings in four months in 1955, its first year of publication.[98] It was the lightest of light reading and told the story of a village in the Cotswolds, Merriford (which, in itself, shows the tone of the book), full of eccentrics living in a rural world where all its hierarchies – the church, the squire – had dissolved through lack of money and changing values. Into this fading idyll arrived the USAF, which built an enormous airbase and runway over its ancient fields. Misunderstandings between the two cultures arose and were resolved through goodwill and romance. It was predictable stuff, but where Arkell excels is in his descriptions of the Americans, whom he portrayed as fully rounded, ordinary people, mystified and bored about being in England. It was a useful antidote to the hyperbolic representations of Americans in British movies of the period.

Americans' Prejudices about Britain and the British

American views on what used to be the Mother Country reflected the changing fortunes of Britain and the United States, but were underpinned by some fundamental ideas based on the United States's conception of itself as a new and revolutionary nation. For example, Richard Pells notes that Americans have long seen Europeans as decadent, pessimistic, and warlike.[99] Nevertheless, the two nations (or, at least, large numbers of their citizens) identify with the idea that they have a shared heritage. This belief has a long history, dating back to the nineteenth century. During the American Civil War, the British elite identified the leaders of the Confederate states as sharing its own aristocratic traits, but were suspicious of continental European influences on the northern states.[100] After the Civil War, Abraham Lincoln, who had previously been portrayed in Britain as a backwoodsman, was reclassified as an exemplar of Anglo-Saxon traits.[101] In the northern states, concerns over immigration of Catholics and Jews led to an increasing interest in Anglo-Saxonism and ideas of shared heritage between the two countries.[102]

These warm feelings did not survive much beyond the First World War, when US isolationist policies and the rise of domestic Irish-American and German-American influence led to increased public Anglophobia, which was a strong sentiment in American society up until the 1940s. In the 1920s it was driven by the belief that the United States had sacrificed its men to support the British Empire in the Great War. The idea reached an apogee in debates over the power of the relative size of the two countries' navies and Britain's continuing ambitions to be a world power. British responses to Indian independence and the Japanese invasion of Manchuria also prompted further criticism in the United States. Condemnation of Britain's actions was also a way to mobilize Irish-American and German-American voters.[103] As historian John Baxendale has pointed out, this was another way for Americans to define their relationship with Britain that competed with the shared-heritage idea. It had a strong appeal to Anglophobes and posited that Britain was a home for a monarchical despotism, seen most recently in its imperialism, and this was the very reason for the formation of the United States.[104] There was a third, hybridized way of seeing the relationship, which acknowledged the break and difference in ideologies from 1776, but harked back to Shakespearian times to provide a cultural link between the two countries.[105]

The shared-heritage concept was revived out of political necessity during the Second World War as a response to the difficult relationship between Britons and the "occupying army" of American troops.[106] This was troubling to both allies, with much bad feeling resulting from the relative wealth, boastfulness, and lack of discipline of some Americans and the resentment and cheating of some locals. Attitudes toward sexual conduct and racial separation were also an area of contention.[107]

One way of resolving the harsh words and sentiments was to emphasize how the two countries shared a common culture, while still acknowledging the reality of the many disparities. An important contribution was made in popular British author H.L. Gee's *American England*, first published in Britain and the United States in 1943, which explored the historical connections between the two countries, through figures such as John Harvard and George Washington. Gee considered that the binding links between the United States and England rendered the differences of opinion insignificant:

We speak the same language – the language of the English Bible. We glory in a common heritage. We have one literature. The fundamentals of the law are alike in Washington and London, each capital the home of representative government. Our common love of freedom goes back a thousand years; and in spite of an amazing intermingling of races in America, the thought and feeling of the United States is largely inherited from the vigorous yeoman-stock of Merry England.[108]

Much of this was true, but these sentiments did not make sense to Irish-Americans or second-generation Polish Jews. Muriel Beadle, speaking on their behalf, noted:

> I'd had a worse case of nostalgia than either of them. Not that Britain was in any physical sense a homeland to any of us ... so the only explanation for my feeling that we were coming home to England was sentiment. A good many Americans feel so, even if their names are Martinez or Stepanek. Through school, almost the only non-native literature we are exposed to is English.[109]

At the end of the 1940s and the start of the 1950s much of the historical content that Gee had explored was reiterated, but without the wartime emotion, by the eminent founder of the English-Speaking Union, Evelyn Wrench, in *Transatlantic London*.[110] Historian William Kent's *London for Americans*, soon followed, which then appeared in summary form in an illustrated pamphlet distributed to American visitors.[111] It is clear from trip reports that this approach was attractive to many tourists. The shared cultural-heritage trope that was so prevalent in the 1950s continued to have currency throughout the rest of the twentieth century.[112]

In the mid-twentieth century, American opinions on Britons were collated and analyzed by both American and British writers, such as Henry Steele Commager, an American and Professor of American Studies at Cambridge University, and British historian Robert Mowat.[113] In 1948, Commager wrote his own summary of the English character as a conclusion to his edited collection. Like many writers, he conflated the terms English and British, or perhaps he met only English people at Cambridge.[114] Commager concluded that "the English character is not only stable and uniform, but various and heterogeneous; it is at once obvious and elusive, and almost every generalization must be not so much qualified as confounded."[115] Commager's exposition of the paradoxes of British culture – for example, polite but on occasion incredibly rude – sits well with the accounts in the trip reports used in this book. Mowat's account from a

decade earlier is more conventional in its identification of the strong
shared heritage between the two countries: "the two people have their civil-
isation and culture in common" – an idea that would have been easier to
believe in 1935 than it would have been in 1948.[116]

One Gallup poll from 1953 reported that about two-thirds of Americans
had friendly feelings for the people of Great Britain.[117] This single point of
data, taken at a time when British troops were fighting alongside the US
forces in Korea, provides the insight that, even at this comradely time, a
third of Americans couldn't bring themselves to say that they liked Britons.
British newspapers were obsessed with the United States and Americans
in the 1950s; revealingly, research in popular US news sources from this
decade produces little about American opinions of the British.[118] The material that is available is consistent in its views; the term "aloof" comes up
regularly. It's not a commonly used word and seems reserved by American
writers for this topic. In 1952, a reader of the *Los Angeles Times* wrote to the
editor rejecting this common way of portraying Britons: "We go all out for
criticism of the English in utter trivialities – how they talk, how they eat,
how aloof, even snooty, they are when traveling, how 'different' from our-
selves in attitude, behavior and manners."[119] A USAF booklet produced for
newly arrived American officers, grounded in a decade of experience, also
described Britons as "traditionally aloof, rigidly conventional."[120] This
bold, unqualified statement was perhaps describing the British officer
class, not the people USAF airmen would meet in an Ipswich pub. Trip reporters also mentioned aloofness, describing the usual views of Britons
shortly before demolishing the sentiment by explaining how nice they
were. Elderly Minnesotan newspaper editor Edward Barsness took the opportunity of setting out for his readers the unwarranted prejudices Americans had about Britons: "Many who go to England go there with the
impression that they are going to find people with much reserve and aloofness. You may have heard about the British being stand-offish."[121] Much-
travelled Anglophile Emily Kimbrough, writing for a wider audience, took
the same approach: "they say the British are aloof, almost unapproachable."[122] Bud Freeman, a jazz musician, reported that "for years on end
we Americans have been saying that the English are a stuffy, unfeeling
people."[123] In 1950, Robert Duffus, a veteran American commentator on
Britain, explained this misunderstanding:

> The British not only talk like foreigners, they act like foreigners. In other words, they don't do things the way we do. It is not necessary to repeat the old libel about British haughtiness towards strangers. They are not now as haughty as they used to be. Some of them never were. Some of them today will positively start a conversation with strangers ... but British manners proceed from a passionate respect for personal privacy.[124]

Duffus proposed here that the confusion about Americans and Britons being "cousins" worked both ways and set unrealistic expectations for each group.

Some prejudices about British manners emphasized the more positive aspects of their conversational restraint. Two female trip reporters made the same point. Ruth Lois Matthews noted that "The English are considered [by Americans] to be very polite."[125] Phyllis Stock, a young book editor from Long Beach, California, thought her American Express guide was a precise and courteous man, and was "exactly like I thought an Englishman should be."[126] The anonymous writer of *In Focus* also acknowledged some positive British characteristics: "he hopes for the best, but takes what comes and refuses to let his inner fears show up in conversation or behavior."[127] By "British," American writers usually meant not just English but English middle-class men. They have little to say about the working classes, Scots, the Welsh, or women.

When asked about their experiences sixty years later, Americans who had travelled to Britain as teenagers with their USAF parents acknowledged that all they knew about the British before their trip was what they had read or what they had seen in the movies. One former student remembered *The Red Shoes*, a 1948 film set in the south of France but with plenty of British accents, as her main source of information on what the British were like.[128] America's idea of the British, and more specifically, the English gentleman, sometimes mirrored P.G. Wodehouse's Bertie Wooster. This trope was sufficiently strong for *Fielding's Travel Guide to Europe* to warn "don't let a trace of these absurd stereotypes [monocles, stammering, buck teeth] linger in your mind. When you get there you'll find a healthy, handsome, sturdy people."[129] In reality, British stars in Hollywood in the 1940s and 1950s were good looking (James Mason, Laurence Olivier, and Vivian Leigh come to mind). To this roster might be added the now-obscure figure of Commander Edward Whitehead, who promoted Schweppes tonic water in its American television advertising from the mid-1950s into the 1960s. Schweppes used his good looks, full beard, and plummy English accent – "Darling, don't tell me. Was it Hong Kong?" – to suggest an international jet-set sophistication.[130] He was such a well-known caricature of Englishness that Malcolm Muggeridge, the editor of *Punch* magazine, referenced him as a model of those Englishmen who became even more English when they visited the United States.[131]

These long-held views about the British were very persistent and did not disperse until the appearance of the Beatles on American television showed there was more than one sort of Briton. For example, as late as 1960, the *London American* newspaper printed a cartoon summing up the most obvious characteristics of an Englishman. The figure in the cartoon wore a hat which combined a bowler and a teapot and sported an old school tie and a blazer badge. It defined his character as being straight-laced, with a stiffening upper lip, who looked down his nose and rarely cut up.[132]

In the 1950s, Alistair Cooke, born in Britain but now a US citizen, mounted a one-man campaign to explain American ways to his former countrymen. He was best known for his long-running *Letter from America* radio program, but he was also a regular correspondent for the *Manchester Guardian*.[133] In 1959, Cooke summarized how Americans and Britons saw each other. He pointed out that both countries' views were one hundred and fifty years old. He concluded that the impressions that most travellers carried away or brought with them had not varied much over all this time, and echoed those they had picked up in childhood.[134]

Cooke analyzed what Britons thought of Americans, which reflected the ideas discussed so far in this chapter and are not repeated here. More unusually, he also documented what Americans thought of Britain and its people, after consulting a straw poll of "students, bankers, textile men, economists, housewives, newsprint salesmen, glamour girls and airline hostesses." Cooke's unscientific summarization is worth repeating in full:

- A quaint old land pierced by cathedral spires and roofed with thatch
- Soldiers in musical-comedy uniforms
- Adorable Regency crescents
- A prim and formal people, but exceedingly polite

- Quaint taxicabs that turn on one wheel
- Good Scotch and poor food
- Something vague and admirable called "tradition"
- Green, green countryside
- Churchill (courageous and tough).

Cooke made another good point, which the research for this book reflects, that Anglophiles loved Britain and said so, but Anglophobes just went to France instead.[135]

Conclusion

The American view of Britain was often ill-informed – if they had formed an opinion at all. Most Americans had never met a Briton; all their information about them, came from politics, literature, and the movies. Two million American soldiers were in Britain during the Second World War, but their unusual experience was outweighed by the impressions of a hundred million adults who were not.[136] Britain or England, seldom the United Kingdom, was often thought a suspect nation, propping up its ailing empire at the expense of American money or American lives – a theme that reached its full realization during the Suez crisis of 1956. Schools and colleges presented Britain's traditional literature, amplified by America's conventional culture, as the basis for a proper education. In movies, some British actors in Hollywood were modern, transatlantic stars, while others were happy to play along with old-fashioned stereotypes, sporting stiff upper lips. One thing most Americans agreed on was that Britons were "aloof"; apart from this they had little impact on Americans' lives.

In contrast, Britons were overinformed about the United States and its way of life. Their knowledge of Americans came from a wide variety of sources, the most direct being encounters with them when tourists or on military deployment, although this most often applied to southern England. The impact of thirty years of Hollywood movies was more artificial but much more widespread across the entire country and all classes. British newspapers provided in their commentary and cartoons a continuous and prejudiced appraisal of the United States and its people. This coverage veered widely, conflating Americans with their government and criticizing them, while simultaneously being in thrall to transatlantic fashions, culture, and modernity.[137]

Movies provided Britons with the most information about the United States. For gullible moviegoers, this torrent of information may have led to the belief that American men were gangsters or cowboys, but in thousands of films ordinary Americans drove cars, ate in cafés, and worked in offices.[138] British film critic Philip Norman remembered a childhood centred on the movies, where he watched American films every week and saw "A parallel world where people lived in long, low white houses, and drove long, low white cars, and drank black coffee."[139] This cinematic projection of life in the United States was reinforced by the domination of British popular culture by American music, from ragtime, to jazz, to big bands, crooners, and rock-and-roll.[140] Finally, there was the less-universal, but important, influence of transatlantic novels, detective stories, thrillers, and comic books on British readers.[141] There was no equivalent transfer of modern-day culture across the Atlantic from Britain. British movies and modern writing gained little traction with American audiences in the 1950s.

Opinion polls in both countries show the extent of this asymmetric relationship. In the 1950s, surveys of British attitudes regularly included questions about the United States, its politics and culture. This was not reciprocated. American polls seldom mentioned Britain, unless it was in the form of "should America have a royal family?"[142] Visiting Americans, the subject of this book, were often ignorant about life in Britain, which is one reason it came as a shock.

❖

CHAPTER THREE

Demographics of American Visitors

Historian John F. Lyons proposes that "in the immediate postwar years, British views of the United States were rarely shaped by direct contact with Americans."[1] This was true for many, but, during the 1950s, 2.25 million American civilians made the trip over, and the US forces deployed 220,000 personnel to Britain.[2] In London, Edinburgh, and Stratford-upon-Avon, in villages near air force bases, workers in hotels, pubs, restaurants, and tourist attractions, taxi drivers, and residents were extremely familiar with real-life Americans. They could make informed comparisons with the archetypal representations in Hollywood and British movies and newspaper cartoons. Meeting actual Americans who spoke almost the same language as the locals provided Britain with a direct form of Americanization.

The number of American civilians coming to Britain rose steadily throughout the decade, reflecting increased incomes in the United States, cheaper and quicker methods of transport, and improved facilities in Britain. In 1951 there were 127,000 American visitors to Britain; by 1959 this had risen to 356,000.[3] A total of 89 per cent of these visitors were tourists, 10 per cent were in Britain for business, and 1 per cent were diplomats.[4] It is reasonable to assume that even a keen businessman or diplomat also went sightseeing. Americans usually accounted for roughly a quarter of all foreign visitors in any one year. The year 1952 was a high point, when they reached 30 per cent of all arrivals.[5] In contrast, many fewer Britons travelled to the United States, particularly in the early part of the decade. By 1958, 125,000 were making the trip.[6]

There was a prejudice in British intellectual circles and elsewhere that visiting Americans were provincial and gauche. For example, *Spectator* editor Brian Inglis, writing in 1957 under his pseudonym Leslie Adrian, thought that "the great majority of visitors from the US are small-town tourists, making the Grand Trip of a lifetime."[7] In 1955, American authors

Ruth McKenney and Richard Bransten also typified tourists as provincials hailing from Mishawaka, Indiana, or Des Moines, Iowa, although they may have chosen these unlikely candidates to demystify the idea of travelling across the Atlantic.[8] American government records, which include embarkation and arrival statistics and US passport applications, provide useful information on where US visitors actually came from.

The most precise information comes from the early years of the decade. This was when the vast majority of travellers to Europe departed by ship or air from New York, either from the great wharfs in Manhattan or from Idlewild Airport. Statistics are available for New York departures and arrivals that recorded the state of origin of American travellers. The figures show that, in 1952, just under a half (48.5 per cent) of those going to Europe came from the states of New York, New Jersey, and Pennsylvania. A surprising third of all travellers resided in New York State. These prosperous eastern-seaboard states were disproportionally represented in the numbers compared to their overall populations. There were two forces in play here: wealth and distance from the port of New York. Wealth determined whether a European trip was possible, and the nearer to New York, the cheaper was the overall cost. There was also the time involved. In the first years of the decade, travelling from coast to coast was a journey of fifteen hours by air or three days by train.[9] California provided the second-highest number of travellers, despite the distance from New York. Its wealth enabled its citizens to travel to Europe, but the extended travel times put some of them off the journey (see Table 3.1).

A broader analysis of passport application and renewals over the entire United States backs up the data on the concentration of American travellers coming from the prosperous northeastern states. This data needs cautious interpretation, but roughly three-quarters of all America's passport applications were for travel to western Europe, and Britain and France were its most popular destinations.[10] Despite some reservations, it is likely that information gathered by the US government on its citizens who took out or renewed passports also applied to visitors to Britain. The US government recorded the state of origin and the profession of each applicant, providing us with a useful insight into the demographics of American travelers.[11] This shows, consistent with the New York statistics, that the propensity for US citizens to hold passports was overwhelmingly in the wealthier coastal states (see Table 3.2).[12]

Table 3.1

Percentage of travellers returning from Europe via New York, 1952

State/District	%	1950 Census %	Under/ over representation
1 New York	33.7	9.8	3.4 x
2 California	8.2	7.0	1.2
3 New Jersey	8.0	3.2	2.5
4 Pennsylvania	6.8	7.0	1.0
5 Illinois	5.9	5.8	1.0
6 Massachusetts	4.4	3.1	1.4
7 Ohio	3.7	5.3	0.7
8 Connecticut	3.3	1.3	2.5
9 Michigan	3.0	4.3	0.7
10 District of Columbia	1.7	0.5	3.4
Other states	21.3	52.7	0.4
	100	100	

Source: United States, Bureau of Foreign and Domestic Commerce, *Survey of International Travel*, Table 7 – Selected State of Residence of United States Residents Returning by Sea and Air at The Port of New York from Europe and the Mediterranean Area, Third-Quarter, 1952 and 1954. US State Populations from United States Census, 1950 at https://usa.ipums.org.

New York State accounted for 32 per cent of all passport applications in 1950 and 25 per cent in both 1954 and 1958 respectively. New York City took 24 per cent, 18 per cent, and 19 per cent on the same basis. By 1958, fifteen major American cities accounted for 42 per cent of all passport applications.[13] This evidence puts an end to the belief that American tourists were from small towns. It is most likely that they were residents of the major cities of the states shown in Table 3.1 or lived in outlying suburbs of those cities. In marked contrast, Alabama, an impoverished state, had a population of three million in 1950, and those three million made a grand total of 806 applications and renewals between them (i.e., 2.6 per 10,000). McKenney and Bransten were mistaken in their choice of Indiana and Iowa as the typical homes of tourists to England, as less than one person in a thousand applied for a passport each year from these states.[14] As the decade progressed, there was greater representation from the more

Table 3.2

Number of passport issues and renewals per 10,000 population, for states
with populations exceeding 1 million

	State	1950	State	1954	State	1958
1	New York	64.4	New York	74.3	New York	99.9
2	New Jersey	42.5	Connecticut	69.5	Connecticut	66.7
3	Connecticut	40.0	New Jersey	55.2	New Jersey	63.9
4	Massachusetts	38.1	Maryland	40.0	California	55.5
5	Illinois	24.1	Massachusetts	37.2	Massachusetts	52.2
6	California	21.7	Florida	34.1	Florida	40.4
7	Pennsylvania	18.6	Washington	32.2	Washington	38.5
8	Florida	18.3	California	31.6	Illinois	36.6
9	Michigan	18.2	Illinois	30.0	Pennsylvania	32.2
10	Minnesota	17.4	Minnesota	29.3	Maryland	32.1

United States, Bureau of Foreign and Domestic Commerce, *Participation in International
Travel – 1959*, Table 47 – Passports Issued and Renewed by State of Residence of Recipients.
US State populations from United States Census, 1950 (used for 1950 and 1954 comparisons)
and 1960 (used for 1958 comparisons) at https://usa.ipums.org.

prosperous states with large urban populations, such as California and
Washington, and, more generally, from the Midwest.

The map in Figure 3.1 shows the geographical domination of the Northeast and the Midwest in the propensity of Americans to apply or renew
their passports. There are two outliers, the sunshine states of Florida and
California. Florida was not particularly affluent in the 1950s, as it was, apart
from the coastal tourist resorts, dependent on agriculture for its wealth.[15]
It is probable that tourists visiting pre-revolution Havana for short visits
took out many of the passports. In 1958, for example, Florida residents
made 36 per cent of all trips to Havana.[16] One might think the same relationship would hold for Californians crossing the border to Tijuana, but
Americans did not need a passport to visit Mexico.[17] As has been shown,
despite the problems of getting to New York in the first part of the decade,
Californians made up the second-largest group of travellers. Its citizens'
wealth, which was unevenly distributed between its urban and rural population, provided the means, in time and money, for the long railway jour-

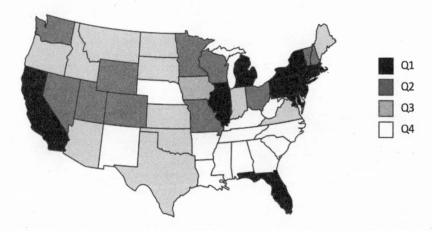

Figure 3.1 Propensity to have a passport in 1950, by US state, by quartiles.

ney or multi-stop flight between Los Angeles and New York, followed by a transatlantic voyage. This suggests that most Angelinos were obtaining their passports to travel to Europe.[18]

The US authorities' analysis of the occupations of passport applicants reveals much about the type of people crossing the Atlantic in the 1950s (see Table 3.3).[19] It is intriguing that, in 1950, Americans receiving a new passport were also issued with a plea to behave well when abroad. The State Department asked that "our citizen travelers will ... deport themselves in a manner *befitting their station and training.*"[20] This wording was a hangover from the interwar years, suggesting that only wealthy, college-educated Americans applied for passports. Indeed, in the first few years of the decade, middle-class Americans made the most passport applications. Little changed until the mid-fifties, when professionals replaced students to some extent. This reflected a bulge of ex-servicemen graduating college and then moving into professional and business jobs. In the second half of the decade, the key change was the growth in skilled workers travelling, which rose from 26.5 per cent of those applying for or renewing their passports in 1954 to 46 per cent in 1958.[21] These occupations included, alongside a generic "skilled" category, the following: clerks, barbers, nurses, technicians, tradesmen, and contractors. This movement toward the lower-middle and working classes was one of the reasons why the 1950s was such a significant period for American tourism.

Table 3.3

Percentage of those applying for or renewing their passports, by occupation

Occupation	1950	1954	1958
Independently wealthy	6.0	5.6	7.2
Retired	4.4	5.9	6.6
Professional and business owner	31.4	39.0	19.8
Creative	2.7	3.2	3.1
Skilled worker	28.7	26.5	46.0
Unskilled worker	6.9	6.5	6.4
Student	12.2	7.6	8.6
Religious/missionaries	4.1	3.0	2.2
Miscellaneous	3.6	2.7	0.1
	100.0	100.0	100.0

Source: Statistics for 1950 and 1954 taken from United States, Bureau of Foreign and Domestic Commerce, *Survey of International Travel*, Table 13 – Passports Issued and Renewed by Occupation, 1950–55. Statistics for 1958 taken from United States, Bureau of Foreign and Domestic Commerce, *Participation in International Travel – 1959*, Table 42 – Passports Issued and Renewed by Occupation of Applicant, July through December 1958.

The arrival of less-wealthy and perhaps less-sophisticated Americans was commented upon at the time. Novelist John Steinbeck, who lived in Paris in the 1950s, summed up his view of the typical American tourist coming to Europe in 1956. "The myth that all or even most traveling Americans are rich is a complete myth. The great majority have saved and stinted for this time."[22] One example of this was evident in a British journalist's account of a sightseeing trip around London from that same year, when she accompanied a group of twelve American tourists who hailed from New York, Chicago, Cincinnati, Cleveland, and Kalamazoo, that is, from major cities rather than small-town America. The article revealed some of their occupations: bank clerk, insurance salesman, and student.[23]

These new tourists to Europe may have come from unremarkable backgrounds, but their economic capital distinguished them from most Americans, who were getting by day-to-day but had little in the way of savings or the ability to take on instalment payments. Phyllis Stock, who advocated low-budget travel in her trip report, calculated in 1958 that "first you must

have a thousand dollars, so if you now have that amount of money well ...
you've got it made." In a reflection of the buoyant American economy, she
advised, "About that job you have. If you can't get a leave of absence, give
it up. There will be a position open when you come home."[24] In the same
year, the *Times* newspaper recorded that "half [of American tourists] have
incomes of less than $10,000 a year, not at all the handsome amount it
sounds."[25] In fact, $10,000 was at the eighty-sixth percentile for US in-
comes in 1960; having less than that would still place most tourists in the
top quartile.[26] The overall conclusion was correct, though: these late-1950s
tourists were not as wealthy as the visitors from earlier in the decade.

The high number of student visitors, coupled with the greater proportion of Americans going to college, meant that Americans in Britain were
likely to be better educated than Britons of the same age and relative
wealth. Only 2.7 per cent of the eligible population of Britain in 1938 (and
therefore about thirty-four years old in 1955) were in college, the numbers
made up equally of men and women (the latter were accounted for by a
small number at university and the majority in teacher training).[27] The
American equivalent for 1940 was 6.6 per cent in college, with slightly
fewer women attending than men.[28] Younger white American women
tourists were about three times more likely to have gone into higher education than British women of the same age.[29]

In 1960, by a small majority, the typical tourist was now a prospering,
skilled, lower-middle-class, urban/suburban resident from a northeastern-
seaboard state. Most of these visitors would not have a college degree and,
as a consequence, would be less acquainted with English literature and
British culture.[30] It is likely that their lower cultural capital and relatively
short vacation entitlements made organized tours of Britain a very attractive way of travelling.

Going on Vacation

American tourists' dollar spending rose steadily throughout the 1950s, as
disposable income, savings, and vacation entitlements increased. Total
numbers travelling overseas rose from 676,000 in 1950 to 1.4 million in
1958, which represented 0.8 per cent of the population of the United
States.[31] These figures excluded travel to the country's two neighbours,

Mexico and Canada. Americans could travel to these destinations without a passport, typically popping across the border to, for example, Tijuana or Vancouver, rather than using them as the base for a long vacation. The US authorities considered that most visits were from citizens living near the border who repeatedly crossed it for purposes of work, study, and shopping, so they did not qualify as tourists. Fewer than one American in a hundred travelled abroad in that year, which shows that, despite the rapidly widening access to this type of vacation, it was still a highly unusual, if not elite, experience. It suggests that the less wealthy who made these trips to Europe did so as a once-in-a-lifetime vacation.

For overseas destinations, the most popular area for travel (but for very short trips) was the Caribbean, closely followed by Europe. The Caribbean was favoured for its climate and proximity to the airports of the eastern United States; the Bahamas, Bermuda, and Cuba were all easily accessible from Miami. Pre-revolutionary Cuba, with its gambling and its reputation for licentiousness had an even greater attraction for American citizens. Weekend visits to Havana were very popular. As air travel became dominant, the duration of visits to Cuba reduced. For example, by 1958, 59 per cent of visitors stayed less than four days.[32] These were short, indulgent trips based around hotel pools, casinos, and the beach. European travel provided a very different type of vacation.

Holidaymakers who travelled to Europe went there for many weeks and typically visited several countries before returning to the United States. Those making the trip across the Atlantic by sea in 1958 (a minority, many of whom were elderly) were away from home for an average of fifty-one days. Those travelling by air came for a still-lengthy thirty-three days. Only 9 per cent of visitors took a trip that lasted two weeks or less (see Appendix 4). The US Department of Commerce concluded that both Britain and France were gateway countries, which offered a start and a finish to European vacations. This makes sense, as the geography of Europe made arrivals at the ports of either Southampton or Le Havre the logical spots to conclude a transatlantic sea voyage. When air travel superseded sea travel, these two countries remained the jumping-off points with arrivals at Heathrow and Orly.[33] Britain was the most-favoured destination in Europe in the 1930s.[34] After the war, France overtook its neighbour in popularity, with just under 59 per cent of Americans who came to Europe visiting it in 1958, compared to Britain's 53 per cent (see Appendix 5). These statistics are muddied by the impact of former European emigrants returning to their home countries to visit friends and families, who formed an important category of visitor. The largest in number were German-Americans, followed by Italian-Americans. Scottish-Americans had a proportionally greater influence on visitor numbers than Americans of English descent, while France had many fewer of these types of returnees.[35] It is likely that non-native Americans visiting Italy and Germany for the first time in decades also visited France and Britain. France's lack of an American diaspora suggests that Paris was even more popular than the raw statistics show.

USAF Servicemen and Their Families

In the 1950s, the United States Third Air Force, headquartered at South Ruislip in Middlesex, occupied thirty-four airfields across Britain.[36] Of these, the better-known were Brize Norton (Oxfordshire), Greenham Common (Berkshire), Lakenheath and Mildenhall (Suffolk), and the giant European logistics base at Burtonwood (Cheshire). The return of the USAF affected its rural neighbours, who faced land confiscation, disruption, the noise caused by airfield expansion, and the lengthening of runways to accommodate jet-powered bombers.[37] They were also on the front line of Anglo-American relations that echoed the concerns of ten years earlier, though the behaviour of the newly arrived USAF personnel was better than that of their predecessors, because many were family men and were not readying themselves to invade Europe.[38]

This number of American service personnel and dependents in Britain waxed and waned during the 1950s, but roughly totalled 250,000 individuals (see Appendix 6). There were 47,000 personnel in Britain in 1953, which was something of a high point of international tension due to the Korean War and threats from the Soviet Union. The Communist Party in Ipswich exaggeratedly claimed the actual number was more than 60,000,[39] but the official figures showed a peak of 63,000 in 1957. Married servicemen brought their families over to Britain to live with them, while 60 per cent of single US servicemen married British women, and many of these couples started a family. By 1960, there were 40,000 wives and children of American servicemen in Britain.[40]

Personnel of the USAF were very different to American tourists. Statistics on the age of adult American tourists are not readily available today, but can be inferred from occupational data. Retirees and students made up approximately 25 per cent of the total; the remainder was dominated by skilled workers and business owners, which suggests income accumulation, with the majority of tourists being in their forties and fifties. Officers of the USAF were far younger and more educated than the average tourist.[41] During this period of conscription, if you had to go into the US armed forces, the USAF was an attractive choice. It was more glamorous than the navy and had a much lower mortality rate than the army. As a consequence, it attracted the best and brightest to compete for places. This was such a problem that the rival services complained to the future president, Senator Lyndon B. Johnson, who wrote, in 1951, that: "The loss to the Nation is incalculable ... Men of high intelligence who might have made invaluable officers for the Army are now consigned to the ranks of the Air Force as privates ... The Air Force's apparent unconcern for the other services is ... an attitude detrimental to the best interests of the Nation."[42]

The USAF was staffed by young men; the median age of the 937,000 personnel in the USAF in late 1954 was twenty-four years. Officers (14 per cent of the total) had a median age of thirty-two years and airmen (86 per cent) twenty-two years.[43] For Britons to meet an officer over forty or an airman over thirty was a rare event.[44] USAF officers were very well educated. In May 1955, aided by the GI Bill, which encouraged returning wartime servicemen to go to college, 46 per cent of officers had an undergraduate or higher degree. For second lieutenants (the most-junior commissioned officer) the figure was 66 per cent, reflecting widening access to higher education after the Second World War. Airmen, largely selected from working-class backgrounds, could count only 1.3 per cent of their number as college graduates.[45] As almost nine out of every ten in the USAF were airmen, most with a lowly vocational status and education, it is likely that about 80 per cent of USAF personnel in Britain were working class.[46] As far as state of origin was concerned, airmen and officers were more representative of the overall population of the United States. Although a disproportionate number came from New England, the air force's recruitment was otherwise spread fairly evenly over the rest of the United States.[47]

Categories of Visitor

British-American writer and broadcaster Alistair Cooke identified five main types of American visitors: businessmen, tourists, educated and wealthy Anglophiles, homeland returners, and spies and flaneurs. Cooke thought businessmen were the group who, because of their daily interactions with their British counterparts, got a "true picture of a working society." His second category of tourist "arranges his itinerary at home and digests travel pamphlets" and looks for a picturesque Britain seen in the movies. Cooke had little time for Anglophiles, whom he typified as being only interested in Britain as an elite and regressive society, and he had no interest in homeland returners. He facetiously placed himself in the very small, superior, fifth category as a "student of other people's behaviour."[48] In reality, American tourists in the 1950s, putting aside their relative wealth and whiteness, were heterogeneous. The trip reports offer clues to the types of visitors and their motivations for travelling.

As Cooke noted, American businessmen and women were frequent travellers to Britain in the 1950s. Their visits were often made in connection with the Marshall Plan and its campaign to modernize British industry or as part of American industrial expansion into European markets through British subsidiaries.[49] Business travellers are often typified as seeing little more than airports, taxis, and hotels; in reality, many also added tourist activities. Cooke's belief that direct interaction with British colleagues provided a deeper understanding of Britain is probably correct, but the quotidian nature of their travels didn't lend to much self-reflection, though there were exceptions. For instance, Edward G. Wilson, a senior executive of leading US advertising agency J. Walter Thompson, provided one such account for his colleagues, which recorded his impressions of trips to Britain, during which he experienced the best that it had to offer a visitor.[50]

Tourists travelled as families, with friends, on their own, or as members of a large group. Many family groups made the trip across the Atlantic to Britain. When children joined the party, it became an expensive trip, with at least twice as many hotel rooms and liner cabins required. Authors with an academic background wrote three of the most comprehensive trip reports featuring family groups, perhaps explained by their costs being funded by their college or by a scholarship, making their trip more attainable.

These families were part of a community in which publishing was expected and normalized.

Of course, not all of these trips were funded. One such academic group was the Lyon family from Claremont in suburban Los Angeles, California. The head of this household was E. Wilson Lyon, president of the prestigious Pomona College and a 1925 Rhodes Scholar, who was returning to Britain in 1953 for that institution's fiftieth anniversary.[51] Accompanying him was his wife, Carolyn, an academic editor, and their two teenage children, Elizabeth and John. Carolyn kept a diary throughout the 1950s and, helpfully, made a daily record of their ten-week vacation to Britain, France, Germany, and Italy.[52] Their younger child, John, still sharp and energetic in 2017 at seventy-eight, was interviewed for this book in Washington, DC, near his home in suburban Maryland.[53] Another example of a tourist family was led by Paul Roberts, a Fulbright scholar, who took the opportunity of his move to an Egyptian university to take a vacation in Britain on the way. Father and mother and three children aged eleven, nine, and six bravely travelled to England in 1959 to take a cycling tour of the Home Counties. His amusing memoir, *And the Children Came Too*, described the perils and pleasures of cycling on Britain's "A" roads and byways at a time when they were increasingly being dominated by the car.

Friends travelled together. One such journey was recorded by Ethel Moller Arwe. In 1953, she was forty-nine years old, well-off, and lived in New Jersey. Her husband had once been to Panama and Havana, but she had never left the United States, or travelled much within the country; her furthest trip, so far, had been to Michigan. Together with two friends they had planned their own trip to Europe rather than take a conducted tour. Like many suburban housewives of this place and time, Arwe was likely to have possessed a college-level education, but not to have had much opportunity to use her learning. As historian Elaine Tyler May noted "many college-educated women [resented] their college training for raising their expectations, and [felt] frustrated and bored because their desire for intellectual and creative work … was unfulfilled."[54] Arwe wrote a self-deprecating account of their trip, which also showed that going to Europe on vacation was a very special and unusual event: "We start the day like a third-rate comedy act … stuffed into [a] station wagon, we try to protect our brave new hairdos, orchids and new clothes from being crushed beneath the ear-high welter of suitcases."[55]

More women than men applied for or renewed their US passports in the 1950s. In 1958 there was a 52 to 48 per cent split. When figures for military personnel and their dependents are eliminated, the figures diverged further, to 54 to 46 per cent. The largest category of women visitors were housewives, followed at some distance by students, retirees, secretaries, and teachers.[56] Categorization as a housewife suggests a woman accompanying her husband on vacation, but in 1950s America, where women were not encouraged to take a career after marriage, this term included independent married women travelling in all-female groups or on their own.

For women to travel on their own to Britain and other European countries seems, looking back at the conservative attitudes of the United States in the 1950s, to be an unlikely prospect, but it was a reasonably common occurrence. Edith Patterson Meyer's guidebook to Europe, *Go It Alone, Lady!*, aimed specifically at single women, provides support for this idea. Two of the trip reports were written by women travelling on their own. Phyllis Stock's *Eight Pence a Mile* described the adventures of a book editor from Long Beach, California. Writing in 1958, she addressed the "white-collar traveller" who didn't want to stay in tourist hotels with other Americans and wanted to see a more authentic version of Europe.[57] The second was Germaine Haney's *No Reservations*. Both these books, unusually for this genre of writing, found commercial publishers. Presumably, the topic and author were distinctive enough for them to make the mainstream. Haney was a part-time lecturer and journalist from San Fernando, California, who was married, with a grown-up son. She appeared smiling and perky with a gamine haircut on the dust jacket of her book, very much the capable traveller. She found her single status in Britain a problem, attracting the wrong sort of attention from overfamiliar British men.

Travelling to Britain as part of a large group was popular. This approach had advantages. It was a cheap way to travel, as a many of the costs could be shared; it lent itself to coach tours and guided travel, which also kept the costs down; and it also minimized the risk of something going wrong or being dangerous, since their guides protected group members from the unpleasantness or disappointments of travelling alone. The disadvantage was that tourists in groups all saw the same clichéd sights and were far less likely to meet the locals. Tour parties had long excited criticism in Britain as they raced from one attraction, city, or country to another. Groups were formed from shared associations, such as churchgoers, keen on cathedrals and going to Rome, or businessmen's clubs, such as Rotary. In the 1950s, American women joined clubs and associations like never before, so it was a high point for women's groups to travel to Europe together.[58]

A good example of this category of trip report was Larry Mersfelder's naive self-published book, *We Were the Foreigners*, its title indicating that Larry (who was in his seventies) had worked out that there was more to the world than Oklahoma. Mersfelder travelled to Europe in 1957 with fellow members of the Civic Club of America, who hailed from thirteen different states. His account is full of tales of visiting Madame Tussauds, seeing the Tower of London, and travelling by coach to "Shakespeare Country." Despite its literary limitations, this type of account is very useful in describing the responses of uncelebrated Americans. In its way, it is more productive than the accounts from well-known writers. Another example, written in a similar vein, is the far smarter and more likeable Juanita Stott's unpublished account from 1954, *Our European Tour*, which records the experiences of a party of women from North Carolina who were travelling together.

As was shown in the passport data, students made up an important category of those travelling across the Atlantic to Britain and continental Europe. This group was most prominent in the early 1950s, as men who served in the armed forces in the Second World War enrolled in college.[59] After this demographic wave subsided, one in twelve of all travellers were students. Students, travelling with friends or in a large party, were almost always on a budget. This meant that they chose the less-glamorous and older ocean liners to make their way across to Britain, and they stayed in cheap hotels or hostels when they arrived. Hitchhiking, which was a popular way of travel in the 1950s, provided free transport across the country. One such hitchhiker was Carol Hummel, a young woman from Florida, who travelled with a male friend up the eastern seaboard of the United States by getting jobs returning rental cars and hitchhiking, and then in Britain by hitching lifts from city to city.[60] Students often travelled to Europe as part of a university-organized tour. They were required to submit short dissertations describing their experiences; an example was Julia Burrell, a master's student studying at Peabody College in Nashville, Tennessee. She submitted her dissertation in 1958, describing in gushing tones her visit to Britain, having listened to and absorbed the local guide's shorthand explanations of British history.[61]

Cooke's third category of visitor consisted of Anglophile Americans who didn't think of themselves as tourists, but as travellers searching for authenticity. This idea permeated Phyllis Stock's travelogue, which was aiming at independent-minded lower-paid Americans, but was also present in elite accounts.[62] A need to enjoy authentic travel can be viewed as a consequence of modernity and as a replacement for the role that religion used to play in Western lives.[63] It is a self-defeating, fruitless exercise, as the very presence of travellers in search of authenticity attracts the many, eventually destroying its promise.[64] Writer Emily Kimbrough was a good example of this type of American visitor. She wrote journalistic pieces for the *New Yorker* and *Atlantic Monthly* and book-length memoirs of her travels for a middle-class American readership.[65] In *And a Right Good Crew*, Kimbrough describes her "roughing it" vacation spent on a narrow boat on the English canals. Sketches of her activities illustrate the book, one of which is very telling. Kimbrough, her husband, and a married couple who were to travel with them are pictured poring over brochures and guides at home, all of them in evening dress. On their travels, rather than join a tour, they paid an independent visit to a stately home in their scruffy narrow-boat outfits, which provoked mock-shame at their behaviour, while simultaneously advertising their knowledge of antique books and their bindings. In this type of memoir, the authors present themselves as so urbane that little surprises them, except for the quaintness and indeed authenticity of the working-class people they meet. Kimbrough was the archetypal sophisticate Anglophile, moving easily between the two cultures.

As Cooke identified, an important reason for Americans to visit Britain was to explore their family trees and to find ancestral connections back in the "home" country. Unlike German, Irish, and Italian Americans who still felt strong cultural and family associations with Europe, the ancestors of Anglo-Americans and Scottish-Americans typically arrived in the United States a century or two earlier than those from the continent, so these visitors to Britain often came with a search for historical distinction. Two trip reports fall into this category. Esther Hilton Dundas, from Chicago, was in her late fifties when she travelled to Britain to research her husband's ancestry. The Dundas clan's claim to be one of the most noble in Scottish history added to the visit's allure. Her account, *So We Went to Europe: An Ancestral History*, is a very dull read. The personal nature of this book ensured that it would not find a conventional publisher, so she commissioned a privately published and beautifully printed and bound book, which she sent as a gift to friends and relatives. Another returning American of Scottish descent was wealthy Nebraskan William Ritchie, who recorded in his *Diary of a European Trip* how he "went to Forfar, the county seat of Forfarshire, from which shire my Ritchie ancestors emigrated to America in 1743."[66] This memoir was also self-published for distribution to friends. Less glamorously, Etta Payne and her husband travelled from Wyoming to a poor part of industrial Middlesbrough, in the northeast of England, to find the street where her father was born.[67]

In addition to Cooke's categories, many thousands of military families also made the journey across the Atlantic. As has been shown, most of these were the dependents of USAF personnel. A few were from the other services, such as the Rumble family. The father was a captain in the US navy, and in 1954 took up a post as a naval attaché at the US Embassy in Grosvenor Square in London. Captain Henry Rumble, previously based at a naval shipyard in Vallejo, California, brought his wife and three teenage boys with him to London, and they all lived in a Knightsbridge house, built a few decades before the Declaration of Independence. Their new lives in London presented many contrasts: they had a beautiful house in a smart part of the city, but it had no central heating, employing, like most houses in Britain, coal fires and paraffin heaters against the bitter winter cold. On the plus side, the children enjoyed a free-and-easy lifestyle in London. The Rumble boys were taller than the locals, so they could pass as eighteen-year-olds, allowing them access to pubs and to travel on their own by tube and taxi.[68]

Americans staying in Britain as longer-term visitors often brought their children with them, which provided them with a different way of meeting and understanding their hosts – one that was not available to tourists. The trip reports contain two similar, overlapping accounts of life in Oxford in the 1950s, written by visiting American academic families. The much better known of these is journalist Muriel Beadle's *These Ruins Are Inhabited*, which revels in the eccentricities of Oxford University and its colleges. Covering the same material, but written in a far-less-knowing manner, is Margaret Griffith's self-published *Unconventional Europe*. These books also record the families' experiences when travelling in Britain as tourists.

Appendix 2 sets out a full catalogue of the trip reports used in this book.

Conclusion

The cartoon images of large men wearing cowboy hats seen in British newspapers proposed that the typical American tourist in Britain was male, Texan, and wealthy. However, the analysis of 1950s traveller data set out above points clearly in a different direction. More women than men went to Britain, and most visitors came from the states nearest to New York's port and airport. Throughout the decade, New York City provided a high percentage of visitors to Britain, and New York State had the highest proportion of citizens who travelled abroad than any other, although New York's neighbouring states also supplied many American visitors to Britain. California was the only important exception to the domination of the northeastern states.

In the first part of the decade, ocean liners departing from Manhattan were the most popular means of travel to Britain. This meant that Californian residents had to add a tedious railway journey or a bumpy multi-stop flight to their schedule just to get to the dockside. For Californians, this disincentive made Hawaii an attractive alternative, but visiting Honolulu did not confer the classy feeling that going to Europe provided. Liners attracted retirees and students, parties of housewives, and the wealthy, who were not restricted to a maximum of three weeks away from work.

In the second half of the decade, flying was the dominant way to get to Britain. Of course, many still came by liner, but the passengers who were attracted to it were conservative, elderly, or those attracted by the low costs of Third-Class berths. Lower-cost, speedy flying produced demographic changes in those wishing to visit Britain, attracting well-paid, lower-middle-class Americans, who now got their opportunity. Better, faster internal flights also made travel from more-distant states practicable, so there was a gradual widening of the geographical origin of American visitors. Rather than the ignorant rube defensively suggested in British criticism, most visitors were urban or suburban and, on average, better educated than their hosts. Those on USAF deployment were different, demonstrating a wider range of Americans. Its officers were young and well-educated, while its airmen were very young and unlikely to have been to college.

CHAPTER FOUR

Selling Britain's Heritage and History

A common language – and, for some, heritage – coupled with the still-fond memories of military alliance in the Second World War suggests that marketing Britain as a vacation destination to Americans would be a simple task. However, putting aside the cost and time involved in travelling across the Atlantic, Britain's relationship with the United States was, in reality, more complex than this. As has been discussed, many Americans with backgrounds in Ireland, Germany, and other European countries were not naturally warm to Britain. Many Americans considered Britain to be either a fading and devious imperial power, whose rigid class system was the antithesis of the American ideal, or, in the early 1950s, a worryingly untrustworthy socialist state.[1] As a leading guidebook put it, Britain was a country that "is complicated, much more obscure and difficult than Brazil or Abyssinia."[2] As a result of these difficulties, the British tourist authorities needed and then delivered a persuasive campaign to attract American visitors; their brochures were a strong influence in making Britain desirable.[3] Along with the British tourist authorities, there were three other important groups working on this project: air and shipping lines, newspapers and magazines, and travel agents. Subtler influencers, such as guidebooks, writing that promoted a shared heritage, and popular movies and music, also made Britain more attractive to Americans.

Marketing

The British government recognized the importance of American tourism in the late 1940s and early 1950s, as it was one of the most important sources of US dollars for Britain's struggling economy. The government-sponsored British Travel and Holidays Association (BTHA) noted the outcome for 1951: "One third of total receipts [from tourism] came from the USA and Canada. US visitors alone ... spent £26.4 million, a sum greater than any of the country's visible exports to America and equivalent to 20 percent of all physical exports to the USA."[4]

In 1949, the British Travel Association (a predecessor to the BTHA), in conjunction with the *Times*, produced a special newspaper for one of its first postwar marketing campaigns aimed at American travel agents and tourists.[5] It was dull fare. Alongside advertisements for Harrods and Austin Reed raincoats, it offered learned articles, such as architectural scholar John Summerson's "English Cathedrals," and less-interesting features on, for example, "Industrial Centres." Two years later, the BTHA was delivering a professional and comprehensive service from the British Travel Centre on Manhattan's Madison Avenue.[6] Amongst its activities, it promoted Britain by arranging for three "real" London buses to tour the United States from New York to Los Angeles and back, calling at most major cities en route. It fitted one of the buses out as a travelling exhibition, presenting Britain to American travel agents. Its displays focused on London, a connection that the buses themselves strongly emphasized, and Britain as a "land of historic and scenic beauty," themes which were consistent with much BTHA marketing in the 1950s.[7] Illustrations of a yeoman warder from the Tower of London and a Rowland Emett poster also highlighted the capital in the exhibition. Emett, a cartoonist and designer, was at the height of his fame at this time, a result of his work on a bizarre model railway, one of the most popular attractions at the Festival of Britain.[8] The poster showed a bus with two top-deck male passengers, one wearing a top hat, the other a monocle; its bus driver and conductor were pictured as elderly and uniformed. A second bus featured another top-hatted gent, but this time accompanied by a nineteenth-century policeman waving a truncheon. Emett's ironic take accidentally reinforced many American's prejudices about Britain, which saw it as Victorian and class-bound.

The BTHA was proud of the results of its marketing, which included, in a single year, the distribution of 1.5 million brochures and other pieces of literature across the United States, although most inquiries came from wealthier states, such as California, Illinois, Massachusetts, New Jersey, New York, and Pennsylvania.[9] Its brochures delivered a simplified version of Britain that promoted London, Edinburgh, and areas of regional beauty or historical interest. As cultural theorist James Buzard has noted, "[each] place [in these brochures] is imagined as a totality so densely packed with significance that a step in any direction sets off historical and affective resonances."[10] This approach was so successful that, when tourists actually saw Britain, they were startled by the reality. Margaret Griffith, an American temporarily resident in Britain, noted this when she met a tourist friend: "Janet was surprised by the prevailing Victorian architecture at Oxford. I had been too; I suppose the British Travel Association ads were at fault, for they emphasize thatched-roof cottages, half-timbered fourteenth-century inns, and Scottish baronial castles."[11] Drew Middleton pointed out this misrepresentation:

> This picturesque, rural England has not been a true picture of the country for over a century. But the guidebooks and the British Travel Association still send tourists to its shrines, novelists still write charmingly dated pictures of its life, and on both sides of the Atlantic the movies and stage continue to present attractive but false pictures of "Olde Worlde" England.[12]

Despite the inaccuracy, this marketing created a powerful agenda in many visitors' minds; they felt that their vacation was incomplete if they had not visited these areas of "heritage" Britain.

In 1953, the attraction of Britain's heritage and history for Americans was amplified by the glamour of the coronation of Elizabeth II. As tourism from the United States grew, with increasing numbers of first-time visitors making a trip, the Royal Family and Buckingham Palace became strong draws.[13] Happily for the BTHA, Queen Elizabeth's coronation was, despite many Americans' suspicions about imperial Britain, a very popular event in the United States. Forty thousand Americans made it to London for the coronation, and back at home fifty-five million (about a third of the population) watched it on their televisions. Media coverage in the United States was extremely positive about the event, with anti-British sentiment mostly confined to readers' letters.[14]

In the BTHA's marketing, individual regions in Britain were linked with well-known literary figures. A good example was a brochure for Scotland, which divided the lowlands of Scotland into three: the [Sir Walter] Scott Country, the Western Borders, and "The Burns Country and Galloway, made famous in the writings of John Buchan."[15] As might be expected, it placed great emphasis on Edinburgh and its array of historical sites and nearby beauty spots. It devoted many pages to the capital and an equal number to the Highlands and the Isles; in contrast, Glasgow did not get a single mention.[16] Scotland was an important part of the BTHA's marketing campaign and was often included in material produced by others operating in this field. Its appeal combined beautiful scenery and heritage with an appeal to those Scottish-Americans wishing to return to their mother country. In 1956, 46 per cent of all visiting Americans made the trip north to Scotland.[17] Despite the BTHA's reluctance to include Glasgow, a third of all American visitors also went there.[18] Carol Hummel did so and noted that she had already "seen a rivalry between the English and the Scotch [sic]. We had nice quarters in a boarding house in this drab city. People seem to have a more ruddy complexion and more sturdy build than Americans."[19] The blotting out of a major city also occurred in brochures on England that did not refer to Birmingham or Manchester. In response, Manchester City Council made its own brochure for American visitors, which optimistically claimed that "Like Pittsburg [sic], Manchester is surrounded by genuine 'tourist country' and the scope for excursions and tours cannot be matched by any other city in England either for extent or variety. Many transatlantic visitors have said these same words after spending a few days in Manchester."[20] The brochure might have made a stronger impression on Americans if it had spelt Pittsburgh correctly.

The BTHA also used indirect marketing techniques, for example placing editorial pieces into newspapers from its target states such as California. The Los Angeles Times carried this type of material throughout the 1950s. One 1953 example, "Come Visit Britain in Royal Autumn," implausibly claimed that "Britain's temperate climate is gentle enough for comfortable year-round sight-seeing."[21]

The Los Angeles Times and other major American newspapers such as the New York Times also featured Britain as an appealing destination in their regular travel pages. For instance, in August 1952, the Californian newspaper presented a feature on the attractions of Devon and Cornwall as a suitable late-season base for a vacation. It explained that Americans were welcome in the West Country because the US armed forces located there in the war were "remembered with affection." It identified Plymouth as especially attractive to Americans because of its association with the Pilgrim Fathers.[22]

The *National Geographic* was one of the most influential magazines for potential American vacationers in the 1950s. Although its worthy articles and prurient images of "natives" aimed at a readership with a wide set of interests, its features on vacation destinations were similar to those in guidebooks and brochures. Britain was the subject of occasional long-form essays, with an emphasis on historic and literary traditions. The addition of interesting and beautiful colour photographs must have convinced many travellers to select Britain as an essential part of their European trip. Britain also featured regularly in the specialist monthly magazine *Holiday*. This magazine, "a favorite chronicle of café society," was, in essence, an upmarket consumerist version of *National Geographic*, and also included beautifully rendered photographs. It set out the exotic travel possibilities for America's wealthiest citizens, featuring articles from well-known writers.[23] Its target audience is most easily identifiable today from its advertisements for pricey resorts, clothing, and accessories. Certainly, its editorial assumptions were that its aspirational readers could travel around the world without any financial constraints. Each month it featured a small number of destinations that combined slick and urbane journalism with well-photographed colour and monochrome images.

Holiday's approach to Britain was similar to the BTHA's, as it connected famous authors and their works to areas of historical interest and beauty. For example, it produced a literary guide to Britain that directed Americans to suitable parts of the country. The article paired Dylan Thomas with a trip to Wales and reassured prospective visitors that "English is spoken everywhere in Britain."[24] Lord Byron was linked with his ancestral home, Newstead Abbey, with an explanation that many of Britain's stately homes were now open to visitors. Of course, nowhere was the connection between literature, history, and natural beauty stronger than in Stratford-upon-Avon, an important destination for Americans from the nineteenth century onwards.[25]

Airlines were naturally keen to make flying part of the vacation plan of every American. In the 1950s, two American airlines, Trans World Airlines (TWA) and Pan American, and the British Overseas Airlines Corporation (BOAC) flew across the Atlantic to Britain, competing for domination of this key route. Pan American was the initiator of the scheduled transatlantic flight in 1939; after the war, TWA excelled by concentrating on customer service, which contrasted with Pan American's colder efficiency.[26] Both airlines produced marketing material to promote Britain to Americans. In 1956, TWA launched their *Vacation Guide and World Atlas*. Priced at $7.50 (quite a sum at the time), it promised "hours of enlightening and entertaining reading about the places you'd like to see" for both the armchair and real-life traveller.[27] The TWA guide featured Great Britain and Ireland as its first entry, which ran to twenty pages. France was next and received fifteen pages, a level of coverage that inverted the relative popularity of the two countries as destinations for Americans. The copy for this guide to Britain was prosaic and used a gazetteer format. It compared poorly with the journalistic style of *Holiday* magazine in the same year, which assumed, unlike TWA, that its readers understood what a pub was without further explanation.[28]

Pan American prepared its customers for their visit to Britain differently. Its in-flight magazine, *Clipper Travel*, addressed a wealthy clientele. In a 1954 example, after a few pages of gossip about celebrity passengers (Stirling Moss, Humphrey Bogart), the rest of the issue was largely devoted to consumption. This was in two forms: first, features and advertising of luxury goods from Bond Street shops and, second, restaurants and bars that visiting Americans would enjoy.[29] Late in the decade, marking the transition to jet travel, Pan American produced a thirty-minute movie guide, which, along with promoting rapid travel, marketed Britain as a destination. It hit the usual targets of heritage, pastoral scenes, and capital city splendour, but also highlighted the many leisure possibilities that Britain provided, from seaside funfairs to the racetracks.[30]

Before the Internet, travel agents provided the essential means through which independent American travellers booked their vacations. Those wanting to go on group tours may also have used them, although they could also deal directly with all-inclusive tour companies by replying to one of their newspaper advertisements. Larry Mersfelder explained why: "We felt it would be wise to know before we left the amount of the total expense, so we bought the entire deal in one package – steamship accommodations, hotels, meals, trains, buses, and everything."[31] At the offices of travel agents, prospective visitors to Britain chose their method of transport and got advice on the pros and cons of sea and air voyages. They then booked their accommodation and any guides or tours they might need. A warm relationship with an agent could make the difference between a good or a bad experience in Europe. Carol Hummel recorded her gratitude to her agent. She noted, "Wednesday, Bob and I ... met Mrs Brong our faithful travel agent. Such an unselfed [*sic*] person, so sincere and so alert for her age."[32] Agents, informed by BTHA marketing or by their personal knowledge, pushed potential travellers toward a generic encounter with Britain. London meant Buckingham Palace and the Tower, Scotland meant Edinburgh, and heritage meant Stratford-upon-Avon.

Influencers

Alongside the direct marketing that targeted American visitors to Britain, there were other influencing factors, which made Britain seem more attractive than going to Florida, the West Indies, or France. One of the most emotionally powerful of these was the idea of Britain and the United States sharing the same cultural, literary, and legal heritage.

Although it is incorrect to describe it as marketing, the sustained public discourse from British writers on the shared heritage between Britain and the United States in the first years of the 1950s, as seen in Chapter 2, also encouraged Americans to make the trip across the Atlantic. Anglophile American travel experts took the concept of shared heritage and transferred it without much dilution into guidebooks aimed at the growing number of vacationers who wanted to visit Britain.[33]

In the late-nineteenth century, guidebooks were instrumental in the growth of middle-class tourism, which debased the elite and distinguished world of the Grand Tour visitor into another form of modern consumption. They had and still have a reductive effect on tourists in that their lists of predefined sights to see and things to do drove increasing demand for the same limited experience.[34] Historian Rudy Koshar has identified that early popular guidebooks such as Murray's Handbooks for Travellers and Baedeker Guides focused on "statues and monuments, historical buildings such as Gothic cathedrals and castles and ruins [that] were the prized sites in the tourist's itinerary."[35] This was still true in the 1950s, making it easy for American guidebook writers to adapt the shared heritage ideals for their purposes. Their concentration on heritage and history left little space for any discussion on, for example, the recent destruction caused by the Blitz or the effect of the Second World War on the British character.

For instance, Anna Thayer's early-1950s guidebook, *Invitation to England*, described England's towns, cities, and buildings through the stories of the people who made them famous.[36] Although Thayer's account was romantic and simplistic, it was persuasive for many Americans. Thayer wrote for those readers who had enjoyed the type of English history and literature taught in US schools in the 1930s. For this generation (the trip reports imply that most were women), Thomas Gray and William Shakespeare remained key figures in their intellectual lives. Thayer addressed this idea directly: "I am going to suggest only a few of the outstanding delights of a stay in England and perhaps will jog your memories of things you have read and studied."[37]

Ruth McKenney and Richard Bransten's *Here's England* covered much of the same ground as Thayer, but with a lighter touch. The "blurb" pasted into the inside front cover captured the essence of the book: "[it] is aimed squarely at American tourists – it's replete with history, architecture and practical travel information, but first and foremost it's a book to read for sheer enjoyment. History comes alive in these stories of Thomas Becket, Old Sarum and the Wars of the Roses."[38] McKenney and Bransten offered a different take to Thayer, recognizing that not all American tourists wanted to take their history lesson in a prescribed tablet form.[39] They encouraged independent thinking and snobbily disparaged coach tours – and, in one example, ladies from Indiana who showed off their knowledge of Shakespeare.[40] Their book was aimed at well-intentioned middle-class Americans, smart, but not well-educated in British history and English literature, who wanted to get the most out of their trip across the Atlantic.

These books also offered straightforward guidance on Britain's major tourist sites. The Tower of London was the most prominent attraction, as it combined ease of access in central London with a long and bloody history. Most guidebooks provided visitors with a simplified view of the capital. For example, Thayer saw a visit to the Tower as a must: "one of the most interesting places in London is the Tower of London, a gloomy gray building that antedates our friend William the Conqueror by 1,000 years!"[41] McKenney took a more personal view: "Richard and I fell in love with the Tower one dark, gloomy afternoon in December, and since then we have many times returned, enchanted by this stone memory of the past."[42] This presentation of Britain as the sum of its history and heritage short-changed Americans. A trip to a pub for an evening would have shown them far more.

Tourist marketing positioned heritage and landscape as the key reason why Americans should come to Britain, but there were others. A 1959 American Express survey revealed how American tourists' preferences were much wider than this. The most-often-stated reason was meeting people, followed by: scenery, architecture, museums, and night life.[43] This wish to meet people speaks to the idea that American visitors were looking for more than castles and lochs and wanted to understand more about contemporary Britain.

As has been shown, some women travelled to Britain and continental Europe on their own, and there were at least two guidebooks that specifically targeted independent American women travellers.[44] Fodor's *Woman's Guide to Europe* was an odd mix of essays on the European male, the role of the single American woman abroad, and practical advice on British society and shopping. It featured an article by Olivia Meeker, a recently divorced American journalist, which was so hip that it hurt in its attitude to "modern" dating games, and is in marked contrast to the didactic Stratford-upon-Avon type of guidebook.[45] Émigré Hungarian humorist George Mikes wrote a further article presenting a genial explanation of why Americans were unpopular in Europe in the 1950s and why, despite this, it was worth persevering with European menfolk.[46] Throughout, the guide assumes its readers were stylish and wealthy, and travelled regularly to Britain.

Popular writer Edith Patterson Meyer's 1957 take on the topic, *Go It Alone, Lady!*, was far less "knowing" than Meeker's and far more practical than Fodor's guide. The sixty-one-year-old Meyer adopted a breezy can-do attitude throughout, and proclaimed, "London is said to be a man's town, but don't you believe it!"[47] She explained how to manage all the little details of travelling to Europe and gave illustrations of what to expect. Meyer thought that Britain should be the first stop of any European vacation because of the strong understanding forged between it and the United

States during the Second World War.[48] Her advice for the tyro female tourist travelling alone was generally good, but it understated the level of resentment felt in Britain toward the United States in the year after the Suez crisis.

Meyer recommended that the single woman travelling on vacation in Britain should get in touch with the American Woman's Club of London or the International Federation of University Women to meet like-minded women in London. This indicated that the type of women she was addressing were likely to be college graduates. She advocated going to the theatre and concerts alone, "knowing that you'll see plenty of 'single' women there."[49] Meyer approved of the London Underground, and explained that it was efficient and, most importantly, that it was safe to walk a block or two from it back to one's hotel, as long as, Cinderella style, it was before midnight.[50] The trip reports compiled by single American women on vacation in Britain, which describe the unwanted attention they received from British men, suggest that her advice did not always hit the nail on the head (see Chapter 9). Much of the rest of the section of her book on vacationing in London explored the possibilities of shopping in the capital.

Guidebooks to Britain in the 1950s fall into two types and periods. In the early 1950s, the shared-heritage approach prevailed. Enthusiasm for the coronation ensured that 1953 marked the height of this type of tourism. After this point, the emphasis of most American guidebooks to Britain changed to a more modern and consumerist tone. They now portrayed Britain, and particularly London, as a cultured city that provided famous buildings and history, but also shopping, theatre, and night life. Shared-heritage tourism had begun to look passé, just at the point when Britain was throwing off austerity and rationing and starting to become fashionable.[51]

In the popular imagination, the mid-1960s was the time when England became "swinging," a period in which Americans began to think that Britain and London were "cool."[52] Historian Frank Mort has argued that this way of viewing Britain in the 1960s had its origins in the previous decade.[53] Some of the earlier view of London as a fashionable destination was due to the influence of popular music on American audiences. In 1954, Frank Sinatra recorded the evocative "A Foggy Day in London Town" for his album *Songs for Young Lovers*.[54] Mel Tormé sang it in 1957 on

the nationally televised Nat King Cole Show.[55] That year, Sinatra released
"London by Night," a song on a similar theme, featured on his *Come Fly
with Me* album, the epitome of 1950s sophistication and modernity. It was
a number-one and Grammy-award-winning album, which pictured Sinatra on its cover as a super-worldly traveller at a modern American airport
saying goodbye to his girl.[56] In its lyrics, the song hinted at something other
than tradition and heritage:

> London by night is a wonderful sight
> There is magic abroad in the air
> I'm often told that the streets turn to gold
> When the moon shines on Circus and Square.[57]

The Hollywood version of Britain most familiar to American moviegoers
usually reflected the clichés of heritage and tradition, but occasionally
there were films shown in the United States that portrayed London as a
centre of intrigue and danger. One such, *Night and the City* from 1950,
featured American star Richard Widmark as a small-time hustler trying
to make it big as a wrestling promoter in London.

❖ ❖ ❖

France which was the most popular destination in Europe for American
tourists, received much more consistent and assured publicity than Britain
in the American media. Although Britain had the advantage of a shared
language and, to some extent, culture, it was difficult for London to compete with un-Blitzed Paris, with all its beautiful buildings intact and ready
for visitors. While London emphasized history in its marketing, Americans
thought Paris offered glamour, a far more attractive proposition.[58] Hollywood reinforced this glamour. The earliest and most obvious example of
this was the 1951 movie *An American in Paris*, starring Gene Kelly and Leslie
Caron.[59] This romantically themed musical showed Paris at its best to
audiences all over the United States. Other successful American musicals
featuring France were *Gentlemen Prefer Blondes* and *Gigi*, from 1953 and
1958 respectively.[60] Vincente Minnelli, who was, it would seem, a one-man
European marketing campaign, directed all these movies. Rome, also un-

bombed, was promoted in *Three Coins in the Fountain*, a movie that combined romance and travelogue in a story of American women abroad.[61] Another of Minnelli's pictures, *Brigadoon*, a popular musical from 1954, displayed Scotland in the most romantic of guises: Gene Kelly once again played a visiting American. The movie proposed, among sillier things, that Kelly could, on the spur of the moment, take a TWA Lockheed Constellation over to Scotland to claim his bride. This last idea was realistic by the mid-decade, however, and must have triggered visits to Edinburgh by Americans, resulting in the purchase of much cashmere and tartan.[62]

Some guidebook writers offered information to visiting Americans about the parts of British life (mostly London) that were not half-timbered and steeped in dense and obscure history. One example from the start of the decade was Francis Aldor's *The Good Time Guide to London*.[63] Aldor was a Londoner, an author and publisher of slightly risqué titles. His book was published both in Britain and in the United States, and, although this is not specifically mentioned, was aimed at visiting Americans. Aldor hinted at this early in the book when he described meeting an American in Venice and setting him straight on that city's attractions. More obviously writing for an American readership, he explained that, in London, "your best bet is to take the Underground (English for 'Subway')."[64] Aldor mixed a lot of conventional guidebook material on London's topography and social conventions with some unusual – for the time – observations on night life. He set out the position on prostitution in Britain to both male and female readers. For men, he warned: "Prostitution is sternly discouraged in this country. But please don't make a mistake: The young lady smiling at you after dusk in the deserted streets around Bond Street ... is not the daughter of Lord X or Lady Y." For women: "My dear young lady – don't take your dog out at night on deserted streets."[65] He then described the whys and wherefores of London's semi-legal clubs: "The 'dives' vary a good deal. Some have specialized clientele – artists, coloured folk, poets or crooks. Some play be-bop all night; others prefer poker. A sniff of marijuana. Not all of them places to go with your wife. Whatever happens, you've been warned!"[66]

He also disdainfully explained the lack of sophistication of more conventional nightclubs such as the Allegro, where "at the tables, small and dimly lighted, lords and ladies find themselves next to businessmen from

Bradford with girlfriends from Bow, and tourists from Chicago."[67] The conceit here was that his readers were erudite people he had put in the know, not mere tourists, an idea which allowed the middle-classes to resolve their search for authenticity in their travels.

Many visiting Americans were keen to enjoy London's nightlife. For them, pubs were a tourist attraction suitable for a quick visit rather than a night out. Most pubs, which had local customers and served warm beer, did not try to accommodate tourists. Those Americans who enjoyed a drink despaired at restrictive licensing laws, which meant that refreshment late at night or on Sunday was hard to find. Aldor wrote his explanation of the pub scene for a male readership. He proposed an extended pub crawl in his well-named "Pubography," which took the intrepid male tourist down the Old Kent Road and the Mile End Road before trying some famous pubs, such as The Prospect of Whitby. Aldor suggested that all visitors would be met with a welcome and genuine bonhomie.[68] Wartime and 1950s USAF experiences suggest visitors might have been well advised to keep their voices down.[69]

London's West End theatres, which were at a peak of success in the 1950s, proved very appealing to visitors from the United States, who of course could understand the language and could get seats for transferred American hits, to which they did not have easy access if they did not live in New York.[70] The BTHA noted that praise of Britain's legitimate theatre was also often recorded on visitors' comment cards. Americans were also keen supporters of the Edinburgh Festival and of opera at Glyndebourne and Covent Garden. The Royal Opera House estimated that, in the summer, 10 per cent of their clientele were American.[71]

Some commentators suggested that male visitors were attracted to the racier theatrical attractions offered by Paris, and to a lesser extent London, because these were not available in the more conservative United States. For instance, writer Joseph Wechsberg described a typical male American tourist as carrying "a popular guidebook telling him where to go after 11 p.m. while his wife stays at the hotel."[72] London's Windmill Theatre, which featured tableaux of static nude female performers, was popular with Americans, some of whom had visited it as GIs during the war. They distinguished themselves from the local voyeurs by wolf-whistling and cheering.[73]

The 1959 American Express survey didn't mention it explicitly, but one of the most important pursuits of wealthy Americans in Britain was shopping. This habit reflected domestic priorities, since the United States had taken widespread consumerism to previously undreamt-of levels.[74] It was inevitable that this practice extended to vacations, where souvenirs and gifts for friends acted as conversation pieces and ensured that everybody knew they had come from Europe. The British government certainly hoped so. American visitors did not have to pay stringent purchase taxes on luxury items, and dollars exchanged for sterling to buy British goods were a key contributor to the Exchequer.[75]

Rhona Churchill, writing in the *Daily Mail*, identified the tastes of wealthier Americans. "He seldom buys pictures here [France being the best choice] but he buys leather suitcases to carry his purchases of antiques, china, cashmere and gent's stay-up, without braces or belts, trousers."[76] Antique furniture was also a popular choice,[77] and TWA directed American visitors looking for antiques to the very-early-morning Caledonian Market in Bermondsey for its glass, china, and silver.[78] For big spenders, old English silver was at the top of the list. It had several properties that appealed to American buyers. It was antique, so was a material keepsake of a vacation based around history and heritage. It was a great bargain, as sterling silver in Britain was the same price as silver plate back in the United States. Finally, it provided the purchaser with a cachet that they could not get by buying a new dishwasher or Cadillac. As a result, Americans were the favourite customers of London silversmiths in the 1950s.[79] Violet Sone and her roommate, Gladys, made the almost obligatory trip to Chancery Lane:

We took a double decker bus, then the "Tube" as Londoners call the underground railway. The silver vaults were also underground – room after room full of gleaming silver bowls, pitchers, trays, tea sets. I never knew that there was so much silver in the world! I browsed while Gladys bought. She arranged to have her purchases shipped back to Waco.[80]

In the middle of the decade, the BTHA sponsored a short advertorial for insertion in newspapers. It was aimed at persuading Americans to visit Britain, not for the heritage or landscape, but simply to shop, and pointed out the helpful exemptions from local sales taxes and the incredible bargains to be had because of the favourable exchange rate, which, combined with low wages in Britain, made for very cheap prices. This, together with enthusiastic, courteous sales assistants, was a winning proposition: "The clerks all speak English." For women, the article recommended jewellery and cashmere as great deals. For men, the emphasis was on sports equipment (fishing rods, guns) and formal wear (suits, hats, and shoes).[81] Advertisements for traditional clothing filled Pan American's in-flight magazine, highlighting Scottish products such as tartans, tweeds, and kilts.[82]

Fielding's travel guide devoted a good portion of its contents to shopping; its attitude was that this was one of the key forms of enjoyment for wealthier Americans. That this group was the guide's target market was clear from the hotels it endorsed.[83] Fielding recommended "Liberty silks, leather (super quality, but super expensive), cutlery, silver, shotguns, children's clothes and antique bric-a-brac."[84] These luxury items were much cheaper than in the United States, the guide emphasized, estimating that in hats "A $25 Brooks Bros. job might run to $8 here."[85] It dismissed the Pall Mall Deposit and Forwarding Company, a leading provider of bargain furniture, as being "geared for the tourist trade."[86] In this way, Fielding's proposed that its readers were not mere tourists, but sophisticated, international travellers.

Fodor's guide for women travellers was no less consumerist or unrelenting in its assumption that its readers were from an elite section of American life. It assumed that the primary interest of any wealthy American woman visiting London or Edinburgh was to shop, with sightseeing taking a far lower priority. Although it is a puzzling and distasteful idea for the modern reader, the role of most American women in the 1950s, despite many of them having college degrees, was to provide a beautiful home for their husbands, so Fodor's instincts may well have been correct.[87] Page after page showed how to find the right beauty parlour or hairdresser: "At 27 Basil Street [just behind Harrods], Simon has a sweet salon where Michael will design a becoming coiffure especially for you."[88] Harrods itself got a strong mention, playing on both wealth and the American interest in the Royal Family: "In this enormous and beautifully decorated store, you are quite likely to see the Duchess of Kent doing her shopping accompanied by Princess Alexandra, or an American film star adding to her wardrobe."[89]

Conclusion

Marketing Britain to Americans in the 1950s required a high degree of selectivity to portray it in the best possible light. Even anglophiles might have felt some concern at visiting a country that was on its uppers, with bomb sites, damaged buildings, and widespread rationing very much in evidence. An active network of marketing organizations worked together to project a consistent image of Britain that emphasized its history and natural beauty. The British tourist authorities provided the lead with a well-executed advertising campaign, placing advertorials in American newspapers and providing travel agents with point-of-sale advertising. American and British airlines also wished to present Britain favourably. They were aided and abetted by influencers such as guidebook writers, who explained to their discerning readers how to get the best out of a vacation to Britain. This network used the idea of a shared heritage to attract Americans who wanted to see Shakespeare's birthplace or the churchyard where Thomas Gray wrote his elegy, an interest that school and college had indoctrinated in them. Movies and popular songs that nominated Scotland or London as romantic destinations offered a different influence, even though they were always behind Paris and Rome in this aspect of their appeal.

A key element of the marketing campaign was achieved by rendering Britain's complex geographies and ways of life into simplistic brand names such as "Shakespeare Country" and by emphasizing London and Edinburgh at the expense of industrial cities such as Manchester and Glasgow.[90] Although this practice was reductive and did not show Britain in the round, it was a realistic approach to take with Americans, most of whom were making their first and only trip to Britain and continental Europe. This was especially true in the late 1950s, when the majority of visitors arrived by air and were staying in the country for a shorter period than those who travelled by ocean liner. They wanted Britain's greatest hits – and got them. As the decade progressed, and Britain's infrastructure recovered, its marketing changed in emphasis to promote London and Edinburgh's luxury shops, high-quality cashmeres, antique dealers, and top-class hotels alongside its traditional heritage attractions.

Throughout the decade, Britain signalled to tourists that they should interpret their visits in specific ways. When visiting London, they were experiencing a thousand years of tradition and history, or, later, shopping for gifts in one of the world's most sophisticated capitals. When in Shakespeare's Warwickshire, tourists were seeing a living version of Tudor history and understanding the roots of the literature they were taught in school. The extent to which Americans complied with this direction and understood the relevance of its claims is discussed in Chapter 6.

CHAPTER FIVE

Crossing the Atlantic

For some, crossing the Atlantic to Europe is now a boring preliminary to a vacation. In contrast, for Americans coming to Britain in the 1950s, the Atlantic journey played an important role. If they were travelling by sea, they could experience a glamorous and thrilling five-day journey, packed with great food and activities, and with the possibility of meeting people and making new friends. As a Cunard promotional film put it, "For sailing is a thrill, one of the many things about ocean travel that makes folks say 'getting there is half the fun.'"[1] When travelling by air, particularly in the first half of the decade, Americans were pioneers in experiencing transatlantic flying's dramatic time savings. Rough weather affected both modes of transport, adding an underlying sense of anxiety or excitement to these significant journeys.

The 1950s was the decade when the dominant method of travelling across the Atlantic changed from sea to air, with dramatic consequences for American tourism to Britain. As early as 1949, the British government was already clear on what the future would hold. A briefing note for president of the Board of Trade Harold Wilson observed that crossing the Atlantic by sea presented no problems, as there was plenty of capacity on British and American liners, although more could be done for student visitors. Its position on air travel was prescient: "A reduction in the cost of transport is of first importance so that a trip to this country may become a practical proposition for the large numbers of middle and working-class Americans who have not a long enough holiday to come by sea, nor enough money to come by air at present rates."[2]

Cutting the time of an Atlantic crossing from the fastest scheduled voyage of five days to one of twelve and a half hours was a drastic time/space compression.[3] The tipping point was, for Americans, about 1956 and was driven by changes to prices, journey times, and levels of comfort. *Flight* magazine examined this phenomenon and identified two types of passengers who found crossing by plane particularly attractive: "The businessman making several quick transatlantic journeys per year is one obvious example of this new class of traffic. Another is the wage-earner who can afford the transatlantic fare but whose vacation period is limited to two or three weeks."[4]

In the early 1950s, most Americans crossed the Atlantic by ocean liner. Although flying was much quicker, it was often a bumpy experience. One man, who flew across as a teenager, later recalled, "We went over and back by plane. Old prop jobs that just droned on and on and shook at every little wind."[5] The most popular ships used by trip reporters were the RMS *Queen Elizabeth*, the RMS *Queen Mary*, the SS *America*, and the SS *United States*. Atlantic liners offered three classes of travel: First, Cabin, and Tourist. To travel First Class on a prestige ship such as Cunard's *Queen Elizabeth* was an exclusive, leisured experience. It offered the chance to experience fine dining and impeccable service and to mingle with powerful and prestigious fellow guests.[6] Cabin Class was, despite the lower price, still a very comfortable way to travel. Young people may have enjoyed Tourist Class, but for older visitors, the cramped quarters must surely have made the journey less fun. *Life* magazine celebrated the high point for ocean liners in the summer of 1955. It pictured Manhattan's wharves crammed to capacity with American, British, and French ocean liners waiting to cross the pond. It also noted, but did not understand, the implications of the increasing importance of transatlantic flights.[7] At the end of the decade, it was clear that airlines had won the battle for Atlantic supremacy; by 1958, airplanes carried 64 per cent of Atlantic traffic.[8] Planes became larger and faster, with more tourist seats; flight frequency increased, and prices tumbled. The future for liners lay in luxury cruises, where speed was not the aim and slowness added to the sense of relaxation and calm.[9]

❖ ❖ ❖

The International Air Transport Association (IATA), an airline cartel, controlled the prices of transatlantic flights. Three of its members, TWA, Pan American, and BOAC, flew to and from Britain.[10] They charged identical one-way First-Class fares of $375 in 1950 ($5,000 in 2017 money), rising to $440 by 1956. If passengers required sleeping accommodation, then this

Table 5.1

One-way fare, London–New York, 1955

	By Sea	By Air
First Class	$325	$450
Cabin Class	$220	$400
Tourist Class	$160	$290

Source: *Flight*, 28 October 1955.

fare rose to $490. A round trip for a couple therefore cost $1,960, although it was slightly cheaper in the off-season. This equates to a 2017 value of about $20,000.[11] As transatlantic planes grew in size, IATA's members agreed from 1952 onwards to provide travellers with less-luxurious, smaller, economy seats,[12] although these were still relatively expensive.[13] In late 1955, *Flight* made the comparison shown in Table 5.1.

Cabin Class on a plane provided passengers with a large reclining seat and a foot rest. The extra fifty dollars for First Class offered a bunk bed in a separate part of the plane. Tourist Class seats were very expensive in comparison to today's low-cost flights. Instalment credit plans made the cost more manageable – "only $52 down, if you use Pan Am's original 'Pay-Later' plan."[14] Payments were 10 per cent up front, with the balance plus interest spread over twenty months.[15]

Airline advertising in *Holiday*, the up-market American travel monthly, reinforced the modernity of flying. Shipping lines responded defensively and had, clearly, recognized that their passengers were mostly older and staider than those who now travelled by plane. A 1956 full-page colour advertisement in *Holiday* described the ss *United States* and ss *America* ships as offering "time for rest … space for action … speed that spirits you to Europe in 5 fast days."[16] The advertisement featured pictures of distinguished passengers, such as Mr Ward Canaday, former chairman of a transport company, who was seventy-one, and Mr Sinclair Weeks, secretary of commerce in the Eisenhower administration, who was sixty-two. These elderly and well-known figures emphasized the solidity and respectability of this company's ships.[17] At the bottom of the market, older and slower liners used very low prices to attract passengers.[18]

In contrast, Pan American advertised their air service to Paris by featuring glamorous and relatively youthful Broadway star Mary Martin. The advertisement reassured potential Tourist-Class passengers that the thrifty "Rainbow" service across the Atlantic had the "same experienced crews as on First-Class President flights."[19] By 1956, 75 per cent of seats on Pan American were for tourists. Flying was even more appealing for those who lived far from New York, as direct flights across the Atlantic were now possible from as far afield as Chicago and Detroit.[20] Toward the end of the decade, the domination of air travel was complete.[21]

There was a distinct seasonality to American tourism to Britain. The four months from May to August accounted for 54 per cent of all departures, with June being the busiest month of all.[22] It was completely understandable that American vacationers (who were most likely to visit rainy London and Paris) were interested in travelling during the northern-European summer, providing, as it did, longer, warmer outdoor days and smoother crossings by air and sea. This concentration of visitors presented a problem for the British hotel industry, which, at the start of the 1950s, faced a shortage of beds, since many hotels had been taken over for government use during the war, and had not yet been returned to their owners.[23] It also placed Britain's transport infrastructure under strain.[24] One early proposal from a visiting American official was that Britain should try to attract the twenty-seven million people living on American farms, who preferred to take their vacation outside the summer months.[25] Airlines and shipping companies offered discounts for travelling in the off-season. In 1952, Canadian Pacific, for example, advertised its First-Class cabins for a fall sea crossing via Montreal or Quebec in the *Los Angeles Times* for as little as $230. The copy dealt awkwardly with the difficulties of a late crossing of the Atlantic by stressing that the first thousand miles at least were close to shore. Adjacent to this advertisement were several others for sailings to Hawaii, which must have been an attractive prospect for Angelinos.[26]

The BTHA and its predecessor, the British Travel Association (BTA), were, of course, keen to increase the number of high-spending American travellers. In late 1949, John G. Bridges, the director-general of the BTA, visited California to build a campaign to encourage those who had the money to come to Europe but, because of the American practice of limiting vacation days, had only two to three weeks for their trip. Bridges, with some foresight, pointed out that it was now possible to fly from Los

Angeles to London in two days, making short European vacations for the salaried possible for the first time.[27] By the following year, Britain's long-distance flag-carrier BOAC specifically advertised to those Americans who had only fourteen days to spare for their visit.[28] In 1952, traveller and author Lowell Thomas estimated that thirty million middle-income Americans now had access to vacations with pay and could afford a trip to Europe.[29] By 1956, the overwhelming majority of workers who were paid hourly (the group least likely to receive benefits) were getting more than two weeks' vacation allowance.[30] As we have seen, journeys across the Atlantic taken by ship required five days each way, plus the time needed to get to New York. This method of travel required a vacation of at least four weeks, and was, therefore, largely confined to those who had no restrictions on their time – retirees, the very wealthy, those with no occupation, or those who, because of their professional status, could negotiate a longer vacation. For students, these rules did not apply. Denis Johnston, writing in the *Listener*, considered that:

> These young people, who in some respects are the most important of our summer visitors, are the reverse of the conception of the American tourist. To begin with they are not rich. They come over at the equivalent cost of about £20 each way ... They do all sorts of chores around the ship to earn a little extra cash. And a large proportion of them work for the rest of the vacation.[31]

Some of these students took their voyage very seriously and while on board attended lectures on British politics and economics to prepare them for what seemed to be earnest vacations of discussions on the United Nations and meetings with members of the Fabian Society.[32]

Flying Early in the Decade

In the first half of the decade most travellers to Britain came from the northeastern United States, and would have to journey to Idlewild Airport in New York City to catch a flight. If you were, for example, travelling from Pennsylvania, you might catch a train to Manhattan. From Penn Station, a taxi or bus ride took you to the East Side Airlines Terminal, where you could get an airline bus to the airport. This allowed travellers to check in their baggage (a maximum of sixty-six pounds for First-Class passengers) at the large, functional building on the corner of 37th Street and 1st Avenue, which had fast access to the Queens midtown tunnel. This was a sensible choice, as the plane wouldn't leave Idlewild until the bus had arrived.[33]

At the airport, well-wishers accompanied passengers right up to the departure gate to say farewell, a practice that was commonplace for ocean voyages and a reflection on how relatively unusual flying was in the early 1950s. This was followed by a walk down some narrow corridors and across the concrete apron to the airplane. Passengers could ensure that they were on the right plane by checking a small sign on the steps up to the aircraft. For some, contemplating flying across the Atlantic for the first time, or, perhaps, flying for the first time, would occasion some nervousness. As Edith Patterson Meyer put it, "as you climb the steps they shake a little under you. Is it the steps, you wonder, or you?" Meyer also described the thrill of the takeoff for those who had not flown before: "Now the great plane moves ... there's a wait ... with the motors alternately speeding and idling. When you think you can stand the suspense no longer you feel a great surge of power and the plane races down the runway."[34]

If you flew with TWA, which was a popular choice, you may well have travelled in a Boeing 377 Stratocruiser. It was a four-engined plane, 110 feet long with room for sixty First-Class passengers. It had a flight ceiling of thirty-three thousand feet with a pressurized cabin and usually flew at about three hundred miles an hour (about half the speed of today's planes).[35] Leaving Idlewild at 4 p.m., TWA's London service arrived at London Airport the following day at 9:30 in the morning. Because of limited flying ranges, planes stopped to refuel once on the journey across the ocean. Popular spots for this were Gander in Newfoundland, Keflavik in Iceland, Shannon in Ireland, or Prestwick in Scotland. The Stratocruiser was a bulbous-looking plane with two decks. Its main cabin was on top, with sixteen rows of seats in a two-by-two configuration. A lower level featured private bunk beds and a "beverage" lounge (see Figure 5.1). Businessman Edward G. Wilson, a trip reporter who travelled in 1954 on a Pan American flight, paid extra for his downstairs sleeping berth.[36]

Ruth Lois Matthews, a forty-two-year-old single woman, provided a full account of her flight from Idlewild to London in 1953. Her seat was at the back of the plane, which, before the advent of jet engines, was the quietest

Figure 5.1 Boeing Stratocruiser, beverage lounge.

place to sit. After a stewardess had taken her coat and hung it up. Matthews removed her hat and jacket and put them in the overhead rack. She wore a comfortable old skirt and had a light wool sweater to slip on if she got cold. Every passenger had a reclining seat and a large, soft pillow. The four powerful engines roared, and the plane gradually rose into the sky, presenting a great view of the Manhattan skyline in the late afternoon. Matthews ignored the stewardess's explanation of how to use a lifebelt, although the other passengers looked under their seat to make sure that they knew where it was. The Boeing airplane reached cruising altitude and the pilot turned off the seat-belt signs. Matthews removed her shoes, adjusted her chair, and lit a cigarette. About an hour or so into the flight, dinner was served: steak, vegetables, bread, milk, and a light dessert. Matthews noted, "I ate heartily. My thoughts were gayer now, my spirits higher."[37]

The steward announced that, because of bad weather at Gander airport, they would land at Sydney in Nova Scotia instead. The plane touched down at this isolated spot, and everyone had thirty minutes to disembark, get some refreshments, and go to the bathroom, while the plane refuelled. Off they sped again, now no longer hugging the coastline, but over the dark Atlantic. Matthews spent the time talking, while the passenger in the next seat took many photographs of the moon, hoping that they would come out. The captain, who had left his cockpit to his first officer and engineer, came down the aisle to chat to the passengers. Following some sleep and chat, Matthews used the restroom at the front of the plane. After a bump-free flight, Ireland, then Wales and England, came into view and the descent into London Airport began.[38]

As has been shown in Chapter 4, not everyone started their journeys from the East Coast. In the latter part of the decade, foreign correspondent and author Willard Price, a Californian, wanted to go to Britain. He had two choices: he could either fly domestically to New York and pick up a transatlantic flight from there, or he could take the polar route. Scandinavian Airlines (SAS) operated this service, which flew from Los Angeles to Winnipeg, where it refuelled, and then crossed over Hudson Bay, Baffin Island, Greenland, and Iceland to Denmark. A short connecting flight then dropped passengers in London or Paris. This route was a thousand miles shorter than travelling via New York, but in the pre-jet age still took twenty-four hours.[39] Susie Butler, a student from Arizona, studying at Brigham Young University in Provo, Utah, had planned a low-cost trip to Europe, crossing the Atlantic on one of the less-expensive liners that specialized in student travellers. To get to New York to join her ship, Susie took TWA's low-priced "Sky Coach" stopping service, which flew from Phoenix, calling at Albuquerque, Wichita, Kansas City, Chicago, Pittsburgh, Philadelphia, and finally New York. This must have been simultaneously an exciting and a very tiring prelude to a first trip overseas.[40]

Flying at the End of the Decade

The development of faster planes during the 1950s shortened journey times across the Atlantic. In 1957, the fastest Pan American flight left New York International Airport at Idlewild for London at 4 p.m. and arrived, non-stop, at 8 a.m. the next morning, a total of eleven hours in flight.[41] Leona Running, with her party of Seventh-Day Adventists, flew on just such a flight, travelling in a BOAC DC-7C, one of the last piston-engined planes. The following year, the introduction of a jet airliner service using

Boeing 707s completely transformed flying over the Atlantic. The new Pan American service in November 1958 offered a flight leaving New York at ten in the morning, which arrived in London at just before half-past nine at night, a journey time of just under six and a half hours.[42] This speedy travel, encouraged wealthy travellers to make repeated fast, short trips, and they became known as the "jet set." At the end of the 1950s, editor and publisher Fleur Cowles, the wife of a British millionaire, noted that "it sounds awfully dashing, but I used to fly over from America just for the weekend."[43] This dramatic reduction in travel time over the course of one decade signalled the era of modern travel that is so familiar today. Six and a half hours is still, since the demise of Concorde, a short time for today's travellers.

Pan American had a product that sold itself. The speed of travel was breathtaking, and the contrast with the previous generation of piston-engined planes was equally dramatic. Along with increased speed came higher cruising altitudes, much quieter engines, and far less vibration. The journey became much more relaxing. Little imagination is required to visualize this experience of flight in the late 1950s, because it was so similar to flying today. Moving through the airport was rather different, with little automation, paper tickets, few security checks, and visitors able to wave travellers off at the boarding gates. Idlewild (by then New York International Airport) had failed to respond to the massive rise in air passengers, and by 1957 its terminals were too small and out of date. It constructed a huge, new modern arrivals building and asked individual airlines to build their own departure terminals.[44] Pan American was one such airline and, as the decade drew to a close, it drew up plans for a new "Worldport" terminal building. Its promotional film *Jet Terminal* contrasted the previous scruffy and difficult experience of checking in to a flight, with the queues and long corridors, with a modernistic view of flight from a terminal full of light, space, and automation.[45]

Arriving in Britain

Flights from New York arrived at London Airport at Heathrow. At the start of the decade, this was little more than a collection of tents and sheds, reflecting the shortage of money, men, and materials required to build a proper airport. Passengers, weary from a long, noisy, and often-bumpy flight, must have stood blinking and disappointed as they queued to get their luggage through customs in one of the larger tents. After they cleared the formalities, buses and taxis whisked them off to the centre of town.[46]

Within five years, the situation had improved considerably, with the opening of a new terminal building at the airport. It offered a modern, efficient service, with escalators conveying people from their planes to meet their luggage, which was brought to them on conveyor belts. Arriving passengers could use a smart, bright restaurant overlooking the runways. In all, it was an experience that promised well for a vacation in Britain.[47] Ethel Moller Arwe, described it in her trip report, while sitting in the departure lounge waiting for a flight to Brussels. "The air terminal is strikingly modernistic. I sit on a bench and take a color picture of it without a flash – the light pouring in from the glass ceiling between the beams makes a lovely exposure."[48]

On the Big Liner

The most popular choice of trip reporters for the transatlantic route from New York was Cunard's RMS *Queen Elizabeth*, a vessel with a British sensibility.[49] Even cynical Lois Glick, an organizer with the American charity International Medical Relief, thought it "a beautiful ship, the appointments are lovely and modern. It reminds one however of a cosmopolitan hotel, with the mixtures of people coming into the United States, and of its tremendous size."[50] A Cunard promotional movie from the early 1950s demonstrated the level of luxury and the wide variety of facilities available on this ship. It is not clear how and where potential visitors might have seen this film (perhaps at Civic Club meetings or the like), but it was impressive in its demonstration of the size and sophistication of this famous ship. It showed that all three classes of passengers had access to libraries and exercise decks. First and Cabin Class customers had a wide selection of restaurants, food, and entertainment. The liner emphasized its Britishness with shops that sold English woollens, Scottish cashmeres, and Savile Row ties. In this way, Cunard promoted the sense that the voyage extended a British vacation from the moment the ship left its pier in Manhattan.[51]

Larry Mersfelder travelled with the competition:

We sailed from New York, on April 25, 1956 on the ss *United States* and returned on her sister ship the *America*. Both are wonderful ships and have every luxury and convenience one might desire, including several lovely dining rooms, movie theaters, swimming pools, a barber shop, a beauty parlor, and other things too numerous to mention … It is in reality a floating city, yet, it is the fastest ship afloat.[52]

In 1952, the ss *United States* had the prestige of winning the Blue Riband for the speediest transatlantic run.[53]

Early in the decade, other much-cheaper options were available to those who could not afford the Tourist Class fares on the grand liners, such as Canadian Pacific's service from Montreal and Quebec, which advertised its service with "see more – spend less – to Europe, White Empress style."[54] Cunard provided an alternative of their own, the RMS *Franconia*, an ancient and slow ship, which carried as many as eighteen hundred passengers from Quebec to Greenock and Liverpool at a steady sixteen knots, about half the speed of a major liner.[55] Carol Hummel chose this inexpensive vessel to begin her hitchhiking tour of Britain.[56]

Departure

Cunard made much play in their promotional film for the *Queen Elizabeth* on how accessible the ship was to travellers and well-wishers alike. Based near West 50th Street in midtown Manhattan, its pier was an easy taxi ride from Penn and Grand Central railway stations. When passengers boarded the ship, it offered open house to visitors seeing off their friends, a great opportunity for those making the voyage to show off. Modest and friendly Juanita Stott was not that way inclined, but the departure of the huge vessel made a strong impression on her (see Figure 5.2):

People were swarming all over the boat – friends of those sailing, and others who just wanted to see the big liner. We were free to go anywhere – even up in the First-Class section! – until sailing time … After we had waved goodbye, until those on the pier were mere dots, we went down to our cabin again to find several letters and telegrams from friends who had remembered us on this great occasion.[57]

Figure 5.2 *Queen Elizabeth* docking in New York.

Student Susie Butler travelled on a modern, new liner, the ss *Constitution*, which was less than two years old in 1953.[58] "We were going Tourist Class, so we got the room assigned to us and put our suitcases in the room and then we all walked on deck. [My friends] stayed and walked around and took pictures until about fifteen minutes before the signal was given for everyone to get off the ship except the passengers."[59]

Leaving New York by ocean liner was a memorable experience for those who were lucky enough to have enjoyed it. A huge, majestic liner slowly moving down the Hudson River to the open sea presented a remarkable spectacle. The sight of the Statue of Liberty, just a few minutes from departure, added some poignancy for patriotic Americans, many of whom were leaving their country for the first time. Another student, Julia Burrell, gathered with her friends: "We went out on to the Sun Deck and watched the New York skyline fade in the distance as the ship moved slowly but steadily into the Atlantic."[60] Susie Butler "waved and waved until the ship pulled out of sight. When I went back to the room ... there were three great beautiful bouquets of flowers ... one from the Nobility Club from Phoenix."[61] Carol Hummel recalled the departure with some literary flourishes: "We sailed a little after 10:30 a.m., excited little tug boats hanging onto our apron strings until we got past all the skyscrapers, piers and their variety of firms – a real international meeting ground, and of course the majestic Statue of Liberty. By noon there was only water. America was over the hill."[62]

The gift of flowers for Susie Butler indicated the significance of such a vacation in the early years of the 1950s, an unusual trip of a lifetime for such a young person. The distinction between those who travelled and those who stayed behind was quite distinct at this time. Those left behind waved from the wharves and sent telegrams and presents for the lucky privileged few who could travel to Europe. America disappeared, and a new person emerged, one who had *been* to Europe, knowledgeable and cultured compared to the parochial stay-at-homes. It is noticeable from the trip reports, particularly of those who sailed, that they often found the sea voyage more exciting and fulfilling than the vacation itself.

En Voyage

Cunard and its rivals made it clear that, once the Statue of Liberty had disappeared over the horizon, the primary objective for its passengers was enjoying themselves, by relaxing, exercising, watching movies or shows, playing games, and above all, eating and drinking. Of course, the variety of things to do was much greater for First- and Cabin-Class passengers. On the *Queen Elizabeth*, these two classes of passenger could visit the ship's cinema; Third-Class passengers had to rely on a good book from their own library.

John Wilson Lyon, recalling his trip to Europe sixty-four years after the event, was a little disappointed with the accommodation. "We went over on the *Queen Elizabeth*, unfortunately Second Class, Dad always wished we had gone First Class. The circumstances of the Rhodes scholars varied. My sister and I shared a room on the *Queen Elizabeth*, it was a small room with bunk beds."[63] Some class transgression was possible. Carol Hummel noted that the liner permitted young people a little flexibility in moving around the ship. "Yesterday was the greatest! Stayed up late Saturday for a singing and tale-telling show by the male crew, including our waiter ... We were allowed to go to the First-Class side. Found other kids and had fun with the upper crust ... Stewards say that First-Class passengers are not as friendly as Second Class and buy their way into superficial happiness."[64]

Julia Burrell, travelling on the *Queen Elizabeth*, appreciated the standard of food and entertainment: "Three regular meals were served each day plus tea in the morning and again in the afternoon. At lunch and dinner, we had from nine to eleven pieces of silver at our plate, while at breakfast we had only seven ... My first real treat came when I was carried on a tour of the ship ... There were two swimming pools, a theater, a library and many other things too numerous to mention."[65] Journalist Mary Branham, who also travelled on the *Queen Elizabeth*, had an eye for detail, noting in her self-published account of her trip what she had for lunch: "Braised Chump Chop Champvallon, which consisted of several thin slices of potato, a slice of tomato, and a slice of onion, all baked on top of a mutton chop, with spinach and jacket potatoes."[66]

Although watching movies and reading books provided some passive enjoyment, the ship's entertainment staff expected and encouraged passengers to make some of the fun themselves. Juanita Stott recorded that "after dinner, we played bingo in the lounge. Our Cabin Class lounge was very crowded every night. 'Horse Racing' was a favorite game of many of the people. Saw Alastair Sim in the English movie *An Inspector Calls* in the morning. That night there was a 'Balloon Dance' in the Main Lounge."[67] Cunard's promotional movie made much of the "horse racing," which involved passengers betting on toy horses racing on a track, their progress determined by throws of a die.

Passengers also expected to join in; they were, perhaps, much less insular than today's middle classes. Stott, despite being a devout Methodist, was happy to take part in the fun, aided and abetted by "Tony, our cabin steward, [who] helped me with my 'jeweled turban' for the fancy dress parade. I put all my earbobs, necklaces, ornamental pins etc. plus some red roses on a towel and made a turban of it."[68] Mary Branham was definitely up for some fun: "Last evening, we dressed specially for dinner. Each person was given a party hat and a mask. The men wore false noses. Later one could play bingo in the lounge, with prizes ranging from 15 to 35 dollars a game ... just got back from the promenade deck from another laughing hour with our table companions of the dining room ... we are the jolliest crowd."[69]

The liners' orchestras provided the opportunity to listen to live music and to dance, both of which were important preoccupations in the 1950s. Youthful Susie Butler, the Mormon from Brigham Young University, received her introduction into the adult world on board ship. "About 3 o'clock we went into the lounge to a cocktail party that was being given for the passengers. It was the first one I had ever been to. There was a good orchestra and it was interesting. I drank ginger ale."[70] Hummel was worldlier and understood what the liner's orchestra members were up to between performances. She was happy to cross over class barriers and dance with the staff: "We had a time dancing, trying to keep from tumbling over when the boat swayed. Our fine little English orchestra played with the usual frequent rests. Fortunately, it was still sober after the last 'rest.' At 1.30 we cut up in the crews' lounge with a 'tin pan' piano."[71]

In the 1950s, the United States was conventional and constrained, and, in different ways, so was Britain. Travelling by airplane was becoming increasingly conventional and was extremely constrained, most passengers confined to their seats for the duration of their flight (the lucky few could go to a downstairs bar). Crossing the Atlantic on an ocean liner had its class segregation, but, putting that to one side, the ship's entertainment staff encouraged passengers to behave recklessly and enjoy a carnivalesque atmosphere distanced from the confines of normal time and space. Passengers could make short-term relationships, dance, gamble, and drink in ways that inverted what would have been permissible in their regular lives. It is intriguing that in one of the hit movies of the decade, *An Affair to Remember*, a transatlantic liner is the setting for an unconventional romantic liaison.[72]

For those who didn't want to let their hair down, gentler pursuits were available. Academic editor Carolyn Bartel Lyon recalled in her diary that she "had an early morning appointment with the ship's hairdresser. Saw the immigration officer and had picture taken at dinner. [We] went to a Church of England service in the main lounge, which was conducted by the ship's captain. I watched Danny Kaye in *Hans Christian Andersen* [at the cinema] then had cocktails. Salon dinner was delicious, went up on deck after dinner."[73]

For younger and first-time travellers, the excitement of being at sea could be overwhelming. Many trip reporters noted in their accounts the thrill of seeing a nearby liner speeding in the opposite direction. Carol Hummel, looking out at the dark sea at night, spotted a ship. "Suddenly I noticed a ship passing by and went to the window to watch it. The mass of tiny piercing lights was so pretty. Soon everyone in the room and on deck were scurrying to see it – what excitement!"[74]

Bad Weather

Crossing the Atlantic by ship in the 1950s was relatively safe and, prior to the arrival of jet planes, usually more comfortable than flying. Mary Branham experienced some discomfort and apprehension travelling in a thick fog on the *Queen Elizabeth*: "when the evening fog increased, a real pea-soup fog, we knew we were on our way to England. During the whole night the foghorn sounded every few minutes. There was a feeling of apprehension – remembering the recent tragedy of ... the luxury liner *Andrea Doria*."[75] Branham was referring to a 1956 collision between an Italian liner and a Swedish cargo ship, in which the liner had sunk. It was unable to launch its lifeboats, because it was listing so much. Luckily, it was just off the coast of Massachusetts, so helicopters could rescue all the passengers. If it had been further out to sea, then this accident would have been better known today.[76] Julia Burrell noted that her ship took safety procedures very seriously:

> At three thirty o'clock in the afternoon a gong sounded, and each person went to his or her room. This was an emergency drill and it was very impressive. Stewards were stationed along the corridors and doorways to direct people to their boat station. Each person put on a life jacket. A steward checked it to see if it was securely tied and then the person hurried on to the assigned boat station to wait quietly until the captain inspected the group.[77]

Even when there was little danger, sea sickness was always a possibility; the North Atlantic was capable of unpleasant swells at any time of year. Shipping lines attracted cautious passengers by advertising that they used sheltered routes via the Azores or the St Lawrence Seaway. Juanita Stott recorded that even a massive ship like the *Queen Elizabeth* could provoke sea sickness: "After tea in the lounge I got a shower, forgetting that just before this the ropes had been put up because the liner was rocking in the rough weather. Good trick if you can get by without a fall – taking a shower in a tub while the boat rocks."[78] On smaller ships such as the ss *Constitution*, it could be far worse. Susie Butler reported that "today was Sunday … the sea became rough and it was raining – nearly everyone on the ship was sick. It was rather comical to see everyone running for a place to relieve themselves."[79] Carolyn Bartel Lyon recorded a bad night on the *Queen Mary* in September 1953. She wrote in her diary, "A very rough day. Many passengers were sick, including the four of us. John [her son] made the best sailor."[80]

Arrival in Britain

Although not all transatlantic liners arrived in Southampton (Glasgow and Liverpool were alternatives), it was the leading seaport for visiting Americans because of its quick transfers by rail to London. In 1950, the opening of the new, thirteen-hundred-foot ocean terminal at Southampton provided a much-improved experience for Cunard's clients.[81] Pathé's newsreel commentator reported that "Southampton's new terminal is worthy of the liners who call so regularly."[82] The luxuries of First- and Cabin-Class travel on board were replicated somewhat, with much wooden panelling and leather seats in evidence. Boat trains were ready for departure directly alongside the terminal, carrying passengers to Waterloo station in about an hour. The large-scale investment for this building did not reflect any forward thinking about the future dominance of air travel. The less fortunate travelling on other liners had to use older, shabbier customs sheds. Lord Lucas, speaking in the House of Lords, thought they looked "more like the back door to a fifth-rate down and out country."[83] Before getting on their trains, passengers had to move through the Customs House, where officers inspected their baggage for illegal items. These detailed examinations contrast with the rather cursory checks made today and required an extra hour or so of waiting around, just when visitors wanted to get on with their vacations.[84]

Conclusion

The trip reports show that many visitors found crossing the Atlantic much more interesting and memorable than their vacation in Britain. The crossing was an event in itself. In the first half of the decade, travelling by ocean liner provided a five-day transformation for its novice passengers. They arrived at the dockside, accompanied by their friends, naive and unworldly. By walking up the gangplank and entering their cabins, they were sea-changed forever. Waiting for them were flower arrangements and telegrams from well-wishers, signifying the importance of the day. The ship's sirens indicated that all non-passengers must leave for shore. Now, separated from their friends, they hung over the ship's rail and waved like members of a royal family at their earthbound subjects. On board, with little to see but sky and sea, there was no alternative but to relax, socialize, and eat and drink their way across the Atlantic. The voyage provided an opportunity for unconventional behaviour and for meeting new people, who were, mostly, never to be seen again.

In the second half of the decade, the big liners became increasingly dependent for their business on older, more conservative passengers. Such was the rate of change that, within a few years, the liners' time was up, and they were relegated to cruising to the Caribbean. From about 1956, air was the thing, projecting a rapid and breathless modernity, endorsed by Frank Sinatra and other opinion formers. For fashionable Americans, taking the *Queen Elizabeth* was now passé. Progress in flight was amazingly rapid during the decade, halving the time required to cross the ocean. Not only did airplanes get much faster; they grew bigger and flew higher, making the journey more comfortable and less frightening.

CHAPTER SIX

Destinations and Travelling in Britain

Visitors to Britain in the 1950s could choose from a variety of modes of travel, most of which were difficult or unpleasant. It is probable that most Americans were members of the much-criticized touring coach parties that plied the country. These people were, by definition, tourists, but that did not necessarily mean, as some thought, that they were gullible, ignorant, and only interested in cathedrals so that they could tell their less-well-travelled neighbours about them. Coach tours provided guidance, security, and camaraderie in a strange and hard-to-navigate country. They took fixed and predictable routes that ensured American visitors got to see all Britain's greatest hits, their guidebooks reassuring them that they were in the right places. On a visit to a Cotswold village, a bored tour guide could, despite the television antennas in the thatched cottage roofs, encourage a coach party of Americans to interpret what they saw as timeless old England, a land of tradition. By visiting the Tower of London, a tourist did not just take a good look at an ancient building, her guidebook persuaded her to connect it with a history that was a fundamental part of her high-school education (see Figure 6.1).

It would be easy to think that discerning independent travellers witnessed a more "authentic" version of the country, but the reality was more complicated. Whether they went by rail, car, or bicycle, they still usually stayed in one of Britain's unremarkable and highly conventional provincial hotels, with their heaters on electricity meters and disappointing food. They could go beyond the guidebooks' strictures, see obscure sights, but still had most of their conversations with waitresses and porters.

Figure 6.1 Photographing a guardsman at the Tower of London.

Coach Tours

Tourists in large groups have always attracted disdain and derision from
their social superiors. As sociologist Graham Dann notes, they have been
described (inter alia) as flocks, herds, lemmings, insects, and invaders.[1]
The first three terms imply a brainless and foolish group that moves together, suppressing individual thoughts and actions. "Insect" suggests a
repulsive lower form of life, while "invader" proposes something more
dangerous and othered. In the nineteenth century, tourists on trains were
bad enough, but railway lines provided, at least, some sort of control on
tourist destinations. In contrast, the arrival in the early-twentieth century
of the motor coach enabled tourists to penetrate into the countryside far
from the railway station.[2] As a result, Britain's intellectuals and establishment figures attempted to control tourist behaviour through the imposi-
tion of moral geographies, proposing that only those who knew how to
properly comport themselves at a cathedral or on a country walk should

be allowed to visit.[3] British elite commentators were rude about both British and American tour parties. Joining in, American guidebook writer Clara E. Laughlin found her compatriots' behaviour in Stratford-upon-Avon dismaying, but noted that the locals' bad manners made it even worse: "it is the English factory hands out for a bus-ride and a cheerful (beer-full) holiday [that were repellent]."[4]

Most visitors to Britain travelled in groups and were transported from attraction to attraction by bus. For the older, timid, and less-well-off tourist, coach tours provided a degree of reassurance that reduced the anxiety of being in a foreign country – even though they did know the language. Coach tours assured that you wouldn't be cheated by taxi drivers, get lost, overtip waiters, miss your connection, or stay in a bad hotel. Larry Mersfelder, in his seventies, toured with a party of Civic Club of America members from all over the United States, and was typical of the elderly, more cautious, tourist. He praised his tour:

> Our director, who remained with us throughout the entire tour, was really wonderful. He bought all the tickets, made all reservations, paid all bills, including tips, arranged for special and unscheduled side trips, attended to our luggage, spearheaded for us in customs houses, served as interpreter and trouble-shooter, and smiled all the while ... what more could you ask of one man?[5]

Prompted by their guidebooks or corralled by their guides, coach-tour visitors took similar paths across Britain, seeing the same places and drawing similar conclusions. Travel agents often sold these tours as part of all-inclusive vacations that included the crossing by sea or air, accommodation, and transport in Britain. These tours rushed visitors from one city to the next and from country to country. For example, in 1952, the Southern California Tourist Bureau offered an air vacation, with visits to eleven European countries in forty-eight days.[6] McKenney and Bransten were dismissive of coach tours, recording a visit they made to York when: "A Guided Tour, forty-four strong, came sweeping in. A lady, dusty, dreary, drooping, overflowed in my direction, and enquired in a shaken Indiana accent, 'Pardon me, but I didn't catch the name when we got out of the bus. Is this Fountains Abbey or Durham?'"[7] This story may well be the product of a condescending imagination. A fat lady from Indiana seems an overdrawn example, indicating a distinction between the authors (knowledgeable East-Coast Anglophiles who travelled independently by car) and ignorant parvenus from the Midwest who could only go where they were told.

In 1958, the *Times* reflected on this phenomenon on a visit to "Shakespeare Country," where its special correspondent joined a coach party of Americans. They cruised past towns and villages, with a guide explaining every sight. The reporter crudely complained that "we were asked to show about as much initiative as in a mental home."[8] On arrival in Stratford-upon-Avon, they encountered three other coachloads of Americans, who all arrived at Anne Hathaway's cottage at the same time; they then moved to an equally crowded Warwick Castle. This account contained the usual snobbery about passive and disengaged American tourists. However, it at least had a sympathetic explanation, which was that the type of Americans now visiting Britain were no longer the "wealthy on the grand tour." In fact, they were mostly folk who were eager to see as much as possible on their only trip to Europe.[9] The following year, Robert Duffus, reporting for the *New York Times*, pleaded for a different form of tourism. He wished to reduce the ignorance of some visiting Americans by helping them understand more about Europe's present, which was a good idea, but unlikely to have been taken up by travel companies.[10] The trip reports consistently included visits to the same tourist sites. It is interesting to note that present-day tours for Americans have very similar itineraries to those from sixty years earlier. A composite coach-tour exploration of Britain distilled from the routes found in the trip reports is shown in Figure 6.2.[11]

Shakespeare Country

Stratford-upon-Avon was one of the most-visited provincial towns. Writer and traveller Willard Price thought that "all tourists who get outside London make a bee-line for Stratford-upon-Avon."[12] *Holiday*'s contributor J. Frank Dobie estimated that 75 per cent of all American visitors went to Stratford.[13] The purpose of "Shakespeare Country" was to associate a quiet part of the west Midlands with key historical events and personalities, tapping into the idea many educated Americans had of what it was to be cultured.[14] By the 1950s, Stratford-upon-Avon had been long established

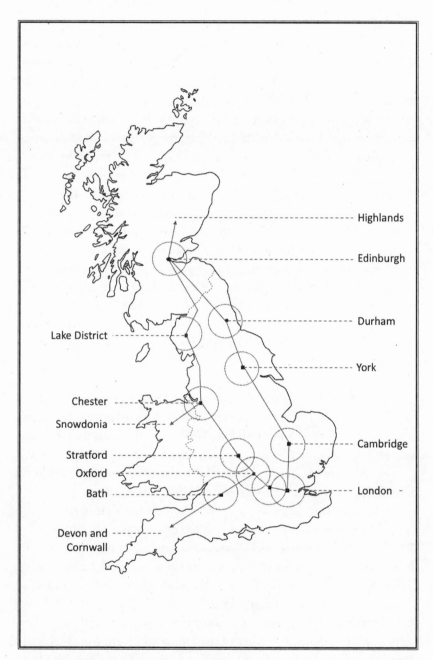

Figure 6.2 Tourist destinations and routes in Britain.

as a centre for tourism. It had become popular in the Victorian era, as in-creased wealth and mobility powered domestic and foreign tourism. Pub-lications from as early as 1894 show its commodification, as it grew from a small market town to an identifiable tourist region that included nearby attractions such as Warwick Castle and Charlecote Park.[15]

Larry Mersfelder, our elderly and pompous correspondent from Okla-homa, recorded the standardized tourist-group experience of the mid-1950s, and followed a path that Americans had trod for many decades:

> Away we went ... on a long trip into the heart of England, through the Shakespeare country with its beautiful countryside of trees, farm, flowers and interesting homes – thatched roof houses of the 15th cen-tury; castles; Stratford-on-Avon – William Shakespeare's old home and place of birth; the church which he and his family attended and where all are buried; the Shakespeare Hotel where we had lunch; the Shakespeare Theatre, still in use; the home of Ann [sic] Hathaway, and her garden, just as they were when she lived there; the cooking utensils used by her and many of them by her parents before her, four hundred years ago.[16]

Mersfelder's reference to the Shakespeare Theatre as being still in use suggests a naïveté in the writer as, at the time of his visit in 1956, the build-ing was twenty-four years old.[17] Esther Hilton Dundas, who, despite being wealthy, had embarked on a coach tour, took a more sanguine view. "We were surprised, or possibly shocked is the word, to see a modern, red, brick theater. Somehow it looks uncomfortable in a Shakespearian setting, but it seats 1,301 persons and every seat commands a full view of the stage. I cannot complain about the type of architecture, at least not with justifica-tion."[18] For Americans, the ticket prices were cheap, with the best seats in the theater costing 14s. 6d. (72½p) and the cheapest 2s. 6d. (12½p).[19] This converted to $2 and 35 cents, respectively, when a ticket for a good seat at a top Broadway show cost about $7.50.[20]

Admiration for Stratford was a common response found in the trip reports. Juanita Stott, the North Carolinian librarian, who was well-educated, but not well-travelled, loved it as much as the gauche Mers-felder: "wouldn't it be wonderful to spend a whole summer at such a quaint little hotel." Stott was not, though, a naive or gullible tourist. She recorded in her account of her trip that some of the furniture she had seen was original, that some was old but from a different house, and that some was reproduction.[21]

The Tour of London

Seeing London was a long-established ideal for Americans; Thomas Jefferson, Mark Twain, and Henry James were three examples of famous names that led the way. For many Americans, whose knowledge of the country came from Hollywood movies, England meant London, home to various versions of Sherlock Holmes. Well-read transatlantic visitors were more attuned to the London of Charles Dickens. Either way, its imagined streets and mysterious fogs were familiar to all. For visitors to London in the early 1950s, fictional London was supplemented with the evidence of the Blitz from a decade earlier, brought home by broadcasts from American reporters such as Edward R. Murrow of the CBS network. The bomb-sites that still surrounded St Paul's Cathedral were a pertinent reminder of London's recent history, but coach-party itineraries ignored them.

Tour-party London was, like trips to Shakespeare Country, a set of well-ordered, unsurprising, and unimaginative visits to the main features of the capital. This allowed Americans on rapid coach tours of the country to say they had "done" London. Tours of London confined themselves to historic and cultural sites whose names most Americans already knew well. In Westminster, they included: the Houses of Parliament, Buckingham Palace, the Horse Guards' Parade, 10 Downing Street (tourists could walk up to the front door), the Tate Gallery, and the British Museum. In the City of London, tours focused on St Paul's Cathedral and the Tower of London. Historian John Baxendale has explained how the curators of the Tower of London gradually reconfigured it in the nineteenth century to make it closer to the expectations of tourists. Its "post-medieval features like sash windows were replaced with fake medieval-style ones, buildings were refaced with more authentic looking stone, and plaster stripped down to naked masonry." This was not explained by tour guides, so as not to distract from the solemnity and significance of visiting such a supposedly authentic and historic building. The custodians of Windsor Castle and Hampton Court made similar efforts to generate fake authenticity.[22]

Guides from American Express and rival organizations led coach tours around the capital.[23] The American Express organization loomed large for Americans in Britain, as it provided banking facilities, hotel, and theatre bookings, train reservations, as well as guides. Fiercely independent trip reporter Paul Roberts cynically summed up their pros and cons, "[American Express] is eager and able, in the major capitals, to organize sightseeing tours by day and night. And, of course, it is ready to shoot you off to Europe on a thirty or forty-five day tour in which you will be intimately acquainted with and attain a profound understanding of the other people on your tour bus."[24] If you could afford it, it could also provide private tours. Wealthy Floridian Ruth Lois Matthews was one trip reporter who did this with a group of friends. She thought her guide unimpressive. "He spent most of the time calling back to the office for relief, as the Americans were asking questions too fast for him. I could not help but feel sorry for him as he stood with his hands in the pockets of his dirty raincoat."[25] Matthews was, perhaps, more reflective than many American visitors. She thought London, on the day before the 1953 coronation, depressing and backward looking, locked into a tourist nostalgia for the distant past. "Down deep in my heart I felt a smugness of my own. Their loyal processions were wonderful [but American] parades had just as much patriotism, I thought, but without any medieval ceremony."[26]

After a tour of the usual sites, she found herself in Westminster listening to the chimes of Big Ben. "Some were saying that we should set our watches by Big Ben, but this would have necessitated turning the hands of my watch backward. I did not want to go backward, I wanted to look forward."[27] Matthews was in the wrong city at the wrong time. The deprivations of austerity meant that there was little or no modernity for the visitor to see. Those arriving in 1951 had, at least, the Festival of Britain to demonstrate the possibility of change, but by the following year the emphasis had returned to history and continuity. On leaving the British Museum, Matthews reflected, "I longed for modern times. I wished I might be shown the rest of London by helicopter."[28]

Juanita Stott was a more conventional tourist than Matthews. Stott travelled with a large party of friends, and on arrival in London submitted without complaint to the idea that they would see the city's sites together, travelling by coach. Americans used to Manhattan, Boston, or Chicago might have been accustomed to navigating a large city on foot or by subway. However, for travellers like Stott, who were used to motorized suburban life, walking long distances in a strange town or using its obscure public transport did not come naturally. One other factor encouraging tourists to use coach tours was that they had already paid for them as part of their package tour. Or perhaps Stott just preferred the companionship of being with friends.

Stott and party travelled around London in a bus, accompanied by their guide, Mr Jackson, and their driver, Les. The distinction in names was typical of the decade. Jackson, who was a guide from the Polytechnic Touring Association (Poly Tours), and was knowledgeable about Westminster Abbey and London's history, had a claim to middle-class status, hence the "Mister." Les sounds a much jollier, friendly, working-class figure. The tour's detailed and rigid itinerary allowed for little spontaneity. Stott was frustrated that they were, in clichéd style, rushed from one sight to another: "Guides sometimes seem to think an American only wants to be able to SAY he saw something! I have a hankering to see all of the event!"[29] Poly Tours advertised in American papers, emphasizing that, once the traveller was in Britain, it would take care of everything: "Full board at comfortable, attractive hotels … payment of gratuities … services of Poly couriers – all for this low, low price."[30] Many Americans used Poly Tours while in Britain, so it is likely that tourists throughout the 1950s often repeated Stott's experience of London.[31] Traffic conditions and parking restrictions were sufficiently relaxed to allow coaches to stop and wait for a few minutes while their passengers admired Downing Street or Horse Guards' Parade. Stott captured the hectic spirit of movement from one sight to another in the capital, sometimes stopping but most often just driving past:

Passed the fashionable Hyde Park Hotel. If our party had piled in there with all our baskets, little bags, raincoats etc. we would probably have been ushered out the back way quicker than we came in! … Soon passed Piccadilly Hotel and then were at Piccadilly Circus which is just some place where the streets cross! Somehow, I had expected [it] to be something bigger – don't know just what. Saw the British Museum as we rode back to the hotel. Regret that I never did get to go in it.[32]

If Mersfelder was most cynics' idea of an American tourist, amiable and suggestible, swallowing half-digested pieces of information related by his coach party's guide, Stott was rather different. She had the education and inquiring attitude needed to separate the simplistic portrayals of "Olde" England from the reality of what she could see with her own eyes. Ruth Lois Matthews was even more critical, finding her tour of London boring and pointless. The accounts of Stott and Matthews demonstrate that not all coach-party tourists were passive and ignorant. Many knew that what they were seeing was contrived and went beyond their guides' simplistic presentations to obtain a deeper understanding of Britain.

Travelling Independently

Successful independent travel in Britain required a visitor to have several attributes. Money was not one of them. The Americans who were disinclined to tour with a coach party were sometimes wealthy or sometimes had little cash to spend. More important than money was a positive attitude, an open mind, and the cultural capital needed to negotiate travel in a complex little country. For those prepared to make the investment in reading them, guidebooks to Britain provided one of the few sources for problem solving; tourists could also correspond with the BTHA's New York office to get suggestions and advice. Travel agents were also vital in making any hotel bookings that were needed on arrival. Without a coach tour, the choice of transport was key. Should it be self-drive, train, and taxi – or, for a very few, hitchhiking or cycling?

Americans, familiar with a motorized society at home, were keen to explore Britain by automobile, despite the difficulties in interpreting road signs and negotiating roundabouts.[33] Visiting motorists displayed a sticker on their cars, indicating that they were "tourist drivers," so that other drivers and the authorities might cut them a little slack.[34] Russell Brockbank's cartoon in Figure 6.3 exemplified the contrasts between driving in the United States and in pre-motorway Britain.[35] As the cartoon proposed, Britons understood Americans self-driving as early as 1950. In July of that year, the New York Times outlined a short driving tour for American visitors to Britain: "Five days and a car – that's an exciting prospect to any American anywhere." The route, from London via Salisbury and Stone-

Figure 6.3 Cartoon by Brockbank #2. *Punch*, 31 May 1950.

henge to Devon and back, expected the adventurous tourist to undertake a hundred slow-speed miles each day. The newspaper encouraged drivers to be back in London before it got dark, such was the difficulty of navigation in the capital. Its unlikely conclusion was that "the only ways to proceed are to follow a bus marked for a street one knows or to consult a bobby."[36] A map would have helped.

Guidebooks promoted self-driving vacations for those who could afford it, allowing them to free themselves from the constraints of railway and bus journeys. Ruth McKenney and Richard Bransten, in their guidebook *Here's England*, suggested that: "Should you have a little extra money to spend, what we call the U-Drive-It system flourishes all over England … Driving in England, if you remember to stay on the left-hand side of the road, is pleasant, and without pain – except for the bicycle menace."[37] Both independent garages and major manufacturers offered cars for rent. For example, Ford promoted their British-made but American-influenced cars, such as the Zephyr, which it could deliver to anywhere in Britain or the Continent and then ship to the United States.[38] The British Motor

Corporation wanted Americans to buy an austerity-styled Morris 1000 for their trip to Europe.[39] They had some success. The *New York Times* reported in 1956 that American visitors who had bought British cars could clock two thousand miles and then either have them shipped to France for more vacation driving or back home to "add chic to the suburban two-car garage."[40] By 1959, the Victor Britain Rent-a-Car System was advertising its nationwide coverage, which delivered rental cars to larger railway stations.[41] Car rentals provided visitors with the opportunity to get beyond the normal tourist haunts (see Figure 6.4). For instance, prestigious *Holiday* magazine recommended an "English Motor Tour, that included unusual destinations such as Bognor Regis, Winchester and Shaftesbury."[42] By the end of the decade, American Express was describing the growth in Americans using self-drive cars as "phenomenal."[43]

Figure 6.4 American self-drive tourists in Sussex.

Willard Price wrote about his experience of picking up a new British car at his hotel in Bloomsbury, London:

> We all get in and I drive around the square. Everything goes well until we reach the east side. Here cars are parked along both kerbs leaving only a little more than enough room for a large lorry – and a large lorry chooses this moment to come along, meeting us just on the bend, where we both come to a halt and I start learning the gear shifts … the lorry driver is very patient while I study, stew and experiment and I am grinding gears and teeth … I am warm for the first time since our arrival in Britain.[44]

Some American drivers found the process a little easier. Stanley Wade Baron, an American journalist resident in Britain, had joined forces with two redoubtable lady visitors from the Midwest for a trip to Wales:

> "Oh no," says Mrs Kemble, indulgent of my ignorance. "We brought a car you see; oh, no, it's the easiest thing in the world. That's what surprised us everywhere we've been, how easy it is. Everybody back home told us all kinds of fairy tales about how we'd have trouble here and there. Why just let me tell you we drove right in to Vienna and had no trouble at all!"[45]

A traffic accident on a narrow Welsh street eventually dimmed Mrs Kemble's optimism. Visitors who brought an American car with them for their vacation unintentionally advertised their nationality, wealth, and difference. American cars, far larger and more glamorous than the domestic product, attracted attention, as they were such novelties.

❖ ❖ ❖

The dilapidated state of Britain's postwar railways meant that they came as a shock to those visiting Europe for the first time. The *Times* noted that Americans were prone to complain about the grubbiness of British trains. One visitor wrote that, because of their dirty windows, he found it "quite impossible to 'See Britain by Train,'" which was the idea proposed by British Railways in its advertising campaigns.[46] *Picture Post* featured an article on the problems recorded by American visitors. One woman from Long Beach, California, asked British Railways to "see that carriage cleaners do their work, the upholstery is generally *terribly* dirty"; a New York woman pleaded for freely available water on trains: "I couldn't get any even when I was ill."[47] American correspondent Don Iddon echoed this thought, complaining that the little things expected by wealthy Americans, such as proper towels and glasses of water, were missing.[48] Other complaints included: accumulation of cigarette butts, litter, and dirty overalls worn by restaurant-car staff.[49] British Railways explained that most of the problems related to the soon-to-be-obsolete steam trains. This all contrasted rather badly with the boosterist claims of the BTHA in their booklet on touring Britain: "that no journey will prove uncomfortable is guaranteed by the finest railways ... in the world"[50]

It is interesting to note that, in its marketing in America, British Railways showed a steam train pulling a long set of carriages; at home, Americans had grown accustomed to seeing diesel trains running their prestige services. Its advertisement in *Holiday* offered a thousand miles of "go anywhere" First-Class train travel for $30. Cheekily, in April 1956, it featured a drawing of Grace Kelly and Prince Rainier (who married in the same month) enjoying an at-seat dinner service, served by an immaculate waiter.[51] Occasionally, British Railways could pull out the stops on its more glamorous routes. A 1953 photograph taken on its Devon Belle service from Waterloo to Plymouth shows some prosperous Americans having a drink. Laughing, these sunglasses-wearing visitors seem to be having a great time on the train (see Figure 6.5).

Despite the occasional success, the problems of Americans' experiences with British Railways proved intractable. As late as 1958, the *Daily Mail* reported that almost every comment card the BTHA received contained an attack on British Railways: "Dirt, discomfort, filthy seats, filthy windows that hide the beautiful scenery, late trains, cold trains ... hopeless railway connections ... the lot."[52]

American students and young people travelling to Europe were usually on the tightest budgets. To keep transport costs down, many resorted to hitchhiking. This practice was far more common in the 1950s than it is today, and provided free travel and an opportunity to talk to British drivers on the way. Joseph Hahn was one such student who travelled around Europe in 1956. He arrived at Southampton and spent his first day hitching

Figure 6.5 American tourists being served drinks on the Devon Belle.

to Preston, Lancashire, to stay with a friend. In his diary, he noted that: "I was really a curiosity standing alongside the roadside, and with the USA showing [in large letters on his suitcase] an eager youthful lad looking for a ride, getting offered a lift was normally an easy accomplishment throughout my trip."[53] Carol Hummel captured some of the freewheeling atmosphere of this type of vacation:

> After several rides, we finally climbed in with a lorry driver going to London … So there we were, three with the driver in this large cab. It was difficult to sleep, and he preferred us talking to him anyway. He was terribly nice and invited us in … when we arrived at his north

London home ... After an unusual breakfast visit we left, still very
dirty, by bus for another suburb, Putney.[54]

An American student, nineteen-year-old future historian Bruce Pauley,
undertook a two-week tour of western England, Wales, Ireland, Northern
Ireland, and Scotland, hitchhiking the whole time.[55] Cycle tours were also
a possibility. Paul Roberts's trip report described his family's tour of southern England by bicycle one summer late in the decade. Suffice to say that
they found the traffic on Britain's "A" roads was a constant danger for them
and their children. Roberts remarked that "thanks to Bartholomew maps
we stayed off them pretty well. We hated them."[56]

Independence and Authenticity

Independent-minded visitors who would not be seen dead in a coach party
were likely to be influenced by guidebooks, magazines, brochures, and travel journalists, who usually associated Britain with its literary past. In 1955,
National Geographic magazine published a detailed account of a literary
tour of Britain. It directed Americans away from the more-obvious destinations. For example, in London, it recommended, along with the good
suggestions of the Charles Dickens Museum and the Cheshire Cheese pub,
that visitors try an evening walk in Limehouse, which "retains much of its
mysterious atmosphere."[57] Two years later, the magazine repeated this idea,
but this time connected Scotland to its poetic past. The article's subtitle reveals its treatment of this topic: "Tam O'Shanter, Macbeth, Rob Roy and the
Lady of the Lake Still Haunt the Lochs and Braes of Bonnie Scotland."[58]

When it considered London, *Holiday* emphasized some of its more
recherché aspects, summarized in a two-page coloured map of "Tourist
London." By noting among seventy-five highlights such destinations as
Wigmore Hall, The Temple, Sadler's Wells, and the University of London's
Senate House, the magazine made it clear that this was not a guide for the
regular tourist catered for by BTHA brochures, but for informed travellers
who wanted to visit places that had artistic or intellectual interest. The
magazine's suggestion for an out-of-town day trip was as distinguished.
Rather than choosing Hampton Court or Windsor Castle, destinations fit

only for first-time visitors, it selected Henley-on-Thames and the upper-class fun offered by its famous annual regatta.[59]

Independent travellers could see different aspects of a town like Stratford-upon-Avon. Phyllis Stock was one such, determined to keep off the beaten path by not staying in hotels that catered for Americans.[60] Stock travelled up to Stratford on the train, going as she described it "the hard way," as it required a four-hour wait in Birmingham for her connection. She had a difficult night at the White Swan Inn, where she found the staff unfriendly (something that she generously put down to her own manner, rather than the rudeness of her hosts). The next day she walked and walked on her own, exploring Stratford's "quaint and lovely" corners. Unlike those hurried along in their coach-tour parties, Stock could meet the locals. After inquiring of an old lady resident where she could get a cup of coffee, and getting the puzzled and puzzling reply "at the coffee bar," Stock got into a conversation and was rewarded by being asked along to watch a procession that was held each year, a week after Shakespeare's birthday. This was so obscure that it had only five onlookers, including herself.[61]

One of the characteristics of independent travellers is their need to assess whether the sites they visit are authentic or not. The Roberts family, who travelled across southern England by bicycle, were the antithesis of coach-party American tourists. Paul Roberts hated Stratford. "Of all the places we visited in England, it was the only one that we thought unpleasant. It's a real tourist trap and, except for the plays given there, about as interesting as Terre Haute, Indiana."[62] Muriel Beadle came to the same conclusion: "it was so full of Ye Old Chintzy Tearooms and Ye Quaint Souvenir Shoppes that we kept right on going until we found a nice, non-touristy two-star hotel in nearby Warwick."[63] *Holiday* magazine, in its feature on the town, was honest about the tatty aspects of Stratford and included a photograph of the Fountain Gift Shop, a tiny establishment emblazoned with postcards, which also sold souvenirs and cigarettes. *National Geographic* magazine acknowledged the town's phoniness, noting that "modern shops add to the effect by masquerading in Shakespearean guise."[64]

Holiday's writer J. Frank Dobie described how his original intention was to write about Stratford without mentioning Shakespeare, but this was impossible, as the playwright was so central to the town's history. The article achieved some of its original aims by describing aspects of the present-day life of the town that were not dependent on its most-famous resident: "the town's weekly newspaper chronicled what was said at the Rotary Club meeting ... and gives country-natured news."[65] In so doing, *Holiday* moved beyond a simplistic portrayal of this important tourist destination, appealing to a readership who already knew who Shakespeare was and were familiar with his works. Dobie showed how a traveller (all readers of *Holiday* were, in their minds, travellers, not tourists) could, by walking around on their own, get a deeper understanding of what life in the town was like.

Sometimes the search for meaning went beyond an assessment of a town's tea shops. One feature of the trip reports is how some visitors presented working-class Britons as authentic. The differences in standards of living between the two countries in the 1950s and Britain's longer history allowed trip reporters to identify a depth in ordinary people and in their way of life that distinguished itself from the consumerist modernity they experienced at home. This phenomenon wasn't confined to Americans; wealthy London suburbanites searched for an authentic "deep" England between the wars, an idea with roots in eighteenth- and nineteenth-century romanticism.[66] As sociologist John Urry put it, "the tourist is a kind of contemporary pilgrim, seeking authenticity in other 'times' and other 'places' away from that person's everyday life. Particular fascination is shown by tourists in the 'real lives' of others which somehow possess a reality which is hard to discover in people's own experiences."[67]

Emily Kimbrough was, as we have seen, a cultured person and part of the literary scene in Manhattan, friendly with well-known actors and writers. Emily and her friends were sufficiently newsworthy for a journalist and accompanying photographer to cover her trip to Britain for *Life* magazine.[68] On her canal-boat trip through the English midlands, Kimbrough met many "ordinary" Britons. Her response was to observe them as if they were in a scene from an old painting. She was very respectful of her subjects and emphasized their purity and simplicity. The contrast between her well-travelled and well-heeled life and the rootedness of these country folk was often present in her writing. For example, in search of a hot kettle of water for their morning tea, Kimbrough and her friend Sophy (who was, back in New York, an advocate for African-American rights) came across a little white cottage, near the canal:

A woman was taking the kettle from Sophy's hand ... she was explaining ... [in] an accent thick and rich as cream, she would put our kettle on at once. She paused to smile at me and say good morning. She was young, slender, with brown skin and pink cheeks ... [her hair] was parted in the middle and drawn smooth into a knot at the back. Her teeth were very white. While we waited for our kettle to boil [over an indoor open fire], we told her about our trip. I doubt that Martians will evoke greater surprise when they visit us ... [after some thought, she said] "Some day I may go to London myself."[69]

Kimbrough evokes a primitivist discourse. In spite of her poverty, the young woman was beautiful and kind, her house (of course) spotlessly clean. Kimbrough took great pleasure in observing the quotidian world of a "real" British woman, with the implication that she had made a connection with her that would have been impossible for a regular American rushing from one tourist attraction to the next. Kimbrough's visit also exemplified the idea that authenticity could be derived from seeing the "back" of a tourist site.[70] By visiting inside the picture-perfect cottage, she had discovered "real life," which earned her a distinction from tourists who saw things only at face value. This glimpse of an authentic and traditional life distanced Kimbrough from her Park Avenue friends.

A further aspect of authentic travel is the wish to be separated from other tourists, their presence disturbing the illusion of exploration and discovery and devaluing the exclusivity of the vacation.[71] There is nothing more disappointing for an American traveller than to find coach-party tourists interfering with their cultured take on Europe.

Germaine Haney, the most amusing trip reporter, turned her fire on her compatriots:

That night, after dinner, an American tour party came in, and they pushed several tables together and sat down at one end of the lounge. They were all noisy about all the places they'd been, making sure that everyone there should know they'd seen Florence and Rome and Paris. The rest of us had to stop talking ... There was one girl in the American group who was the leading comedian, and she kept screaming over and over and over "I speak two languages, English and Obscene" and they'd all go off into howls of laughter.[72]

Haney, smart and literate, a world-weary lone traveller, observed and categorized the vulgar "tour party." A pardonable sin. At least she did not do it under the cover of some bogus Anglophilic imitation; she remained a paid-up American in her attitudes.

Kimbrough epitomized the urbane, much published, traveller, who, when in Britain, liked to disguise her American origins. "If there is one thing that I abominate, it's the sight of Americans abroad swinging along in loud-patterned sports shirts, women in shorts and slacks, and sandals with nothing but a sole and a thong between two toes. I think it is disgusting."[73] Margaret Griffith, resident in Oxford for an academic year, could go even further, because her experience of living with the British had provided her with different insights from short-term visitors like Kimbrough. As she travelled home on the ss *United States*, small-minded, provincial, or wealthy and vulgar Americans surrounded her:

> I'm going to be quite critical of them. Take the two ladies at supper
> … they didn't like Paris because of the rain and the poor hotel; all
> they could say about Nice concerned the food, and they didn't like
> it. Or the man sitting … in First Class, in a great steam because he'd
> lost his [cream-coloured] shoe trunk. Somehow, I feel I've gotten
> so much more out of my experiences this year than this kind of
> traveler.[74]

These attitudes had been tidily summed up just before the Second World War in the Hollywood movie *Dodsworth*, in which Mary Astor plays Fran Dodsworth, an unhappily married American, who, on an Atlantic liner, meets a suave Englishman played by David Niven. Astor observes her compatriots. "Look at those two women. Can't you just see them in Venice with their Baedekers. Why is it that the travelling Americans are so dreadful?" Niven, inverting the conventional view of Britons, replies, "Why is it that Americans are such snobs?" Astor responds, "Do you think it is snobbish to see something else besides one's fellow citizens abroad?"[75] It would seem that an elite American traveller could despise bookish intellectuals who, in turn, could despise noisy vulgarians.

Conclusion

If American visitors had booked an all-inclusive tour, then they would see a rigidly defined set of sights they would understand to be "Shake-speare Country" or "Bonnie Scotland" or "Olde England." Trip reporters who went on coach tours tended to make similar observations about what they had seen. Their usual response to the major sights was sur-prisingly understated. The trip reporters' accounts often serve as a printed *aide-memoire*, with little attempt made to persuade the reader that something of significance had occurred. They regularly described things seen by chance, such as beautiful flowers or a herd of cattle, as more memorable.

Americans who made their own travel arrangements probably had the best experiences. Their assiduous reading of guidebooks and travel mag-azines provided them with much-wider possibilities, such as visiting Devon or Henley-on-Thames at their own speed. People cheated them more often, they ran up some blind alleys, and they had to endure Britain's trains, which were a disgrace, dirty and unpleasant, but these visitors learned the most about Britain and came back with more interesting pho-tographs than those on coaches. Some urbane Americans visiting Britain in the 1950s could enjoy searching for a deeper experience through meeting the British working classes. Emily Kimbrough personified the type: culti-vated, wealthy, connected to metropolitan artistic circles. She was pleased to be allowed into a clean-but-humble home by a young British woman. The opportunity to visit a "real" back room provided visitors with a pre-cious authenticity that they thought would be unavailable to an American on a coach tour of Britain who could see only the outside of a thatched cottage. Americans' disdain for their fellow citizens while abroad could be very sharp. One set of Americans condemned coach-tour party types for their manners, clothing, and voices, while another group might laugh at earnest guidebook-reading history lovers. This wide variety of scorn showed quite a British approach.

CHAPTER SEVEN

Accommodating American Visitors

In the autumn of 1958, the BTHA carried out one of its regular surveys of departing foreign visitors to understand what it had to do to meet their needs and expectations. Despite improvements over the course of the decade, many Americans were frustrated and disappointed with what they found. One such was Mrs Walt H. Bradley from Cambridge, Massachusetts. As a regular visitor to Britain, she was prepared to overlook its infrastructural failings: "Those of us who come each year to Britain wonder sometimes why we do. The hotels are bad ... and the food is impossible."[1]

This was a reasonable summary of the situation in Britain. With some notable London-based exceptions, it was a seemingly intractable problem brought about by the disruptions of the Second World War and the austerity program that followed. Most visitors formed their impressions of the country from their experience of Britain's hotels, cafés, restaurants, and pubs. For Americans, the contrast between home and abroad was very marked. In the United States, domestic tourism was booming as increased wages, longer vacations, wider car ownership, and a well-developed domestic airline network powered growth.[2] American hotels had made a great leap forward, with modern architecture, ensuite rooms, and air conditioning the norm. In Britain, little had changed since 1938 and, even at that date, a lot of the hotel stock was still Edwardian.

Hotels

In 1954, when Britain's problems with postwar austerity were easing, James Brough, an English journalist resident in the United States, writing in the racy magazine *Men Only*, remarked that "The typical American visitor,

Leica at the ready, arrives with some clear objectives in mind. He wants to see Buckingham Palace, sample a pint of bitter, buy a raincoat, and find a room with a bath. By and large, Britain is equipped to satisfy all such ambitions – except the last."[3]

The effects of the Second World War on Britain's hotel accommodation were severe. Hotels of all sizes, from boarding houses to major city-centre establishments, had been requisitioned for government use to house troops or act as temporary offices or had been damaged or destroyed by enemy action. In 1944, one British seaside town reported that 33 per cent of its one thousand hotels were war damaged, 11 per cent requisitioned, and 46 per cent empty or not functioning.[4] Within five years, the impact of these constraints on the British economy and its need for tourist dollars were clear. The British government's Board of Trade led the way, appealing to the Ministry of Works to return requisitioned hotels to the market-place.[5] In 1948, pioneer transatlantic air carrier American Overseas Air-lines described the condition of British hotels to its American passengers before arrival, to manage their expectations. It explained that "Hotels in England are crowded since some of them were bombed and have not been repaired ... Soap is not furnished, sugar is not plentiful, heating is not up to standard." It optimistically advised visitors to respond by being "dignified, courteous, friendly, tolerant, modest, patient, generous, moderate, careful and intelligent."[6]

One early postwar idea to attract American tourists was the construction of a vacation village for less-well-off visitors, who, short of time and not able to afford a top-class London hotel, might still want to visit the capital. Billy Butlin, the originator of this idea, had developed a successful holiday-camp business in Britain just before the war.[7] He had recently bought an establishment on the northern outskirts of London, the Thatched Barn, which had been a successful roadhouse in the 1930s. Roadhouses (quite different to American roadhouses), of which the Thatched Barn was one of the best, had provided Americanized country-club-style entertainment to British middle-class drivers, offering swimming, sports, dining, and dancing around the clock.[8] This former roadhouse was occupied by the Ministry of Works, but a few miles away, one of its pre-war rivals, the Spider's Web roadhouse, was up and running again and attracting a large number of visiting Americans. The *Daily Mail* presented its impressions of the scene in July 1949:

The peeling bodies stacked around the turquoise pool might have be-
longed to Havana ... We get over 1,000 foreign tourists a week, says
Colosanti [the roadhouse's manager] of whom 750 are Americans.
You see we advertise in the "Queens" ... The Americans, indistin-
guishable from the wealthy merchants of Golders Green, sip their
mint juleps.[9]

Advertising on the big Cunard liners was a smart move. Here was one successful place that Americans could enjoy, unaware of the *Daily Mail*'s snobbery and anti-Semitism.[10]

Butlin's idea for an American vacation centre was hardly far-fetched.
His plan was to target airline passengers from lower-income groups, rather
than those travelling on the *Queen Mary*. He wished to charter special
planes to reduce the cost of crossing the Atlantic. A letter from the Board
of Trade to the Ministry of Works explained the project:

> Butlin's have acquired the site with the idea of using it as a Vacation
> Village in time for the 1950 season. They are working out a scheme
> under which inclusive arrangements will be made in America for
> visitors to fly here and spend part of their time at one or more of
> the Butlin camps, but they must of course have somewhere close to
> London ... This scheme ... has the merits of getting visitors away
> from the overcrowded London hotels and of bringing a very large
> class of tourists with short holidays and limited means.[11]

Butlin never realized this innovative project. The Ministry of Works had,
after the war, invested £40,000 in the Thatched Barn to turn it into a build-
ing-materials testing centre and perhaps thought finding somewhere else
to locate this facility would be too difficult.[12]

✢ ✢ ✢

Early the next year, the short-lived, government-controlled British Tourist
and Holidays Board (BTHB) published the results of their inquiry into the
state of British hotels. The views of actual and potential American visitors
informed much of the criticism.[13] It gathered trade views by interviewing

staff from American Express, Pan American Airways, the American Chamber of Commerce in London, Richard Bransten (American writer and co-author of the *Here's England* guidebook), and oddly, Hollywood star Douglas Fairbanks Jr.[14]

The report concluded that the grandest London hotels provided exactly what the most-demanding tourist required, but that, below this level, Britain's hotels were in a parlous state. It identified personal service as a particular problem, with visitors encountering surly staff and cold and diffident receptionists. This was put down to either the effect of recent changes to hotel wage rates that made service for tips less necessary, or a "Jack-is-as-good-as-his-master" feeling that five years of socialism had produced. The report, reflecting the free-enterprise background of its investigators, stated: "There was a lack of inclination on the part of staff to put themselves out in the interests of visitors, and to sell their services in such a way as to imbue the guest with the belief that they positively wished to make him as comfortable as possible."[15]

The report is interesting in signifying a change of mood in the country from state control toward a more free-enterprise style of working. It criticized hotel dining rooms, concluding that head waiters were cold and aloof, served wine at the wrong temperature, and their waiters did not always have clean uniforms. Hotels were often unheated and freezing in winter. Lighting was poor. The committee identified that American visitors "had become accustomed in their own country to having a private bathroom when staying at a hotel and had long since ceased to regard this as a luxury." The alternative, communal lavatories were insufficient, both in number and standards of cleanliness.[16] One urbane American visitor came up with his own system of classifying Britain's simpler hotels, all of which had bathless rooms. "It's my own classification ... 2T stands for two towels in your room. That's pretty good. It's the most we've had."[17]

Despite terrible service, Americans were big tippers. Part of this was due to a difference in practice between the two countries, which remains in place today, but it was also at the time due to Americans' greater wealth and their unfamiliarity with the strange British currency. This raised alarm in conservative circles. Magazine editor Leslie Adrian wrote: "As a consumer, I find their tipping alarming. Can we continue to expect reasonable service from restaurants and hotel staff who know they are not going to get more than 10 percent of the bill, if they also know they are going to get 30 percent from the Americans at the next table?"[18] By the middle of the decade, British waiting staff, now dealing with lower-middle-class Americans, were receiving far smaller tips than they had from the visitors of a few years earlier.[19]

Hoteliers who wanted to increase their appeal to American visitors could not do so, because Board of Trade regulations would not permit the necessary building work.[20] The board was, though, prepared to make minor grants to hotels who attracted American and Canadian customers, providing relief against the purchase tax hotels incurred in improving their facilities. For example, if a hotel's occupancy by Americans and Canadians was greater than 20 per cent, they were, in 1951, entitled to a 90 per cent rebate on any purchase tax they had incurred.[21] This largesse did not last for long; by the end of the decade, hoteliers were complaining of a long-standing lack of support from the government, despite the industry's importance to the country and its foreign-exchange balances.[22]

Both the inquiry's respondents and American visitors condemned the food in Britain's hotels. They considered the five-shilling maximum price for a meal (an austerity measure) a sham, as hoteliers made every effort to make unreasonable charges for any extras. The report assessed breakfast as the worst meal of the day, and it noted that "American visitors are very fond of fruit juices, and … these should be provided on a generous scale … [they] expect to find iced water on the table." Coffee needed improvement, as a matter of "particular importance for our overseas visitors, especially those from America."[23]

Not everyone agreed with these views. For example, politician and socialite Nancy Astor (a US native) thought that "what is really essential is that our American visitors should feel that they are really wanted here."[24] American standards did not necessarily appeal to visitors searching for an authentic European experience. Writer Stanley Wade Baron reported one example:

> Alan eventually speaks to me. "I can't understand Americans who don't like Europe because it's not like America. They're always complaining because there aren't enough showers, the beach is better in California or they can't get pancakes and maple syrup in the morning. What the heck do they *come* to Europe for?"[25]

Alan might have been right, but some British hotels tried the patience of even the most open-minded American. For example, Ethel Moller Arwe, a forthright resident of New Jersey making her first trip to Britain, was astonished by the poor state of British hotels. In a vanity-published account of her 1953 vacation, she provides us with great and surprising detail of her bedroom, bathroom, and toilet at the Great Northern Hotel at King's Cross. Arwe's travel agent booked this unglamorous railway hotel for them, and the choice suggests both the shortage of hotel accommodation in London in 1953 and her mid-price vacation budget. Arwe's enormous hotel room had tatty window dressings, elderly mahogany furniture, and two beds, covered (for a stay in August) with three woollen blankets and a quilt. There was a large sink in the room, with old-fashioned taps, but no soap. There was no central heating, just a coin-operated electric fire in the tiled fireplace. Arwe's search for the toilet at her hotel is one of the best parts of her book:

> I start out down the silent corridor. Under a lighted glass sign reading "BATHROOM" I enter a cavern that is just exactly what the sign says. A monstrous room with shiny tile walls, it has four great booths, each containing a bathtub – nothing more! [Arwe is referring here to the euphemistic use of "bathroom" in American English.] I find a door without a number on it which indicates what lies behind is not a bedroom. Yes! There are two small apologetic letters in black painted high on the frame "W. C." ... I am confronted by a raised dais upon which are two booths ... all elegance has departed. Choose either one, neither is in repair. The seats are viciously grooved ... Turning to leave, I am perplexed by the dismal and unclean towel hanging by one corner from a nail driven into the middle of the door.[26]

Phyllis Stock, travelling on a limited budget, recorded her stay at a hotel she had booked without advance knowledge. "[B]ehind [its] dingy portals ... a Somerset Maugham story came to life ... You may get bread and breakfast for about two dollars a day. There are shilling heaters in the room ... and bathtubs complete with rings."[27] Some visitors did their best to get used to British standards. Wealthy William Ritchie phlegmatically noted that "the hotels of Scotland are a little hard to take, especially the food, but when you adjust yourself they are bearable."[28] Bill Maudin, a humorous writer for *Life* magazine, also travelled to London in 1953 to see what Americans had to put up with. He avoided the obvious choices of Americanized hotels made by his compatriots, such as the Cumberland or the Strand Palace, booking himself instead at an old-style place off Piccadilly. He came up against an employee who made a virtue of his hotel's lack of facilities:

> When I had inspected my room ... I went to the desk and asked if I could change to one with a bath ... all the clerk in the white tie at the desk said, after a long pause and a lifted brow, was this: "Sorry, sir. Nothing like that available at the moment. We are not a new hotel." Somehow, he made a virtue of no bathrooms. He conveyed to me that rooms with private baths are where the *nouveaux riches* go, where Americans go.[29]

The clerk had cleverly engaged the fear of many upmarket "travellers" of travelling inauthentically. As the 1950s progressed, hotel standards improved under the influence of American visitors, although an interview in 1957 with Marguerite Allen from an American hotel organization showed that some long-standing problems were still evident. They included: absence of shower cubicles, soap, and face towels, unheated bedrooms, double beds (Americans preferred twin beds), and, of course, British coffee.[30]

Not all Americans disliked cheap British hotels. Muriel Beadle, taking a vacation away from her stay in Oxford, noted: "we had travelled on some terrifying highways and beautiful byways, had fallen in love with pagan Britain and pub signs, had eaten incredibly uninteresting food at amazingly cheap and well-run hotels."[31] Beadle left a detailed account of her visit to a good two-star British hotel, which reflected her desire not to be a tourist:

> One enters them through a small dark foyer, in no sense a lobby, and often even bereft of chairs ... buried deep in a closet-like cubbyhole is a trim little woman in a flowered dress and crinkly perm ... [she] politely takes no notice over the bemused expression on the faces when she says that the price of their rooms will be twenty-one shillings each. That's approximately three dollars and includes

a hearty breakfast … A porter, summoned by a bell, pops in, wiping his hands on an apron. Since there are no lifts … he totes the luggage up several flights. The staircase, which cants to one side, and is carpeted in turkey red, has as many turns as an English road … the porter indicates the location of the public rooms which are on the first floor (the first floor *up*, of course). [We get] a high-ceilinged room with flowered wallpaper, a washstand, an enormous mahogany wardrobe, one straight chair, and a magnificently comfortable bed with four fluffy pillows. Somewhere in the room is the only source of illumination, a forty-watt lightbulb, and a gas heater. If fed a shilling, this latter will yield enough warmth to damp-dry socks draped on the rungs of the chair. The bath and the toilet – separate rooms, these – are somewhere down the corridor. They, like the bedrooms, are immaculately clean.[32]

Wealthy Americans travelling to London in the 1950s could choose from many luxury hotels. Advertising executive Edward G. Wilson favoured the Connaught Hotel in Mayfair for his visit in 1953, finding its distinguished style and location attractive. "The Connaught, a very British and very nice hotel, where I stayed is only about two blocks from the office."[33] He also used its restaurant and cocktail bar as a location for entertaining members of J. Walter Thompson's London office.[34] *Fielding's Guide* from 1955 recommended the Connaught as one of their top hotel choices. "Its flavor is unique. If you're after spacious rooms, excellent food, period furnishings, carpets that are shabby in a genteel way, no orchestras, no dancing, no radio, no television … this is perfect."[35] The Connaught was, in this way, the ideal solution for the classiest American visitors, who wanted all the comfort of a US hotel, but with a distinguished European twist that increased its cachet. Wilson might have chosen other first-class hotels. Fielding selected his recommendations to appeal to American visitors. He included Claridge's, the Dorchester, Grosvenor House, and the Berkeley, but, in his view, the Savoy (at £6 per night minimum) reigned supreme. "If you're an American in search of the grace of old England combined with a charming décor and facilities which work in the American way, the Savoy is the place for you. Highest recommendation of all for the discriminating US voyager."[36]

Among these luminaries of the London hotel scene, Fielding added a different type of hotel: The Westbury. This was brand-new, the first constructed in London since the war.[37] It was built in fashionable Mayfair for American hotel group, the Knott Corporation, using a British architect, Michael Rosenauer, at a total cost of $3 million. Rosenauer had also been responsible, three years earlier, for another important Mayfair project for an American corporation, the Time-Life Building. The Westbury featured facilities that were already standard in modern American hotels, but were uncommon in London, including air conditioning in all the public rooms and 219 bedrooms maintained at a temperature of 67°F (20°C). Each of the bedrooms had a radio, and could convert into sitting rooms when guests wished to entertain visitors. All the bedrooms were ensuite and offered both a bath and a shower and adapters for American-style electric razors (see Figure 7.1). Room service provided food as a norm, rather as an exception, which also reflected American preferences. The emphasis on private rooms over public areas was unusual in British hotels, and the Westbury's bars and dining rooms were far smaller than in the British equivalent.[38] Other American touches were a shoeshine boy in the men's dressing saloon and an "Iceflow" ice-making machine that could produce sixteen thousand ice cubes per day.[39]

The hotel's Polo Bar was based on an original in the New York Westbury and was in a modern international style. It was very green. It had a jade-green carpet, banquette seating in green and gold, and green velvet curtains.[40] The dining room was in Regency style, in contrast to the hotel's otherwise contemporary look. Not everyone liked its appearance. The *Guardian*'s correspondent thought the dining room "cheerful and rather vulgar, but far less vulgar than the crockery."[41] Atticus, the *Sunday Times*' diarist, noted, "The visiting [American] executive will not find (and will not miss) the erratic luxury and splendid wastefulness, which are the mark of the older European hotel. His taste buds will not flower unexpectedly, for much of the Westbury is hideous, but he will be perfectly looked after."[42] Fielding concluded that "in spite of its much-advertised US planning and US techniques, we still feel that the English know how to do it better. Very expensive."[43] The Westbury's prices were certainly at the top of the range, with double rooms from £4 10s (£4.50p) a night at a time when an ordinary provincial hotel was charging £1 1s (£1.05p) for bed and breakfast.[44]

Figure 7.1 A bedroom at the Westbury Hotel.

Fielding's well-travelled readers might have preferred the quiet dignity of Claridge's, but as the decade progressed, the Westbury reassured wealthy but unchic visitors. As Marguerite Allen remarked, these new tourists wanted "to see the sights and observe the quaint local customs in the daytime; but at night they want to feel at home. So, the newest hotels – like the Westbury, off Bond Street – are designed for that purpose; they are being built with low ceilings, smaller rooms and modest décor."[45] The Westbury positioned itself at the centre of a new world of transatlantic connections and offered two special services to its clients. The first was the ability to book rooms at Knott Corporation hotels in New York and across North America with instant confirmation, which was not an easy thing to achieve in the 1950s.[46] Second, it featured a BOAC office in the foyer that could provide tickets for flights to New York on demand.[47] These two offerings provided instant travel bookings for those whose schedules required it, many decades before they became widely available. These were the first signs of a burgeoning jet-set lifestyle that fully developed in the 1960s and 1970s.

The British hotel industry made little response to Knott's introduction
of this new, American-modern hotel. In fact, excluding the Westbury, it
built only four new hotels in Britain from 1945 to 1959.[48] One was the Leofric
Hotel in Coventry, which was constructed for Midlands brewer Ind Coope,
and was a key component in the rebuilding of Coventry's blitzed town centre as a modernist project.[49] The Leofric's owners were aware of the complaints directed toward British hotels and featured, among other modern
ideas, that important American requirement – a flask of iced water on each
bedside table. Its Grill Room had a "steak throne," where customers could
select a cut of meat and watch it being cooked for them, an idea redolent
with American influences. Although Coventry was not on many coach-tour
routes, some came to see its ruined Cathedral.[50]

The second new provincial hotel, the Keirby Park, was built in 1960 in
Burnley in Lancashire, a town not on any tourist routes. Academic writer
Francis Williams described it in shocked tones:

> In the centre of town a new skyscraper hotel rises above the mills …
> One walks through the wide doors into a lobby that might be that of
> an hotel in Chicago or Detroit. The bell-hop takes one up in the el-
> evator to a room that with its sleek functionalism, its private bath,
> telephone and central heating, is a duplicate of thousands across the
> American continent … The dining room has a chef from Monte
> Carlo and stays open until midnight.[51]

Three new hotels were built at Britain's gateways, suggesting that it was visitors, not domestic consumers, who were driving change. The Dover Stage
hotel attracted travellers wanting to spend the night in modern style before
a Channel crossing. The Skyway and Ariel hotels at Heathrow were both
nearing completion as the decade closed. These last two hotels presciently
provided up-to-the-minute accommodation for travellers about to make
a transatlantic flight.[52]

Rosenauer's next outing in London was with an even larger hotel, again
for American owners. This was the Hotel Corporation of America's 318-
room Carlton Tower Hotel on Sloane Street in London's Knightsbridge. It
was the corporation's first hotel outside the United States and was aimed
at business travellers and wealthy American tourists.[53] As its name suggests,
this was London's first hotel with a tower of bedrooms above its public

areas, and it finally opened to the public in early 1961. On its launch, the *Architectural Review* commented on the implications for tourist hotels, echoing Marguerite Allen's thoughts: "The public do not want a new hotel to evoke Merry England but the highest standards of efficiency."[54] There was no quaintness at the Carlton Tower, no "Regency" dining rooms; its launch brochure displayed American-style modernity in every aspect, a style that would dominate hotel design for at least two decades.[55]

Britain's mid-priced hotels did not offer what most Americans expected for their vacation accommodation. The continuing need to attract this market led in the 1960s to a relaxation in building development controls and the construction of further new hotels specifically designed to attract visitors from the United States, such as London's Park Lane Hilton, which was planned in the late 1950s and opened in 1963, becoming an iconic destination for transatlantic visitors. American tourists and their preferences, which came to such prominence in the 1950s, were a key driver for change and an important factor in improving hotel standards in Britain.[56]

Food

Wealthier Americans could choose from not only the best hotels but also the best restaurants that London could offer. William Ritchie dined at Quo Vadis, a famous Italian restaurant. Advertising executive Edward Wilson chose most interesting and highest-rated places, lunching at the Cheshire Cheese pub in Fleet Street, having dinner at the Dorchester, drinking cocktails at the Connaught Hotel, and eating dinner (alone) at the Stafford Hotel. His list of recommended restaurants included famous names such as Kettner's, Simpson's, and Wilton's.[57] One interesting stop for Wilson was lunch at the Colony Club, an infamous London club presided over by Muriel Belcher and described by an habitué as "one of the most outrageous of Bohemian drinking clubs it has ever been my good luck to encounter on either side of the English Channel."[58]

Ordinary British restaurants provided a lamentable standard of food, which American visitors very much disliked. Some problems were understandable during rationing, which lasted until mid-1954. Afterwards there was less excuse. Good food was available in luxury hotels and restaurants, and in foreign restaurants in Soho, but in other establishments, the food and service were often found wanting. For example, reporters at *Picture Post*, a magazine aimed at ordinary British readers, complained when offered a choice of either minced beef or minced chicken at a pricey restaurant.[59] A visiting American professor told a conference in Glasgow that "it was a sad but simple truth that British cooking had the reputation of being the least inspired in the world."[60] Raymond Postgate, the originator of the *Good Food Guide*, described the state of British food in 1951:

> Sodden, sour, slimy, sloppy, stale or saccharined – one of these six things (or all) it certainly would be, whether it was fish, flesh, vegetable or sweet. It would also be overcooked; it might be reheated. If the place was English, it would be called a teashop or caffy; if foreign it would be called a restaurant or caffy. In the second case, it would be dirtier, but the food *might* have some taste.[61]

In 1953, novelist Angus Wilson derided British hotel restaurants: "There is usually a menu offering such cosmopolitan attractions as *Crème Parmentier*, *Filets de Merlan*, *Petits pois* (processed) and *Pêche Melba* (tubs). Many of the more enterprising of these hotels have added *Jus de tomate* to the evening menu to appeal to the American tourist."[62] Bad food met bad service. The BTHB reported a dismal standard in British restaurants: "there is no doubt that stained coats, and dirty aprons and shirt fronts, are by no means uncommon and that they have an unfortunate effect upon the visitor."[63] Postgate agreed, "the first picture that anyone has of British cooking outside the home, is of dullness and incompetence; and of British service it is of ineptness or downright surliness."[64]

Some American visitors were happy, particularly the wealthier or well-connected variety. Emily Kimbrough, who was a woman who hosted black-tie dinners in her apartment for her friends, dined well in London. She recorded on one of her frequent trips that "we lunched at The Ritz. It was gay, crowded, the food delicious."[65] In fairness, she also enjoyed eating at less-fashionable establishments: "then we went on to Rye, where we stayed the night at a hotel, where our two rooms were delightful, though they were under the eaves. The food in the restaurant was good and the town delightful."[66] Margaret Griffith, whose husband was a Rhodes scholar at Oxford, visited London for the day and enjoyed a lunch at the Dorchester, a hotel that attracted visiting Americans. "A most elegant lunch ...

[It was] out of sight – melon, fish, duck, raspberries and ice-cream – and the company wonderfully gay."[67]

Juanita Stott, who visited Britain with other Methodists in 1954, ate in much-cheaper restaurants. She, for one, was happy with the simple food she received in Britain. "At Carlisle for wonderful dinner at Crown and Mitre Hotel. Had bread sauce and stuffing for chicken. Stuffing is brown (similar to ours) while sauce is about the same but without the sage and is completely white."[68] She had to admit though that the food she ate on the *Queen Elizabeth* "was the best we had on the entire trip."[69] Ethel Moller Arwe, a stern but fair critic of Britain's hotel bedrooms and toilet facilities, enjoyed her breakfast at her station hotel. "[T]he eggs are good, and the porridge excellent. Toast is served in a silver rack ... it is stone cold, thick and heavy. I like it."[70] Carole Hummel liked the favourite standby of many Londoners. "We ate at Lyons where we consumed all the delicious salads we could eat for only four shillings, about fifty cents."[71] Leona Running led another tolerant religious party group to Britain in 1958. It had an added complication; they were all vegetarian, so could not have meat, the one thing British cooks were good at. Running reported that their restaurant served "a can of Nutolene [a vegetarian 'meat'] ... with three sorts of potatoes ... the cooks at the hotel did not quite know what to do with us."[72]

Britain's food improved throughout the 1950s, thanks to the good work of Raymond Postgate and Egon Ronay and others, although it remained conservative.[73] Travel writer and illustrator Samuel Chamberlain witnessed a sign of this progress. In the late 1950s he wrote a series of articles on good food in Britain. At first, he thought "this seemed a dubious idea, in view of the forlorn reputation of English cooking, and I hesitated for some time." But he decided to give it a go, and in 1959 he started exploring. He realized that "Cornwall and Devon are swamped with vacationists in summer, but in May the hotels were not crowded. I was able to stay in the best ones and found excellent food and wine. Gastronomy indeed has its place in rural England!"[74]

As the BTHB noted, providing a decent cup of coffee was beyond most British hotels and restaurants, despite the arrival of espresso bars in Britain's major cities. Trip reporters were critical and puzzled by the lack of cold water, and even more so about the coffee. Ethel Moller Arwe noted that her breakfast coffee was "made with an inexpert hand, but the generous pitchers of hot milk help to kill the taste."[75] Phyllis Stock reported from her cheap hotel in west London, "porridge with blue milk, perhaps an underdone sausage, or a sad pale egg served always with cold toast and weak coffee."[76] Margaret Griffith, temporarily resident in Oxford, solved the problem by using instant coffee: "leisurely breakfast with Prof. Hawgood … he loved the Nescafé – any Englishman would, after the terrible coffee they mostly make."[77]

The hotel trade recognized the issue at the start of the decade, but complacency reigned. One explanation offered in a trade magazine for the dismal performance in this area was that Britain "as a nation of tea drinkers, cannot understand why anyone should prefer coffee," a predilection put down to attempts to tax tea in America in the 1770s.[78] In the same issue of this magazine was an advertisement for a massive and complicated boiler. It proposed that hotels should "greet American guests with real coffee served from the Jackson Filtomaton," and noted that "midsummer is again in the offing, and from lands where currency is hard [i.e., US dollars], come thousands of inveterate coffee drinkers."[79] This bizarre device, designed to keep large amounts of coffee warm for long periods, probably did not solve the problem.

Going for a Drink

Visiting Americans who wanted to go for a drink while on vacation in Britain had a choice of two rather diverse options. In the 1950s, drinking alcohol, like many other aspects of British life, was informally segregated by class boundaries. Bars, an idea which thirsty Americans were most familiar with, were usually found in hotels, although London's Soho was an exception, housing many legal and illegal bars and clubs. Outside Soho, hotel bars were the preserve of middle-class British life. To access them, it was necessary to dress well, which provided the informal segregation that its customers preferred. As has been shown, the Westbury Hotel had a smart polo-themed cocktail bar, copied from its sister hotel in Manhattan. This imitation of American sources had, in fact, a much longer history in Britain, beginning with the Savoy Hotel's American Bar in the early part of the twentieth century. This cocktail habit dominated middle-class drinking until at least the 1970s, and was in full sway in the 1950s.[80]

Any American wanting to find a good cocktail bar needed to look no further than Britain's major cities. Rural hotels found it harder to provide a convincing drink. Emily Kimbrough recorded her own solution to this problem. "At an inn, Howard tends bar. He always asks for permission first and he always has a spellbound audience. Howard spoke 'Now then', he said briskly, 'you see that's the way my wife and I like a Martini. If you'll just double it, please.' The bartender answered in the far-off tone of one coming from a trance into an unrecognizable place."[81] Based on Kimbrough's tenor here, there is a suspicion that the locals might not have been quite so keen on this forced tuition as she thought.

The alternative to going to a bar or a club was to visit a pub. As we have seen, James Brough thought this something that American men were keen to do. Pubs were gendered spaces in the 1950s: the rougher type were for men only; the smarter sort confined women to the saloon bar or lounge. Regardless of the pub or its reception, Americans found the weak and unchilled beer served in Britain in the 1950s very different from their cold lager-style beers inherited from German and Bohemian immigrants. Served at cellar temperature, British draft beers were stout, mild, or bitter, or a combination of the latter two. In the west of England, pubgoers could also drink various types of alcoholic cider. They are all an acquired taste, and although it is clear from trip reports that some Americans made the effort and enjoyed British beer, the disgust that some felt became one of the clichés about American visitors' behaviour. Like many attitudes toward Americans, this first came to light with the arrival of many thousands of working-class American males in the Second World War.[82] The idea of newly arrived American men finding warm beer revolting was so pervasive that it formed a key scene in the 1955 British movie *A Yank in Ermine*.[83]

Conclusion

Americans wanting to experience Britain without sacrificing anything of the latest standards adopted by hotels in the United States had just one option, to stay in one of the grandest hotels in London for the duration of their trip. Here they could enjoy luxurious rooms with private bathrooms, world-class facilities, and great restaurants; if you had the money, the Savoy could look after all your needs. Few Americans had the money, or were happy to stay only in London, so almost all of them experienced Britain's stock of eccentric and old-fashioned hotels. Eating in hotel dining rooms, which was the only option for those who had booked all-inclusive tours, was a chastening experience of dull, tasteless food, watery vegetables, cold toast, bad coffee, and, worst of all, no cold table water. Eating out in a restaurant was a hit-and-miss affair. If you had access to a *Good Food Guide* you might eat something enjoyable. If you were in Soho, your chances of a good meal increased. Alcohol in most of its forms was available, but the beer was warm and not all cocktail recipes were authentic. Visitors with adaptable attitudes enjoyed themselves, but those who judged everything by American precedents had a difficult time.

In the last few years of the decade, things changed. American money and expertise sparked the building of important new hotels, the first in Britain since the war. The Westbury showed the way. With air conditioning in public rooms, televisions in the bedrooms, and airline offices in the lobby, the Westbury displayed all the features of modern American hotels. For the most-stylish American travellers, this was a step too far; they didn't want to stay in a hotel exactly like one they could find back home. For them, Claridge's sent the right signals. By the end of the decade, the Carlton Tower Hotel was almost finished, the Park Lane Hilton was on its way, and very modern hotels were in construction at Heathrow, all hinting at the rapid development of new hotels in the 1960s.

CHAPTER EIGHT

Ecountering the British – USAF Families

Some 220,000 individuals from the US Armed Forces visited Britain in the 1950s. Although their tourist compatriots far outnumbered them, their reactions to Britain are worth examination, because their interactions with the natives were much less superficial. They met neighbours and teachers, lived in British homes, and worked with the locals. While American tourists were largely middle class, the majority of USAF visitors were working-class airmen and their families (see analysis in Chapter 3). Their experiences provide a wider set of information to understand how Americans encountered Britain and the British.

Without the shared and immediate dangers of war, British attitudes to US airmen had hardened by the early 1950s. *In Focus: The Americans in Britain*, a USAF publication, explained the antagonism between the two groups. This frank booklet documented American servicemen's perceived crimes as: brashness, anti-social behaviour, associating with good-time girls and prostitutes, and undue wealth. It also proposed that Americans found Britons stuffy, resentful, judgmental, and cold, commenting that many Americans mistook "British reserve for hostility."[1] This was a generous evaluation, as there was a great deal of actual hostility toward the Americans. *Picture Post* also investigated this topic. A local resident stated, "These Americans think we are too superior, too 'goddam snooty.'" One serviceman put it this way: "We're a braggart people – we show off. We're proud of being Americans. But you Limeys never boast about yourselves. What are you hiding?"[2]

This chapter examines the encounters that USAF personnel, and in particular their children, had with the British.

The map shown in Figure 8.1 identifies the parts of Britain that fell under the influence of American airbases in the 1950s. Most of these were in country districts; many were in East Anglia and Oxfordshire, areas that

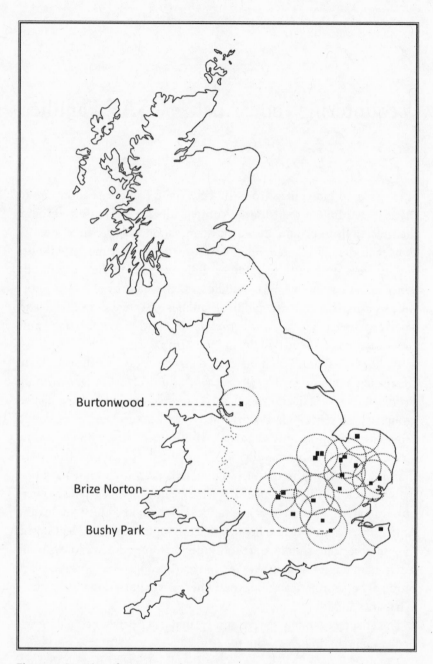

Figure 8.1 Location of major USAF bases in the 1950s.

had become used to Americans during the Second World War. Disputes arose over access to farming land and the noise of planes, but the smallness of the local communities allowed the visitors to see them as individuals. One important exception to rural deployments was Burtonwood, the USAF's most important logistical base in Europe, which was in Warrington, close to the major cities of Liverpool and Manchester. Surprisingly, two of the trip reporters encountered this massive base. Juanita Stott was en route from Stratford-upon-Avon to the Lake District when she saw "American jet planes from nearby Burtonwood [fly] over us."[3] Carol Hummel had a guided tour of the base: "the library, living quarters, offices, flight runways, recreation hall, and the officers' club where we splurged [on] a buffet dinner. Talk about food enough for an army, we had it! Meats and salads, and I had ten green and black olives."[4]

The liberal *Manchester Guardian* regularly featured sympathetic coverage of Burtonwood. Nevertheless, it reported in 1952 how two airmen from the base robbed a Manchester jeweller using a sawed-off shotgun.[5] In the same year it noted how Warrington had, because of the USAF base, become an attractive destination for teenage girls from the area. The town's senior probation officer explained:

> These youngsters are causing us a good deal of concern. It is not the local girls who worry us so much as the "teen-agers" who travel some distance from other towns like Manchester, Stockport and Liverpool. When you talk to them, they admit that their one aim has been to pick up an American. Some of them are girls of 15 and 16.[6]

Britons, not wishing to be outdone, played their part in worsening relations. Local gangs targeted Americans on nights out in Manchester, mugging airmen and stealing their pay, sometimes using underage girls to draw them away from their friends.[7] Servicemen also fell victim to less-violent crimes. Proprietors of shops, pubs, and restaurants raised their prices when they heard an American accent. A reporter described "exploitation [from] property owners and estate agents ... and widespread and unscrupulous short-changing, not only by taxi-drivers and waiters, but even by cinema cashiers."[8]

In late 1952, the *Manchester Guardian*, trying to pour oil on troubled waters, printed an article written by David Lampe, an American airman based

at Burtonwood. This moderate and intelligent piece explained the difficulties as seen from both sides of the divide and concluded that ignorance
drove the problems in communication. The article acknowledged that
only stricter regulation by the local police force and encouraging airmen
to meet "nice" women could control the most immediate problem of amateur and professional prostitution around the base. It seems typical of the
period that British commentators blamed the USAF for the behaviour of
young British women. In fact, street prostitution was an unresolved issue
in British cities, with or without US airmen.[9]

As the 1950s progressed, relations between American service personnel
and their "cold" hosts moderated. This was partly through the actions of
a friendship campaign promoted by the USAF that met with an enthusiastic response from British civic organizations. The USAF eased the problem by sending home troublemakers and through the gradual increase
in enlisted, married servicemen, who, if they lived off base, had the best
chance of meeting and integrating with their neighbours. In 1954, the
British government and the USAF agreed to the experimental deployment
of a British Community Relations Officer at three airbases to improve
inter-community harmony.[10]

The massive bomber base at Brize Norton in Oxfordshire was one location where they tried this approach.[11] Among other duties, the Community
Relations Officer at Brize produced a news bulletin, providing information
on local sports clubs and colleges, and made introductions to British families.[12] Service personnel joining local gardening and darts clubs seemed
to work well.[13] Even considering the need for the USAF to emphasize the
success of these programs, many airmen made connections with the
locals.[14] This airbase already had an established outreach program, which,
for example, encouraged servicemen to play local teams at baseball. Figure
8.2 presents an intriguing image that shows the differences in clothing between the two national groups. The inclusion of African Americans in the
airbase team is evidence of the USAF's early efforts at racial integration.[15]
This mixing of races, which was such an anathema in much of the United
States, would have also been a new experience to many Britons, particularly those from rural backgrounds such as Chipping Norton.

In its July 1952 survey of cultural differences between American service
families and their reluctant hosts, *Picture Post* noted that British racism

Figure 8.2 Baseball – USAF Brize Norton v Chipping Norton, July 1953.

contributed to poor relationships. It reported that at one USAF base, after an early get-together between wives from the base and local women, few lasting friendships resulted. "Take, for instance, the coloured sergeant's wife. She is a good case because we are very quick to accuse the Americans of their intolerant treatment of Negroes ... when she is out shopping she sometimes sees a woman ... give her a half smile of recognition [and] then there is quick and silent hurry past."[16]

Although the USAF concentrated its attention on the troubling behaviour of their male service personnel, others saw the role of their wives and children as key to promoting greater integration and understanding between the host and visitor communities. In 1956, one hundred and fifty USAF wives and an equal number of socially conscious British women attended a meeting to discuss improving Anglo-American relationships. Appropriately, they met at Rhodes House in Oxford, close to the big airbases and famous for building academic ties between Britain and the United States.[17] Lady Dugdale, the keynote speaker, proposed that greater ties could be achieved through harnessing the goodwill of teenagers on both sides, presumably because young people were less prejudiced than their parents.[18]

The rest of this chapter focuses on the attitudes of American teenagers to life in Britain in the 1950s. Although some came on vacation with their parents to Britain – for example John and Elizabeth Lyon, whose mother's diary recorded their experiences – the majority were children of USAF personnel. Many of these children attended British schools, but some, in London and at Burtonwood, went to an American school run by the USAF.[19]

Central High School, London

The shared connection of a school, combined with the importance of social media in the first two decades of this century, has produced a store of reminiscences about life in Britain from Americans who were teenagers in Britain in the 1950s. Now elderly and resident in the United States, their shared interest is their attendance at Central High, a school for the children of USAF personnel.

This school, based in Teddington, Middlesex, taught an American curriculum and maintained the cultural apparatus of schools in the United States, such as football teams, cheerleaders, pep squads, and yearbooks. These teenage students lived an unusual life, moving between their military families and a residential school, while observing and interacting with the peoples and customs of a strange country that was itself experiencing great change. They occupied and shifted among a variety of different roles that included: military brats, teenagers, tourists, expat residents, and cultural ambassadors.[20] Their arrival in Britain came just at the time when the country's own teenagers, who were highly influenced by subversive and attractive American archetypes, were coming to public attention.[21] Their experiences offer further insight into relations with Britons and life in Britain.

As this generation of schoolchildren aged, they remained in touch with each other through regular reunions at hotels in various American cities and by distributing a newsletter by email that collated students' accounts of their time in Britain. Social media has transformed the ability of geographically disparate friends to get back into contact with each other, and the former pupils of Central High have engaged in this successfully. They subscribe to an online newsletter, *Bushy Tales*, which acts as a noticeboard and repository for memories and inquiries.[22] The website has an archive of almost two hundred monthly newsletters from March 2001 onwards.[23] They encompass the leaving classes of 1953 to 1962, so, as of 2017, the students are now between sixty-nine and eighty-two years old.[24] Many of the original subscribers have died, leaving six hundred active readers and contributors.[25] This chapter uses material gathered from the *Bushy Tales* newsletter archive and the results of a survey conducted for this book. The survey had a small sample size, so its results need careful interpretation. Most importantly, these memories are not from teenagers, but from their elderly selves sixty years later, and a hazy nostalgia may well have been superimposed on less-happy memories. An overall response bias is likely to have affected the survey, as those students who were unhappy at Central High were unlikely to have subscribed to the newsletter. Subsequent correspondence with the current readers of *Bushy Tales* provided more direct insights into the students' interactions with the British.[26]

Central High was located in Bushy Park, Henry VIII's former hunting ground, opposite Hampton Court Palace. It occupied an unglamorous set of prefabricated former USAAF buildings, which General Eisenhower and his staff had used for their headquarters before and after D-Day. Central High's students ranged in age from fourteen to eighteen, categorized in their yearbooks as freshmen, sophomores, juniors, and seniors, conforming to American norms. These young men and women were the sons and daughters of USAF personnel working at airbases in the Home Counties. A smaller number of the dependents of other US services and agencies and of diplomats also attended the school.[27] Students could commute each day to their family homes by special bus, or they could board at the school, returning home each weekend. The school began in 1953 with just thirty-eight students, and by the time of its closure in 1962 had reached 640 strong.[28]

The 1953 yearbook offers an insight into the frame of mind of these pioneer students. Sandwiched between a picture of the Statue of Liberty and a portrait of the queen (an apt representation of the students' liminality) was a dedication to the school, which acknowledged ideas of shared heritage:

> It has been our fortunate opportunity in this year of world and national doubts, misunderstandings, and fears to study, think, and plan for our personal futures in a setting characteristic of the highest ideals

in the English speaking, Christian world. We are deeply and respect-
fully grateful for this year's work that our parents ... have provided
for us in this locality of rich tradition – a tradition particularly precious to the young Americans of our great country.[29]

The editorial for the yearbook provided an account of the school's first
year: "Through all the strangeness of new faces and new surroundings
came a realization that although we didn't know each other, we were
all Americans. We all knew what hamburgers, the Fourth of July, and
Thanksgiving were and so with this to build on we could start in making
friends."[30] These two statements sum up the dysfunction required to live
in two cultures simultaneously. While acknowledging a shared heritage
between the Americans and their hosts (which, in reality, only applied
to students from a WASP background), the school appealed to the distinctive transportable culture that Americans carried with them around
the world.[31]

The students undertook much extracurricular work. Central High's
yearbook for 1958 reveals a wide range of activities, reflecting the need to
keep lively teenagers occupied in the evenings after school.[32] The main aim
was to mimic life in US high schools as far as possible. As the editorial
noted, "It has now been six years since Central opened her doors to admit
the first student. Amid the hammering and sawing of new construction,
Central has done much to establish American high school traditions at
Bushy Park."[33] The students could join the Student Court and Patrol which
offered a degree of self-governance. The school band and chorus provided
entertainment at parties and at assemblies; various clubs such as the art
club and the audiovisual club kept students busy with hobbies. Sport was
important in emphasizing esprit de corps, and Central High had a successful basketball team, supported by the school's pep club, which supplied
cheerleaders and pom-pom girls. Central High used sport as one of the
main ways in which they introduced their students to British life. For example, the school ran soccer and rugby teams that allowed students to
meet and compete with local British schools. The 1958 yearbook recorded
"how the American youth has picked up the most English of sports [prob-
ably cricket], the British opponents have given the Centralites high praise
... this has so strongly helped the Anglo-American relationship wherever

they have met a British team."[34] Outside sports, Central High also organized an Anglo-American club which undertook day-exchanges with a local grammar school.[35] Students had a formal dance each year at a local hotel, and those with access to central London could go to the American Teen-Age Club in the basement of a hotel in Lancaster Gate.[36]

In their school life, Central High's students worked and played within a close facsimile of an American high school, apart from encountering the occasional British teacher. Once they left the premises, they entered a more-complex, hybrid world that required a negotiation between British and American culture. Although Central High was keen to cement better understanding between visitors and hosts at school through formal meet-ups, its students were in continuous contact with ordinary Londoners. They met them by going shopping and to the cinema, talking to bus drivers and policemen, visiting their neighbours in their suburban homes, and by making friends with local children.

The Students' Life in Britain

Central High students transferred to Britain from USAF bases located across the United States, often at a distance from major cities. There was a marked distinction between home, with its car-based culture centred on the base, school, and church, houses with refrigerators, central heating, air conditioning, and fitted kitchens, and Britain in the 1950s. Britons were much poorer, their houses simpler, and their food terrible. A student remembered that "there was not the familiar US suburban environment I had grown up in and everything seemed so old and decrepit."[37] Another noted that "Everything [was] antique back then … dark and grey without much color, not like it is today. I do not miss those blizzards, fog and smog."[38] A student from Alabama recalled: "I remember being shocked at the bombed-out buildings left in London – also a very cosmopolitan society in London compared to what I had known living in severely segregated Alabama. I had never seen interracial couples before. It was also the culture shock of going from a small air force base … to a huge city."[39] Surprise at the different attitudes to the mixing of races in Britain and the United States was a common response in visiting Americans. It had produced much bad feeling during the Second World War, when many Britons resented the racial segregation of troops imposed by the US Army.[40]

The survey showed that most respondents enjoyed their time in Britain. They placed emphasis, in descending order of popularity, on Britain's countryside, experiencing a different culture, Britain's heritage and history, and the opportunity to use public transport on their own. After a period of adjustment, most students liked Britain, but not everybody was happy. A female former student made that clear: "Someone mentioned in the last newsletter that they were not too happy about moving to England, but eventually came to love it ... to be perfectly honest I never liked it much. I actually disliked it a lot."[41]

As has been seen, American visitors in Britain often commented on the natives' reserve and unfriendliness, although most of their interactions were in shops, hotels, and restaurants.[42] The students at Central High lived in Britain for two to three years and gained a more complex insight into their hosts' character. They found the adults they did not know cold and reserved, but when they got to know them well, such as with their teachers and next-door neighbours, they thought them warm and responsive. Meeting working-class Britons was a surprise for those whose prior information on the British came from the movies. Respondents thought this group were easier to talk to and more like Americans in their attitude. As one respondent recalled, "There were working class people! I was impressed by how easily one could work into a conversation, how forthcoming they were if you spoke up."[43]

It is clear from the responses that the passing years have softened reactions to encounters with the British, though memories of a few harsh incidents remained, with former students recalling being treated poorly by local shopkeepers. A student reported "buying a model airplane kit with a pound note and getting change for a ten-shilling note. When I reminded the clerk [that I had] proffered a pound, the response was, 'I'm terribly sorry sir, I thought you were a tourist!' and he gave me the remaining 10 shillings."[44] Another remembered his mother's experiences: "she sensed some resentment in the shops and thought the greengrocer made sure to reach down for items that weren't as good as the ones on display. She wasn't a loud or obnoxious person, but surely she was more openly assertive and freer with money than the regulars."[45]

Parental Relationships with the Locals

The students recalled the reactions of their parents to their new neighbours in suburban London. There was a wide variety of responses, reflecting individual prejudices and preferences that applied just as much back
at home. A student from a working-class background (his father was a
master sergeant) remembered his parents adapting to life in Britain:

> My parents frequented the [local] pub in the evenings, where they
> very quickly became friends with many of the other regulars from the
> community. They very much enjoyed the relationships built and the
> exchanges in conversations were about general topics, but especially
> those regarding the differences in customs and perhaps politics in the
> two countries ... the War was a frequent topic amongst the men, I be-
> lieve. The women's topics were full range, from domestic issues, rais-
> ing families, to [West End] productions.[46]

In contrast, a student from a wealthy background remembers a stuffy
visit made to a local family. Two things sprang to mind after a sixty-year
gap. First, that the dining room was so cold he could see his breath, and
second, that when watching television after dinner, the English family
stood up for the national anthem at the end of the programs for the day.[47]
A student whose father, unusually for this USAF school, worked in sales for
an oil company came from a family positioned, from the point of view of
social class, somewhere between those of the two previous examples. He
recalled that his parents:

> made little effort to mix with neighbors, but they weren't great so-
> cializers at home either ... My father became familiar with colleagues
> at work in London and got along well with them I think. He did crit-
> icize their business style. I don't remember specifics but I think they
> weren't aggressive enough for him, the hard-driving American, in
> selling their products to other industrial companies.[48]

Experiences varied. As one student remembered it, "my parents got on
quite well with the British, both those my father worked with and with the
neighbors. We knew some Americans who barely spoke to their neighbors

and [we] could never understand why."[49] This sort of response is not surprising; expatriate groups often deal with the problems of being abroad by only associating with their compatriots.

Friendship with British Teenagers

As a subscriber to *Bushy Tales* has noted, military children made friends quickly, so their experiences differed from that of their parents.[50] The response to the survey showed much agreement on this point. In contrast with the more distant relationships they had with British adults, Central High students often had warm and affectionate relationships with British teenagers.[51] Respondents reported close attachments with the English kids in the neighborhood; sometimes this involved dating, but most were simple friendships. Coffee shops, which were a booming and popular fad in Britain in the 1950s, were a good, neutral place to meet local teenagers.[52] Attending church, still popular in Britain and a majority habit in the United States, also provided common ground for both communities.[53] American teenagers visiting British homes were likely to have been objects of attention and fascination. The students' wealth was one important area of difference.

One survey respondent lived in the London suburbs, which meant that he could get the school bus home every night. This allowed him and his two brothers to meet the locals. He enjoyed all the fun available to a 1950s British teenager: going to the movies, stealing neighbours' apples from their gardens, ice skating, and riding the Underground up to the West End to mess about:

> I got to know many of the English boys and girls fairly close to our age living nearby. We all became fast friends and they were over at our house and yard most of the time. The first thing Dad did, finding out that just about EVERYBODY rode bicycles with bells on them [was to buy] the three of us new 10 speeds from the PX at Ruislip to ride everywhere with our newfound friends ... [They] were always very polite to our parents and very friendly to us all the time. Three of those guys ... became very good friends of ours and they would have lunch with us on weekends.[54]

The px was the Post Exchange, or base shop, at South Ruislip, the administrative headquarters of the United States Third Air Force, an airbase without a runway or planes, where the fathers of many Central High students went to work. At the px, usaf personnel could buy American produce and goods that were otherwise unavailable in Britain.[55] The purchase of three new, top-of-the-range bikes at once would have been beyond most British families.

Americanization

The survey responses show that the Central High students were aware of the more obvious forces of Americanization at play in Britain, identifying American music and movies as the two most important influences. Respondents also noted that their English friends regularly used American slang, with movies and American television series the most likely culprits; several mentioned American products such as cars and clothes. The px and the goods on sale there provided an unusual source of Americanization by revealing the standard of living in the United States available to its ordinary citizens in a most material form. Seeing these things in a Hollywood movie might persuade a cynical viewer that American wealth was exaggerated, but when displayed so close to home, the contrast to life in Britain was dramatic. V recalled the impact of these purchases: "The English kids we got to know were in awe of the goods we could get at the px: 45 rpm records, comic books, Levi jeans, boots, etc. We always gave them what we didn't need any more. They just loved to receive those special things."[56]

The base was also home to "real" American food. One female student remembered that at weekends she "would catch a shuttle to South Ruislip. A good part of the day was spent eating hamburgers, French fries, and shakes."[57] The alternative was a pale British imitation of the American original. A respondent speaks of "Wimpy's in Piccadilly, where we'd have a hamburger – it wasn't the same as an American burger – but it was a burger."[58] Historian Adrian Horn, who lived near to the base as a child, now confirms these American memories:

[The usaf] families appeared affluent beyond the dreams of local children, for whom to see an American car was an awesome experience.

Striking examples of their wealth were the use of seemingly exotic foodstuffs in their ordinary diet such as potato salad and "dips," as well as Coca-Cola ... The American children introduced us to previously unknown commodities as diverse as Marvel comics and felt-tip pens.[59]

Wearing Levi jeans and boots was a way of connecting to the students' lives back home. As well as maintaining a sense of identity, this had a performative element. Teenagers like to be different and conform simultaneously. The self-conscious playing out of the role of an American abroad offered distinction and the display of a powerful American culture, the appreciation of which was at something of a high-point in Britain in the 1950s. As former Central High student, Elizabeth, recalled:

That year, as I walked down the street to go to the movies on a Saturday, the parents of my English friend Jenny didn't recognize me any more, or didn't care to, when they saw me with my rolled up blue jeans, my father's big white shirt, bobby sox and loafers. Somehow, even though we were across an ocean from home, we always knew what they were wearing back home in the States.[60]

Elizabeth could, of course, watch American movies and read American magazines to keep up to date with US fashions. Boys also engaged in this demonstrative behaviour:

My two brothers and I were walking ... to a nearby restaurant for dinner. We decided to wear our ... cowboy hats, which we had purchased in San Antonio, Texas. After dinner [we] walked down to Oxford Street. It created quite a large amount of attention. Clearly in 1954 London, young folks in cowboy hats was a rare sight.

This student described his regular dress both inside and outside of school as "Levis, flannel shirt, leather jacket, with an American flag sewn on the back, and a NRA [National Rifle Association] patch on one shoulder."[61]

Central High students, when old enough, went around in a group, wearing their American clothes and enjoyed going to the West End (see Figure 8.3). The boys who had gained varsity status for their sporting endeavours

Figure 8.3 Central High School students in Bushy Park,
c. 1958.

wore their school jackets with a big "C" school letter.[62] One student essayed
a different American style, "I was soooo cool in those days; 'London Fog-
ger' [a London Fog raincoat], cigarette hanging out of my mouth and a
limey chick on my arm."[63] These teenagers generated an exotic effect, rem-
iniscent, for local onlookers, of the characters in *The Blackboard Jungle*, a
controversial 1955 American film that was popular in Britain.[64] In effect,
they were competing with British teenagers, who were also busy displaying
their distinctive branded fashions and spending their disposable income
"mainly on dressing-up in order to impress other teenagers."[65]

Anti-Americanism

Central High students carried out these performances of heightened
Americanism at just the same time that British teenagers were pouring
much of their emotional energy and spare cash into imitating them. Influential cultural critic Richard Hoggart, writing in 1957, drew attention
to this phenomenon, placing the coffee shop as a locus of cheap imper-
sonation of American mannerisms.[66] "Teddy Boys" were an important
contributing group to Hoggart's thesis. So named because they favoured
modified Edwardian dandy clothes, Teddy Boys outraged 1950s convention
because of their working-class origins, their propensity to violence, and
their interest in American rebel culture.[67] As historian Stanley Cohen
points out, "the heroes of the fifties were cast in the very American role of
the brute and the hipster: Brando and Dean being the most perfect and
Presley the nearest musical equivalent."[68] Adrian Horn makes a further
connection between Teddy Boys and Americanization, by tracing their
drape jackets back to 1940s spivs (wartime black-marketeers), who themselves were imitating the exotically tailored "zoot" suits worn by black GIs.[69]

The survey results show that most students experienced no direct anti-
American behaviour, but for those that did, their dealings with local Teddy
Boys (or Teds) have stuck fast in the memory. Teddy Boys did not view actual American teenagers in London as favourably as their celluloid compatriots. The visitors' wealth, clean-cut appearance, crew cuts, and college
jackets prompted a different reaction. One Central High student remembers his encounter with the Teds:

> [we] were walking together at a small circus in Uxbridge in the late
> evening and were spotted by a rather aggressive and vocal group [of
> Teds] who were making unkind remarks and gestures ... I was quite
> frightened. There were no more that probably five or six of these fel-
> lows, but our instincts told us that it was time to go. We backed off
> the "mid-way" and were cornered against a trailer occupied by a
> member of the circus troupe. The shouting managed to get the atten-
> tion of the trailer's occupant ... He came flying out the door of his
> trailer and dove into the middle of the aggressive chaps sending them
> flying in several directions.[70]

Another remembers a more violent occasion:

> There was a "rumble" at a party, given by a Navy brat whose parents leased a small estate in Harrow. The party was a western hoe-down affair in the barn next to the house. I just remember that half-way through the party several carloads of "teddy boys" came over the fence and through the gate. They were armed with brass knuckles and chains and were ready for a fight. And they got it. Even a few of the girls joined in.[71]

This antagonism toward American teenagers also had a non-violent counterpart, which was part of a campaign against the USAF's presence in Britain and the use of nuclear weapons. Contributors to *Bushy Tales* recall rotten eggs being thrown at and into their bus and "Yanks go home" graffiti painted on a wall on their bus route. The latter insult was removed when Central High students added "and let Britain starve" to the original wording.[72] In fact, both sides had something to be ashamed of, as Central High students "would yell stuff at the English people, make obscene hand gestures, and generally be rude," or occasionally write "IRA" across the bus windows in lipstick.[73]

Conclusion

Central High students were unusual in attending an American school in Britain, but their family circumstances differentiated them even further from most other teenagers in the United States. They were military brats, children who had a peripatetic life moving from base to base, with fathers and sometimes mothers who believed in military discipline, who expected order and compliance from their children.[74] As one alumnus and subscriber to *Bushy Tales*, noted:

> Living in England and going to Central High School was such a unique experience for us and being able to share those experiences and memories with each other is pretty special. Ours is a rich heritage as military brats, because it forced us to make friends easily, be adaptable

to moving often and sometimes, for long stretches of time, having our Dads [away from home]. But we survived and for the most part are better citizens, sharing a love for our country.[75]

The students' ability to make friends was evidenced in *Bushy Tales*, in the survey, and in later correspondence with former students. Their experiences need to be treated with a little caution, as they were far more open to meeting new people and experiencing new cultures than the average American.

The observations of the now-elderly Americans who spent part of their adolescence in London in the 1950s provides a new commentary on that time and place. Some of their memories are unsurprising. For example, these young visitors found London dirty with smog and fog and saw that the buildings were scruffy and interspersed with unrepaired Blitz damage. It is also to be expected that Central High students thought British food disgusting (although fish and chips got a good hearing); most visitors and some residents thought the same.[76] Their views on Britons provide more nuance. They could see, in adults, the British reserve that older Americans were so conscious of, but they could break through it to find warmth and humour in their teachers and bus drivers. That working-class Londoners were warm-hearted and friendly, but also articulate and opinionated, came as a surprise. British teenagers in turn accepted the Americans as ordinary kids who would go cycling or make mischief. As more Americans arrived and Central High students moved into their late teens, going into the West End with their compatriots, advertising their American style became attractive.

The students had a strange and liminal position in Britain. They were part American archetypes, part kicking-around-town London teenagers, never quite being one or the other. Their unfettered consumption of American jeans, music, and food provided confirmation of what their British friends had seen at the movies and was a direct, if small scale, contributor to Americanization. Central High students were a real-life corrective to the images of Americans seen in both Hollywood and British films. The former emphasized glamour and crime, and the latter wealth and naïveté. Some characteristics reinforced the clichés. *Bushy Tales* respondents note that the male students were often taller than Britons of the same age and the female students were better turned out, wearing makeup and jewellery earlier than the local girls. They were all relatively wealthy and had privileged access at the PX to high-quality goods and produce unavailable to Britons. Their consumption and lifestyles showed to their British friends what would be possible in the near future. Other characteristics of the students modified the received view of Americans. Actual American teenagers were spottier than their filmic avatars. When Britons got to know them, they realized that their human strengths and weaknesses were the same as theirs.

CHAPTER NINE

Encountering the British – Trip Reporters

Despite the shared language, many Americans found it difficult to meet British people. As Stanley Wade Baron (an American author resident in Britain) remarked, "most of us Americans move through these foreign countries like a band of Gypsies, cut off from the natives, having only the most superficial contact with them."[1] When they did meet the British, the differences in cultures of the two countries did not help matters.

As was seen in Chapter 4, those marketing Britain to potential American visitors emphasized its beauty, history, and shared heritage. This last narrative held a strong influence over American Anglophiles, who justified Britons' reserved behaviour by relating it to Britain's long history and resultant feelings of superiority. One such visitor was Edward Barsness, making his second trip across the Atlantic. Barsness, who was travelling alone, seems a friendly, uncynical man, who, writing for his friends and colleagues, explained what the British were like:

> You may have heard about the British being stand-offish. If this is what you find, the fault will be your own, as the English people are really friendly and warm-hearted. It is true that the British people have their reserve … It is the kind of reserve that you learn to appreciate in time and understand. Part of it is breeding and old English tradition. Behind that reserve is culture and even pride.[2]

Americans' opinions on the Britons they met differed widely. They appreciated the honesty they encountered. They expected to get cheated by taxi drivers, but usually weren't. They admired policemen for their helpfulness and charm. Some loved the level of courtesy in British manners. On the other side of the same coin, others found Britons rude and unfriendly. A female American tourist described them as "shy, diffident, distant and strange."[3] A student reporting on his travels in Britain had the balance about right when he wrote, "we saw a good deal … of the reputedly cold English. Perhaps, in some ways they are reserved, but they were always generous and helpful to us."[4] Writer Emily Kimbrough recalled one encounter: "they say the British are aloof, almost unapproachable, [but] can you imagine any American inviting total strangers to stay as long as they liked, in a house where the hostess wouldn't even be home to count the silver?"[5] Academic Paul Roberts was also a fan. "As always happened in England when we looked sufficiently disconsolate and hopeless, some Englishman observed our plight and rushed up with advice and comfort."[6] Nathan Sharp, a self-published author and probably a decent person, since he donated the proceeds from his book *Happy Landings* to charity, recorded his impressions of the British in a generous-but-universalizing manner:

> Superficially, English people are rather cold and formal; but when you get to know and understand them better, you will find that your first impressions are wrong … once you have won an Englishman's confidence and liking, you will find him friendly, warm and loyal; and he may surprise you by showing signs of a delightful sense of humor.[7]

Relative Poverty

American visitors to Britain, once they had stopped being distracted by the landscape, heritage, and history, may have noticed how much poorer the locals were than they. The longer the stay in Britain, the more the disparity would have become obvious. In 1950, gross domestic product (GDP) per capita in the United States ran at about three times the level in the United Kingdom. By 1960, a relatively strong economic recovery in the UK reduced the gap, with US GDP at about twice the UK level.[8] American visitors did not reflect these averaged figures; they came from prosperous parts of their country, and had high disposable incomes. For example, personal incomes in California in 1950 were two-and-a-half times higher than they were in Arkansas.[9] These are not precise calculations, and this is not an economic history, but as a rough estimate, most visitors to Britain were probably four or five times better off than the natives at the start of the decade. As was shown in Chapter 2, one of the most persistent prejudices that Britons held about Americans was that they were overmaterialistic. Few in Britain had seen the inside of an American home in real life, so it was the portrayal of American life in the movies that provoked this feeling. Complaining about materialism was one way that Britons dealt with the contrasts between their homes and those shown on the movie screen, which, although idealized, reflected a wide difference in actual incomes.

Margaret Griffith from Washington, DC, visited Britain in 1951, so experienced at first hand the poverty associated with its austerity policies. Griffith, who was temporarily resident in Oxford, placed her child in the local state junior school and was sad to see the lack of decorations in her son's classroom. "Any 'Christmas' in the school is rather a bleak affair – one tree in the downstairs hall, untrimmed, and toys under it, are brought unwrapped." She noted that English children were "a little bleak too … cold in appearance and in fact, with few toys and not much to brighten their lives. They don't have much – and yet they are happy."[10] In the new year, Griffith and her daughter felt awkward about wearing their new winter coats in public. "We feel so terribly dressed up, even conspicuous, in them in this land of anything-but-elegant clothes." She described the experiences of one of her husband's American colleagues, who told Griffith how "the old clothes I brought to wear around Oxford every day are too good for that purpose."[11] This correlates with the experience of British journalist Douglas Sutherland, who could only dress well in the early 1950s by having a tailor remake two discarded American suits.[12]

Ruth Lois Matthews visited London in 1953, having got a prized and very expensive ticket to watch the coronation. She received some of the criticism raised against the United States when she started talking with an Englishwoman who had known better days. "The English are considered to be very polite. Yet I was more polite than one lady with whom I engaged in conversation. She told me that we Americans were too young and inexperienced to know how to lead in world affairs," a commonly-held British prejudice. The lady told Matthews how she had lost her home and all members of her family during the Blitz. Matthews recalled, "Her eyes, hands and facial expression showed me what she had suffered. I dared not mention my luxuries. She did this for me. She said, 'I know what all of you Americans have – you have everything – clothes, homes, and food.'"[13] Floridian Carol Hummel travelled round Europe on a shoestring, hitchhiking whenever possible. Despite her low-cost methods, she came from middle-class suburbia and was surprised by the lack of facilities when she called in on some Scottish friends in Edinburgh, who lived in local authority housing. "They don't know what it is to have a refrigerator, modern sink, shower, ironing board (they use the table), or running hot water. No central heating."[14]

Disappointment

The dissonance between the brochure writers' promises and the varied actualities of 1950s Britain was quite noticeable. Ruth McKenney, co-author of a leading guidebook from the early part of the decade, addressed this phenomenon in her opening chapter. She remembered her first visit to London, when her husband, who had visited the capital between the wars, raised expectations that were not immediately realized. "As we chugged along in our matronly high-slung taxi, he announced in a voice charged with emotion, 'Look Darling! London! The greatest city in the world!' 'Where?' I cried."[15] Despite the work undertaken by other more-selective brochure and guidebook writers and the efforts of tour guides and motor-coach companies, Americans still witnessed the ugly parts of Britain that undercut the promises of history, heritage, and rural beauty.

Many of the trip reports conform to the expected norm. These writers thought Stratford beautiful, Kent the garden of England, and London magnificent. Some, though, looked beyond the brochure's promises and found Britain to be dirty and disappointing. This encouraging feature suggests a veracity in reporting from authors who were not just setting out to impress their suburban neighbours. For example, Ethel Moller Arwe, one of the most interesting of trip reporters, saw the bad and good in Britain in an even-handed manner. She liked London, vowed to come back, but was aware of its greyness and lack of glamour. Rather than go misty-eyed at the sight of Buckingham Palace, she called it as she saw it, noting that it looked "very much like a railroad station." If you lived in New Jersey like the Arwes, you would have been familiar with New York City's Penn Station, which, in the 1950s, was a massive and dirty-faced classical building, not unlike the Palace.[16] Wealthy independent traveller William Ritchie from Omaha was struck by the dirty buildings in London. "They are so grimy with the smoke and fog of London that they are depressing. The tops of the buildings looked, however, as if they had been whitewashed [by the rain] ... I went to Westminster Abbey ... Over all, it was infernally and abundantly filthy with dirt."[17] It took another thirty years and clean-air legislation before London's buildings returned to their original hues. Phyllis Stock, like many others, gained her first view of London from a railway terminus, which experience from around the world shows is never a good idea. She recalled "My first view of London Town! What a disappointment it was! The train came into Paddington Station, which was my stop. I made my way through a dark haze of smoke that hung in the air like a gray ominous cloud."[18] Ethel Moller Arwe, arriving at Waterloo, concurred: "Sitting on a drab bench surrounded by suitcases, I survey the famous station and I find it quite the most dismal I have ever seen in my life. It is a dreary structure of steel and dingy glass with no light but the fading day."[19] Muriel Beadle had a similar feeling driving through Oxford for the first time. It was "a city of dirty, no-period buildings, of narrow streets choked with traffic, of store fronts like those in small towns in Nebraska."[20]

The surveys described in Chapter 2 reveal that the American characteristics most admired by Britons was their modern factories, vigour, and go-ahead attitude. In the interwar years, American companies, such as Hoover and Firestone, led the way in Britain with their efficiency and excellent working conditions. During the Second World War, the British wondered about the US Army's fighting qualities, but admired its smart methods of problem solving. Looking at life in the other direction, Americans saw Britons as inefficient, slaves to hidebound tradition, or just lazy. In the 1950s, American technical advisors funded by the Marshall Plan came to Britain to train its managers and engineers in how to become more productive. It was not always successful, with their British counterparts often keen to explain why the US practices would not work for them.[21] The USAF complained that British workers would do only two to three hours work but expected payment for the full day, resulting in Americans taking over their tasks.[22] As more US companies set up in Britain, their managers noted the difference in office working practices, such as drinking alcohol at lunchtime and not working on Saturdays.[23]

This American tendency to see Britain as a second-rate version of the United States is present in some of the trip reports, which responded to the condition of the two countries, one dynamic and forceful, the other in a state of decay. The visitors conflated Britain's dreary architecture and climate with its citizens' downbeat attitudes to form disappointing conclusions about the country. Ethel Moller Arwe, who was unwell on her arrival in Britain, told her readers how she felt. In effect, she proposed that Britons were subject to an environmental determinism in that a combination of the weather and buildings caused their behaviour. Her comments about this are worth quoting in full:

> There is something here that is puzzling – is it tangible? Is it a somber note? It is not a sadness, nor a humorlessness. There is, of course, the expected English reserve and preoccupation, but in addition to that, there is this *something*.
>
> It must be the grayness. The buildings are gray. The men's clothing is gray, their hats gray or black. The ladies wear dresses of black or a lifeless pastel. Taxicabs are black. Store window displays are dull and uninteresting, houses have their eyes closed, and I see no flowers.[24]

Arwe complained about her jolly "Good Mornings" being ignored in a hotel's breakfast room and put this "unfriendly, unmoved, withdrawn" rebuff down to British reserve.[25] However, the explanation could have more to do with Arwe misunderstanding conventional conduct in a foreign country, a crime of which Britons often accused Americans. Phyllis Stock, who travelled to Britain on a tight budget in 1957, echoed Arwe's sentiments.[26] She visited Cambridge, and enjoyed the city, the colleges, and the beautiful flowers on display. She loved Cambridge, but found the students surprising:

> There is a quietness among the English students ... It gave me a strange, strange feeling as though I was in a movie in technicolor with the sound turned off. Even the clothes of these college youths were drab. A far cry from the gay, careless dress of our own collegians. Quiet, withdrawn, these young men lacked the nonchalant arrogance of our own American youth. It made me feel a little sad.[27]

Lois Glick visited Europe in 1950, just at the point when the Labour government in Britain was facing a mountain of economic and political problems. She made a short visit to London, at the time in the grip of one of the terrible smogs of the period, and then moved on to Southampton to catch a liner home. Her short stay did not deter her from reaching a depressing verdict on Britain:

> Without a doubt, the glamor of England is gone. They remind me of children having been spanked with their heads still dropped in shame. They just can't seem to look up yet ... If the millions in America could see all the unhappy people I saw under real bondage they would do everything possible to protect our government of freedom rather than try to destroy it.[28]

Glick, a supporter of the drive to remove communists from the US government, assumed that the conditions in London were a consequence of socialism, instead of war debts, war damage, and poor investment in industry. Despite her zealotry, her picture of Britain at the start of the 1950s is striking.

Novelist John Knowles, who was resident in London in the early 1950s, realized that he was prone to these prejudices.[29] Early in his first visit to Britain, he watched a beggar on the street outside his window and despaired of his attitude: "when one of the infrequent pedestrians passes, the man extends his cap; it is a limp cap and he holds it out in a limp way." Knowles must have thought an American beggar would have made more of an effort. "As I stood tingling with irritation ... England for the first time really became foreign to me; this was the kind of beggar 'they' had. I also saw in myself for the first time the American disapproval of lassitude, of lack of enterprise, of limpness."[30] Ruth Lois Matthews felt the same: "I almost felt myself becoming lazy as I observed the slow pace with which the typical Englishman goes to his work."[31]

Class

Britain's historical class system was still in place in the 1950s. Some in Britain might have imagined that after the shared experiences of the Second World War and five years of socialist government Britain might have thrown off its class consciousness. It was a false dawn. Many working-class voters turned to the Conservatives again, and the country, buoyed by the ceremony and tradition of the coronation, returned itself to its historical divisions and became again much like it was in the 1930s. Change occurred slowly. The aristocracy was becoming poorer, the middle classes were on their long, slow rise through the twentieth century. By the end of the decade, real working-class voices were heard in British literature and drama.[32] Britons had become wealthier and could afford cars and washing machines, but their social expectations did not change a great deal. Factory workers became car owners, but they did not become managers, although their children would.

Americans did not see the strictly-drawn lines in the way a Briton would, although they were aware of the less-visually-obvious but still real class distinctions in their own country.[33] Floridian Carol Hummel noted, "They say class distinction is more defined here, but we do not see it except in the area of trains."[34] Longer-term resident Muriel Beadle recorded her encounters with Britain's class system during her stay. Her British friend told her it was the "assumption of equality with one's fellow-man that distinguishes Americans in England quite as much as their accents."[35] This flattery was mostly nonsense, as it presumed that Americans were incapable of class prejudice. As has been shown, the disdain of Americans for their compatriots in Britain was commonplace, and like British class distinction, this was about manners and education. Beadle noticed one key difference: in Britain a person's accent immediately announced his or her class. She thought that, for the United States, "It would be stupid to claim there are no classes ... but there is no widely recognized badge of caste comparable to that of English speech. [In America] the educated or the well-born man speaks essentially like the shopkeeper or the telephone repairman."[36] She showed her hand a little by later describing the class/accent dividing lines in British society as uncomfortable, but useful, because they informed behaviour toward people one did not know.

Ethel Moller Arwe, in her self-published memoir, revealed herself to be a gruff, judgmental, but kind woman. Despite her manner, she had an open and enthusiastic mind about the trip and the people that she met. When she fell ill, her descriptions of the doctor and the hotel maid who helped her were stamped with a democratic spirit. She didn't seem to recognize the difference in class between her two helpers. Arwe noticed that the maid was poor, and presented her with a well-received pair of nylons for her work.[37] Arwe was not a self-consciously cultured person and did not categorize her experience with the maid as being anything more than one woman meeting another with a very different background.

John Wilson Lyon from Claremont, California, visited Britain in 1953, when he was thirteen years old, and later recalled the time he spent in Oxford:

> In the Randolph Hotel, I met a boy my own age, maybe slightly older, who was running the elevator there. My family were talking on the elevator about going punting. The boy expressed interest too and so we took him along. In the United States that wouldn't have been an unusual thing to do, but now that I understand the class system in England at that time, it was probably a very unusual thing to do. We did it, and had a nice afternoon. The boy would have thought Americans more open about this type of thing.[38]

Lyon's analysis of this situation is spot on. He was from a well-known family; his father was president of a private college, the *Los Angeles Times* noting their departure for Europe with an accompanying photograph.[39] Lyon describes himself as a "privileged child," and his family were from the upper echelons of the American middle classes, which gives their actions even more contrast with British habits.[40] Historian Ross McKibbin notes that the class interaction Lyon described would have been almost impossible for a Briton: "Although middle- and working-class sociability rarely intersected anyway, middle-class sociability usually kept them firmly apart. Not only did the practice exclude the working class, it was often intended to."[41] Even saying more than the number of the floor required would have been unlikely. British readers of this book can make up their own minds about whether this has changed at all in the subsequent sixty years.

Gender Relations

In 1958, about 40 per cent of the women who applied for passports in the United States were in employment, which was very similar to the national percentages that showed 37 per cent of women were in paid work.[42] Half of the applicants identified themselves as housewives, but many were also college graduates. The American housewife was a rather maligned figure in the postwar years.[43] Journalist Leland Stowe summed it up: "American women are spoiled, self-centred, exceptionally aggressive, unhappy, dissatisfied, very expensive in their tastes, less and less interested in men … restless and bored … The men hug their offices, and the women turn to lectures clubs … [and] trips to Europe."[44]

British sexologist Eric John Dingwall thought American men were "immature, adolescent in outlook" and "pushed around by their female relations and friends."[45] Germaine Haney, travelling alone in Britain and Ireland in 1957, noted this British preconception that American wives henpecked their husbands, a notion that the people she spoke to said came from Hollywood movies and imported novels. However, this was an idea that had a much longer history. Nineteenth-century British visitors to the United States were surprised by how men were required to treat women of all classes with chivalry and politeness.[46] American women's assertiveness and independence contrasted with the more-conservative approach in Britain, so their attitudes stood out as unusual and surprising.

For example, book editor Phyllis Stock had arranged to be met at Liverpool Street station by a representative from American Express. Stock was meeting a friend at the station who was leaving the country to return home, and as a result the two women had three hours to kill. Her guide, Mr Smith, a precise and cautious man, recommended the station tea room, but the women were made of sterner stuff and wanted to try a pub. "'But my dear young ladies,' protested Mr Smith, 'there are no suitable places, really, in this neighborhood.'"[47] Stock had heard about one pub, Dirty Dicks, on her voyage over, so went there, despite the advice, and found it safe but tawdry. Smith was overprotective perhaps, but at least met Stock's expectations about Englishmen.

Stock was successful in finding pleasant Englishmen to talk to, and met one on a train, a lawyer who spotted that she was an American. Following a good conversation about international affairs, he asked if she was travelling alone. Informed that she was travelling as the spirit moved her, he remarked "'An Englishwoman would not do such a thing,' 'Why not?' I asked. 'You buy a ticket to where you want to go to … and there you are.' 'But you won't go to the Continent alone?' he asked. 'Oh yes,' I answered. 'Aren't you afraid?' he inquired. 'Of what,' I countered. 'An Englishwoman wouldn't go alone like that.'"[48]

Unluckier women travelling alone had the unpleasant task of fending off British men who wished to take them for a drink, or a walk, or to "look after" them. However, it was likely that a single American woman would have had a similar experience in Texas or Boston, and that single British women could also expect men to proposition them. For American women, it was the dissonance between the romanticized Hollywood screen image of the British gentleman and the actuality that was problematic and surprising. They were just like men everywhere. Germaine Haney had her fill of this behaviour when a stranger approached her and suggested (imagine a British upper-class type of voice), "Let's take a jolly old walk to the jolly old Lake Hotel."[49]

Haney was as forthright in her condemnation of British Railways waiters, and when invited to have a cup of tea with a nice man she met on a train (who wasn't picking her up) declined. "English train waiters ... bend over you and stick their dirty pale face into yours, and they pretend to be very solicitous, but really they are just trying to get close to you, to brush against your arm, or your breast, or your shoulder. I felt that if one more train waiter even looked at me, I was going to break a plate on his head."[50] Haney's book was titled *No Reservations*, which was a good pun, but not accurate about her experiences in Britain, as she had plenty of reservations about the country. Her account was outspoken for an American publication of that date and brings to mind the salacious accounts in the *News of the World*, which showed that Britain was a sexually repressed nation in the 1950s.

She was also interested in the roles that British men and women occupied, and contrasted this with American life. Of course, she met well-off middle-class Britishers, the sort who could afford to stay in a hotel for a few days. In the mid-1950s, this was a narrow section of society. Haney analyzed, with a good deal of acerbity, British middle-class married life. "The Englishman feels very secure in his position as head of the house, and if that house is built on sand and the foundations shift at times, he chooses not to notice. He calls his wife 'Darling' and Darling may do all the scrubbing ... but she's far from the meek little doll she pretends to be."[51]

Haney was refreshingly objective in her assessment of the English (her visit to Europe included Ireland, and her surname suggests a Celtic heritage, so she might well have been Irish-American) and documented a nasty exchange with a Mrs Darling. "'I know you people say *loo*tenant, and of course that's correct.' But, she added under her breath, 'It's the only thing they *do* say correctly.' [Her husband] gave her a look of concentrated poison and told her under *his* breath to mind her manners." Haney concluded, "Sometimes [an Englishwoman does] this deliberately because she doesn't like Americans. Sometimes she can't help herself, because she is really shy … and the immediate friendliness of many Americans gets her confused." It is likely that the wife mistook Haney's American friendliness and openness toward her husband for flirtation. Most single English women in the same circumstances would have been much more restrained in their conversation than their American equivalents.

Some Exceptions

Soon after his arrival in Britain in 1952, American writer John Knowles joined London's artistic circles, and was surprised by the metropolitan types he encountered. He met literary young men and women and ex-officers suffering from a kind of postwar malaise, circling from party to party. British journalist Douglas Sutherland described this world in his memoir *Portrait of a Decade: London Life, 1945–1955.*[52] Knowles was astonished to see how different this group of Britons were compared to the widely held reputation for reserve. "The English, or at least the Londoners, quickly established themselves for me as nonstop talkers, magpies hurriedly and matter-of-factly unravelling their intimate lives to strangers at parties … nothing stopped them."[53] Drew Middleton agreed. Returning to London in September 1953 he found that wartime experiences had led to much change, with people's superficialities stripped away. A committed Anglophile, Middleton may not have been the most reliable witness, but his recognition of this change is interesting. "I have never found the British cold or taciturn. On the contrary, I have met more real warmth among them than any in Europe … I reckon them a talkative, even garrulous, people."[54] John Crosby, the television critic of the *Washington Post*, noted the same phenomenon on his regular flights to Britain:[55]

I have traveled across the Atlantic on BOAC with the British several times now and it occurs to me that there should be some reconsideration of our traditional attitude towards our British cousins. I'm speaking specifically about this idea that the British are aloof. Maybe they're aloof on other people's airlines but not on their own. It's been my experience the minute we get off the ground they start chattering like magpies at you ... about the most intimate things – their marriages, their business affairs, their ailments.[56]

American visitors who travelled around Britain by train encountered the unusual culture of the British railway compartment. In the 1950s, railway carriages had six or eight separate compartments, which sometimes had a connecting corridor, sometimes not. Even the enclosed and semi-private nature of these spaces did not encourage chatter among strangers. Californian resident Katherine Ames and her husband, visitors in 1954, were enjoying sole occupation of one of these compartments. They were joined by two prototypical British men, who with their silence "seemed to ignore *our* presence [and] put a damper on the freedom of speech, I'd enjoyed for several hours."[57] Ames consigned these intruders to the category of "arrogant" Britishers she had met in the past. "Doubtless they believed, as most Britishers do, that their nation is superior in culture and wisdom to ours." She was surprised to discover that, when they realized the Ameses were Americans, the men were "charming and cultured" and happy to discuss the United States and its politics in a pleasant conversation.[58] Ames, who was elderly and refined, was pleased she had been recognized as a person of quality and learning.

Being Cheated

Americans generally admired courteous British manners. However, if most of encounters were pleasant, there were always some locals who let the side down.[59] Elderly Nebraskan William Ritchie travelled on his own to Britain in the summer of 1950 and encountered a sequence of demonstrations of poor treatment in London. Staying at the Savoy Hotel, Ritchie asked the hotel porter for a recommendation for a restaurant. The porter proposed Quo Vadis, a well-known Italian restaurant in Soho. This was an odd choice for a man like Ritchie (kickbacks from restaurants to hotel staff are not unheard of). It "was filled with many modern works of art and the tables were full of artistically dressed 'haircutted' persons. Some of them, the men of course, wore full beards." Four hours later, which must be a record for dining alone, Ritchie got his bill and left, but, it now being midnight, could not find a taxi for the journey back to the Strand. The restaurant manager recommended a limousine service, which then drove Ritchie around in circles "through rough looking places where drunken men were in the streets, until I finally told the driver that I expected to go to the Savoy right away." For what should have been a very short journey, the driver charged Ritchie £1. A real taxi would have charged two shillings, including a tip.[60] Ritchie unwillingly and accidently had become involved in a more authentic London experience than he would have got by dining in his hotel. Most trip reporters' coach tours carefully moved them from one attraction to another, thus avoiding Soho's drunker, seamier side.

Katharine Ames and her husband were also cheated, but in a more good-humoured way, when visiting Exeter. Their taxi driver took them for a tour of the city and waited with them for an hour for a museum to open, keeping the meter running. After three hours, their bill came to £4 and 11 shillings (£4.55p), about £150 in 2017 money. The next morning this cabbie was waiting for the Ameses to take them to the station. As Katharine recorded:

> Although it seemed pretty clear that he had gypped us neatly the day before, I really liked him. I forgave him for what looked like an excessive charge ... However, in parting, I told him that he was thrown away in Britain, that he belonged to the U.S. that he'd end up a millionaire surely. He seemed delighted – missed the sarcasm entirely – took it all as complimentary.[61]

Translations

The shared-heritage ideal promised, for most Americans, a common language that made travelling to Britain attractive. Everything would be clear. The reality was sometimes different. Jazz musician Bud Freeman, a regular visitor to Britain, felt the need to disabuse his readers of the idea that the English were just as the movies portrayed them. "For years on end we Americans have been saying that the English are a stuffy, unfeeling people. On the contrary they are the warmest, most gracious people I've ever met."[62] Freeman's perspective was perhaps unusual in that many of the people he spoke to were jazz fans and put him on a pedestal. He was keen to acknowledge there was another side to British life. When he was in York-shire for a gig, a domestic argument on the street outside his hotel woke him up at three in the morning. Freeman reported, in the vernacular, "You're nothing but a thieving, fooking busterd; You're a knave!"[63]

Ruth Lois Matthews met a different sort of Britisher when taking a tour of London by coach. She described her guide as "small, purely English ... He had an umbrella on his arm, wore a black English hat, soiled raincoat, and was 'veddy, veddy' happy to be with us for the morning tour."[64] Matthews had transliterated the slight lisp that many Londoners had, which Dickens wrote as "werry, werry." Either way, she gained insight into the wide variety of British speech in southern England before the rise of Estuary English. Paul Roberts, travelling with his family on a train from London to Slough, found the booking clerks at Paddington Station incom-prehensible. He was asked questions, muffled by the glass a little, such as "Plooker flaugh?" or "Yur miving on the raunches?" to which he could not make a response.[65] Germaine Haney was baffled by railway loudspeaker announcements and asked an English fellow-passenger to translate for her. "I never was able to understand anything over a speaker anywhere, it all sounded like pig Latin."[66]

Americans as Celebrities

We are so familiar with the United States and its citizens today that it is surprising to hear how Britons could see Americans as exceptional. This was most likely to occur in the parts of Britain that had seen little of Amer-ican troops during the war or afterwards. For example, Carol Hummel and her brother Bob were travelling around Britain in 1956 and visited Chester and Wales, among many other places in Britain. In Llangollen, they attend-ed the Eisteddfod, and being American made them celebrities of a sort. Hummel recorded that "Bob and I came back to the slope near the mar-quee and watched people for a long time. Several were having a picnic. We took a walk and many children came over to us for autographs, two for snapshots. I don't know how many came over, knowing we were Americans." They were not the only Americans at the festival; they met two girls from Jacksonville, Florida, with whom they had mutual friends, and an American Girl Scout who lent Carol her lipstick.[67] Earlier, Carol's arrival at a family friend's house in Chester was considered of such historical significance that they tape-recorded it for posterity.[68]

Driving a large American car in areas that were remote from USAF bases would draw a crowd of bystanders. Margaret Griffith, travelling in Scotland in 1951, described this phenomenon. She drove a "red American Ford … on Princes Street in Edinburgh, top down full of young people! Of course, the car creates a sensation. Whenever we go, or are – a crowd gathers, and it and we are the object of intense interest. I refuse to put the top up or down when there are people around – I'm afraid they'll mob us."[69] Etta Payne and her husband, who had travelled from Wyoming to Middlesbrough on the trail of her family tree, parked in a working-class part of town. "While I was taking some pictures about twenty-five youngsters gathered around our car. They were really thrilled because never before had they seen such a big American car. They actually patted it and stroked the fenders and body as though it was something precious and they wanted to determine if it was real." One girl asked Payne's husband, Oscar, "How'd you like to live in a dump like this?"[70] It is revealing that Payne couldn't understand that a car like hers might be considered precious, despite it being obvious that it was beyond the reach of most local people.

Conclusion

The differences between Britain's tourist marketing and the reality was often a surprise for visiting Americans. Their encounters with Britons gave them even more pause for thought. The responsibility for this was largely due to the influence of Hollywood movies that presented American moviegoers with a set of British caricatures bearing little resemblance to the real thing. For some trip reporters, this was a disappointment. Women travelling alone bore the brunt of the difference, as the charming, polite archetype was nowhere to be found, replaced by grabby hands, perhaps no different from the rest of the world. British attitudes and character proved disillusioning to some visitors, who expected Stewart Granger or David

Niven, and, in reality, encountered poorly dressed, disappointed, and impoverished Britons. The more perceptive visitors connected Britain's dilapidation to a wider national malaise.

In the first half of the decade, Britain was shabby and dirty. London and other cities such as Exeter, Southampton, Plymouth, and Coventry were badly bombed and had achieved little in the way of reconstruction. The combination of a dependence on coal fires and Britain's weather meant that black soot covered its public buildings, a situation that did not change much until the 1980s. Some trip reporters told it as they saw it. Westminster Abbey was a letdown; Buckingham Palace looked like a railway station.

Visitors' interactions with ordinary Britons were mostly with those working in the tourist industry. American experiences of waitresses and tour guides were pleasant. The trip reporters gave the police a high rating, reflecting a widely held respect for the badge in Britain, contrasting with the more authoritarian figure of the American cop. Some British taxi drivers cheated tourists, but that was the same the world over. Britons were surprisingly heterogeneous, defying the assumption, made in both Britain today and the United States at the time, that 1950s Britons were cold, reserved, and aloof. Some people were, but metropolitan types were happy to defy convention and talk about their finances and love lives to strangers, and many others were keen to discuss politics and the world with visiting Americans.

CHAPTER TEN

Asymmetry and Ambiguity

In the 1950s, the wealth and economic and cultural power of Britain and the United States, and their citizens' knowledge of each other, were highly asymmetric, which resulted in a complicated and ambiguous relationship between the two countries and their peoples.

James Bossemeyer thought that Americans were the most mobile people the world has ever known. While his statement disregards the mobilities of the British Empire, it spoke of the restlessness of modern American society, a key aspect of its modernity that was evidenced by countless domestic and foreign journeys. Americans saw leisure travel as a symbol of their wealth and a form of distinctive consumption in a decade when the United States was at its most conventional and homogenous. The rapid growth in the United States economy in the 1950s paid for higher wages, while a transformation in attitudes to taking on debt fuelled consumption of luxuries such as foreign travel. The percentage of Americans travelling to Europe was tiny, but nonetheless interesting, because of the changing nature of the class of people who could now afford to make the trip across the Atlantic. Europe called out to them after the Second World War, particularly Britain and France, although hyphenated Americans wanted to visit their families in Italy and Germany as well. In contrast, for Britons, if you excluded day trips to Calais, exchange controls made foreign leisure travel difficult for the wealthy and poverty made it impossible for the rest. Only a lucky few got to see the United States at first hand.

High levels of disposable income provided Americans with consumer durables and leisure opportunities for which Britons would have to wait another decade. In the United States, successful skilled workers and those above expected to own a house, a car, a television, and a fridge, have central heating and air conditioning, and to take regular vacations. Britons were more used to rationing, bicycles, radios, coal fires, opening a window, and a week in a boarding house in Scarborough. Alongside their relative wealth, Americans were (although exact comparisons are difficult) better educated than their British equivalents. They were much more likely to go to college, a process accelerated by the GI Bill. Women's higher education was also far easier to access; Britain's intelligent women were directed toward teacher training.

As with their physical mobility, Americans' social mobility was greater than in Britain. American self-help books explained that the son of an American worker had, through hard work and study, the opportunity to become a manager, and in turn the son of a manager could become an executive. Britain's grammar-school system was making some inroads into class barriers in the 1950s, but this was for a few bright boys and girls. At the same time, the class system in the Unites States was more permeable than in Britain and had fewer distinguishing accents, but was still very real, explaining why trip reporters did not find Britain's more overt class structure repulsive or puzzling.

By the 1950s, many Britons had met or seen an American in real life. The US Army's presence in the South of England during the war, the USAF's continuing occupation of Britain's rural airbases, and increasing numbers of visitors ensured their familiarity. These encounters were not always straightforward, and differences in culture, wealth, tone, and attitudes toward race led to differences between the two groups. In contrast, very few Americans had met a Briton. Those that had were likely to have met them in New York or Los Angeles or another major city.

Of all the differences between the two peoples, the most marked was in the nature, direction, and level of cultural transfers. Cultural Americanization had been a concern in Britain for generations, such was the disturbing impact of the importation of music, literature – and, most pervasively, movies from the United States. Despised by both the intellectual left and the establishment right, these influences destabilized Britain's self-image and changed the way that Britons thought and behaved. As scholars have pointed out, this was not always a process of passive adoption. On the whole, ordinary Britons loved American music and Hollywood movies, while still admiring the Royal Family and obsessing about cricket. Britons' knowledge of Americans was, then, formed from a variety of disparate sources. Direct encounters provided a correction to the influence of American popular culture.

Americans' knowledge of Britons was of a different, much-lower, order. They had little opportunity for direct contact, and there were few mainstream imports of British movies to inform them about British life. American newspapers and magazines were interested in the queen and in travel opportunities, but not in everyday British life. There were few British cultural transfers to the United States until the Beatles' appearance on the Ed Sullivan show in 1964 prompted the "British invasion" into American popular music. One exception was the enduring popularity of British film actors in Hollywood movies, who provided Americans with most of their information about Britons.

How Britons Saw Americans

It is difficult to sum up what fifty million Britons thought about Americans in the 1950s. There had been much ill-informed prejudice and much repetition of ideas generated over the previous hundred years. What emerges is a complex set of attitudes that were amplified by British newspapers and magazines that had something of an obsession with the United States, its citizens, and their lifestyles in the decade, and threw their criticism and praise around wildly.

One idea that resonated was that Britons and Americans were members of the same family. This was informed by the shared-heritage discourse and amplified by wartime experiences. It was, in truth, directed at WASP Americans, and excluded African Americans and other minorities. That these groups rarely featured in a meaningful way in Hollywood movies helped Britons' sense of identification with white Americans. The envy, resentment, love, and arguments found in most families demonstrate that this was a good, if incomplete, metaphor for the relationship between the two countries. If one thought that Americans were members of the same broad family group as the British, then the disappointing aspects of the relationship were felt harder than with other countries.

This sense of family disappointment also informed an alternative way of seeing the United States and Americans. In 1945, both the United States and the Soviet Union were admired as close allies engaged in an existential cause. The falling out with the Soviet Union (not family members) was quickly absorbed by most Britons (the Ipswich branch of the Communist Party was one exception). The question of whether Britain and the United States could be allies in an equal sense, or whether Britain was now subservient, was played out in parliament, opinion polls, newspaper articles, and pub discussions throughout the decade. The Suez Crisis brought Anglo-American relations to a boiling point, but Britain's subsequent acknowledgment of geopolitical realities quickly allowed for a more positive relationship by the end of the decade. In opinion polls, Britons readily conflated their views of the United States and Americans, proposing that they were guilty of being boastful, overconsumerist, ignorant of the world, and other crimes. These sentiments were encouraged by cartoon caricatures in popular newspapers. There is some evidence to suggest that working-class Britons, who enjoyed imported American cultural products the most, had a more favourable attitude toward Americans than their middle-class compatriots.

Interestingly, negative British attitudes seem to have rarely spilled over into real life. Britons may have laughed at their media portrayals in private, but were usually pleasant and helpful to actual Americans if they met them. In addition, the good welcome Americans received did not seem to be affected at all by the ups and downs of Anglo-American relations. The trip reporters encountered only a couple of mild examples of anti-Americanism. The Central High School students got some attention from local hooligans, but nothing really different from what well-turned-out Britons might have received in the same circumstances. USAF servicemen received the sort of attention that visiting troops got in most countries.

In summary, some Britons were anti-American in the sense that they resented the power of the United States and feared the consequences of its foreign policies, but most were polite and helpful to the Americans they met. The small number of African Americans in Britain may have experienced some racism, but not in the institutionalized way they were used to at home. Britons told opinion pollsters that Americans were too consumerist, but when confronted with it in actuality were intrigued by their wealth and their possessions, rightly sensing that they were glimpsing their own near future.

How Visiting Americans Experienced
Britain and Britons

The responses of Americans to Britain and its people varied depending on their background. Anglophiles came to Britain as the central point of a European vacation. Typified by Juanita Stott, the Carolinian librarian, they had long seen Britain as a focus in their intellectual lives. To see Westminster Abbey or Anne Hathaway's cottage in person was the experience of a lifetime, placed in context by a traditional education in English literature and poetry. Many Americans who did not have this background still found Britain's heritage and history deeply appealing. Britain, in conjunction with France and Italy, provided them with an evocative alternative to the consumerist and increasingly homogenous suburbanized life at home. Britain's castles, palaces, and stately homes were appealing and photogenic and would stay in their memories forever.

For the more neutral American visitor, Britain was less impressive; some found its cities dirty and disappointing. The concentration on heritage and history in tourist brochures made it hard for an impoverished, post-Blitz country to keep up. Grimy buildings and railways were one thing, but the food and accommodation was also frequently unsatisfactory. Some of the trip reporters were surprisingly downbeat. Their accounts suggest that the most exciting and transformative part of their trip to Britain was the journey across the Atlantic. Travelling by sea offered luxury (apart from those in the cheap berths), companionship, and a carnival atmosphere. Flying presented a different signifier. Its compression of time and space gave airline passengers an exciting journey, in which they left Britain at breakfast and were back in New York before lunch, connecting them to a powerful modernity brought about by new technology.

Britishers turned out to be a heterogeneous people. The trip reports and USAF memories featured in this book recall warm friendships, meetings with articulate working-class men and women, a world-weary metropolitan set happy to discuss incomes and sex lives, and the startling fact that not all Britons were English. One or two of the clichés were true. Some people were cold and hard to read, and Americans could confuse a reluctance to engage with strangers (a behaviour that Britons applied just as much to each other) for mute hostility. Some Americans thought Britons were either depressed, lazy, or both, a sentiment that was at its strongest in the early years of the decade. On a more positive note, even considering that most of the respondents sourced in this book were Anglophilic, the warmth and open good nature of those they met surprised American visitors. Some were cheated or short-changed, but the overwhelming majority of their encounters were pleasant. The variety of British behaviours noted by American visitors in the 1950s suggests that the Britain of the 1960s (working-class voices, openness, obsessions with fashion) were, at the least, in formation during the preceding decade.

❖ ❖ ❖

In the long history of Americans visiting Britain, the 1950s stands out as a decade of change. It saw, in about 1956, the transition from a time when Britain was visited largely by middle-class Americans to one where successful lower-middle-class and working-class visitors were in the majority. That same year also marked (in a not-unrelated event) the transition from sea to air travel. Within ten years, the choice of travelling to Britain by liner was reserved mainly for the elderly. American tourist demands for modern hotel accommodation had begun to change Britain's cities, a process that reached an apogee with the opening of the London Hilton in 1963. As the 1960s progressed, Americans of all social classes came to Britain in increasing numbers, at first for heritage, history, and shopping, and then for a few years from 1966 to see "Swinging" London in Carnaby Street. This short diversion quickly came full circle and once again Americans came to Britain to enjoy its traditional attractions.

Appendices

Appendix 1

Number of American civilian visitors to the United Kingdom

1950	127,830
1951	127,580
1952	163,580
1953	186,400
1954	202,840
1955	239,140
1956	255,440
1957	262,730
1958	325,190
1959	356,540
Total	2,247,270

Source: Medlik, *The British Hotel and Catering Industry*, 156. This book presents a summary of BTHA reports that are not readily available today.

Appendix 2

Book authors – visitors

Author	Occupation	M/F	Title	Date of Trip	Self-published	Age on trip	State
Ames, Katherine Fitz-Gerald	Retired	F	Adventures Abroad	1955	Y	78	CA
Arwe, Ethel Moller	Housewife	F	Bring Your Own Soap	1953	Y	49	NJ
Barsness, Edward	Journalist	M	Europe Calling: A Minnesota Newspaperman's New Adventures in the Old World	1959	Y	68	MN
Branham, Mary	Journalist	F	Good Morning, American Ladies	1956	Y		NM
Dundas, Esther Hilton	Housewife	F	So We Went to Europe: An Ancestral History	1958	Y	65	IL
Glick, Lois	Businesswoman	F	It's Too Late to Wait	1950	N	45	CA
Haney, Germaine	Lecturer	F	No Reservations	1958	N	50*	CA
Hahn, Joseph E.	Student	M	Hitchhiking Through Europe During the Summer of 1956	1956	Y	21	MI
Kimbrough, Emily	Author	F	Forty Plus and Fancy Free	1954	N	55	NY
Kimbrough, Emily	Author	F	Water, Water Everywhere	1957	N	58	NY
Kimbrough, Emily	Author	F	A Right Good Crew	1958	N	59	NY
Matthews, Ruth Lois		F	Come Abroad with Me: On Vacation Tour Through Europe	1953	Y	44	FL

Author	Occupation	M/F	Title	Date of Trip	Self-published	Age on trip	State
Mersfelder, Larry	Retired	M	We Were the Foreigners	1957	Y	72	OK
Payne, Etta	Housewife	F	Home Was Never Like This: A Trailer's-Eye View of Europe Today	1957	Y	50*	WY
Price, Willard	Author	M	Innocents in Britain	1958	N	71	CA
Ritchie, William A.	Politician	M	Diary of a European Trip: July–August 1950	1950	Y	70*	NB
Roberts, Paul M.	Academic	M	And the Children Came Too	1959	N	35*	DC
Running, Leona Glidden	Religious	F	From Thames to Tigris	1958	Y	42	DC
Running, Leona Glidden	Religious	F	36 Days and a Dream	1951	N	35	DC
Sharp, Nathan		M	Happy Landings in Europe	1959	Y		
Sone, Violet West	Poet	F	13 Innocents Abroad.	1959	N	47	TX
Stock, Phyllis Swale	Book editor	F	Eight Pence a Mile	1958	N		CA
Young, Estelle		F	Gone to Europe	1952	N		

Book authors – residents

Author	Occupation	M/F	Title	Date of Trip	Self-published	Age on trip	State
Baron, Stanley Wade	Novelist	M	People and Americans	1953	N	30	PA
Beadle, Muriel	Journalist	F	These Ruins Are Inhabited	1957	N	39	CA
Griffith, Margaret D.	Housewife	F	Unconventional Europe	1951/2	Y	45*	DC
Huntington, John	Diplomat	M	A Bean from Boston	Throughout	Y	34–44	MA
Knowles, John	Writer	M	Double Vision	1952	N	26	CT

Unpublished diaries/memoirs

Author	Occupation	M/F	Title	Date of Trip	Archive	Age on trip	State
Burrell, Julia	Student	F	*European Tour*	1958	Vanderbilt Peabody	22*	TE
Butler, Susie	Student	F	*My Trip to Europe*	1953	BYU Utah	40	UT
Hummel, Carol		F	*Pardon My Thumb: The Author's Account of Her Hitchhiking Experiences*	1957	UNC Chapel Hill	27*	FL
Lyon, Carolyn Bartel	Academic Editor	F	*Diary*	1953	Claremont Colleges	45	CA
Lyon, John Wilson	Schoolboy	M	*Oral History*	1953	Self	13	CA
Stott, Juanita	Librarian	F	*Our European Tour, April-May 1954*	1954	Duke University	48	NC
Wilson, Edward G.	Executive	M	*My Trip to Europe*	1954	Duke University	45	CT

* approximate age

Appendix 3

A planning study for the series of programs "Talking of America" – Opinion of Americans, as volunteered by Londoners.

Percentage of respondents mentioning a characteristic

Negative characteristics	Positive characteristics	%
They are boastful/swaggering		45
	They are friendly	28
They live at too high a pressure (i.e., they hustle too much, they compete too hard)		24
They are unfit to be a world power (in the United Nations sense)		22
	They work hard	20
	They are generous	19
They place too much importance on material things		16
They are immature		15
They are ostentatious (dress the ordinary thing up as the extraordinary)		14
	They are go-ahead and ambitious	14
	They are good company/ cheerful/like fun	14
They think that America is the only country in the world		11

Negative characteristics	Positive characteristics	%
They are politically immature		10
Films give a false impression of American life		9
	The American way of life is very much like our own	8
They treat Negroes badly		7
	They are courteous	7
There is a lot of crime and corruption in America		7
Money is far too important to them		6
Their clothing is loud/spivish/ in poor taste		6
American children are ill-mannered and uncontrolled		6
	They are home loving	5
Politics in America are undignified (mass hysteria)		5
	The standard of living is higher there than here	5
Their politics are corrupt		5
They are noisy in speech		5

Source: Belson, *The Impact of Television*, 85.

Appendix 4

European vacations, percentage duration of stay for American air and sea passengers in 1958

	Sea	Air	Total
for less than 14 days	2.2	12.6	9.0
15–28 days	15.4	28.9	24.2
29–42 days	21.4	21.6	21.6
43–60 days	23.9	17.5	19.7
for more than 60 days	37.1	19.4	25.5
	100%	100%	100%
Approximate median	51 days	33 days	39 days
Average time in Britain	Less than 14 days		

United States, Department of Commerce, *Participation in International Travel – 1959 Supplement to Survey of International Travel with Revised Data through 1958*, Table 28 – Length of Stay and Kind of Travel of United States Residents Returning from Europe and the Mediterranean Area, 1958.

Average time in Britain from Medlik, *The British Hotel and Catering*, 156.

Appendix 5

Proportion of visitors to various European Countries, 1958

	% that left USA and visited each country
France	59
United Kingdom	53
Italy	49
Benelux (Brussels expo in 1958)	45
Germany	44
Switzerland	40

Source: 1958, Department of Commerce, *Participation in International Travel – 1959 Supplement to Survey of International Travel with Revised Data through 1958*, Table 6

Numbers of United States residents travelling in Europe

	1951	1954	1958
France	144,000	244,000	381,000
United Kingdom	124,000	221,000	338,000
Italy	107,000	183,000	248,000

Source: For 1951 and 1954, United States, Bureau of Foreign and Domestic Commerce, *Survey of International Travel*, Table 5. For 1958, Department of Commerce, *Participation in International Travel – 1959 Supplement to Survey of International Travel with Revised Data through 1958*, Table 6.

Appendix 6

Number of servicemen in United Kingdom

	USAF	US Army, Navy, Marines	Total
1950	4,793	415	5,208
1951	18,939	7,374	26,313
1952	42,029	6,000	48,029
1953	41,746	5,672	47,418
1954	44,219	3,060	47,279
1955	40,205	6,707	46,912
1956	38,489	5,670	44,159
1957	37,366	25,642	63,008
1958	31,744	802	32,546
1959	29,487	2,459	31,946

USAF figures: Department of the Air Force, *United States Air Force Statistical Digest – Fiscal Years 1950–1959*, Various Tables – Command Strength Based on Operating Location by Country Outside Continental US.

US Army, Navy, Marines figures: Defense Manpower Data Center. *Worldwide Manpower Distribution by Geographical Area*. 1951 figure is economist Tim Kane's estimate. Actual deployment statistics were not disclosed because of the Korean War and are still unavailable. Kane, "Global U.S. Troop Deployment, 1950–2005." 1952 figure is author's estimate. 1957 figure reflects the temporary arrival of US 6th Fleet for duty in the Mediterranean.

Assuming an average two-year term of duty, this represented approximately 220,000 different individuals (some staff were on three-year terms, others on ninety days). When American wives and children are included, this rose to (even more approximately) 250,000 individuals.

Notes

Chapter One

1 Stott, *Our European Tour, April–May 1954*, 3.
2 Dulles, *Americans Abroad: Two Centuries of European Travel.*
3 Dunning, "American Tourists in Victorian Britain."
4 Baxendale, "The Construction of the Past and the Origins of Royal Tourism in 19th-Century Britain," 29.
5 Jennings, *Them and Us*, Chapters 3 to 6.
6 Dulles, *Americans Abroad: Two Centuries of European Travel*, 164.
7 The number of American tourists in the 1930s averaged 78,000 per annum, see Middleton, *British Tourism: The Remarkable Story of Growth*, Table AV.1 "Estimates of Visits to Britain from the USA, the Commonwealth and in Total from 1921 to 1938," 189. The *total* number of temporary visitors to the United States (mostly from Britain and continental Europe) in the 1930s averaged about 65,000 a year, see United States Bureau of the Census. *Historical Statistics of the United States, Colonial Times to 1970*, Table C 150.
8 Evidenced by the British invasion into American popular culture from 1963 onwards, which reached something of a pinnacle in *Time* magazine's coverage of "swinging" London in its 15 April 1966 issue.
9 I originally thought of these visitors as "ordinary" Americans, but having the cultural and economic capital required to make the journey across the Atlantic made them, in reality, unusual and distinctive in American society in the 1950s. For some, this distinction was the point of the journey. Using the term "ordinary" is also problematic, as it has a variety of negatively constructed meanings (see: Williams, *Keywords: A Vocabulary of Culture and Society*, 226).
10 Williams, *The American Invasion*, 107.

11 Tindall and Shi, *America - A Narrative History*, 823.

12 Cohen, *A Consumers' Republic*.

13 Packard. *The Status Seekers*.

14 Mead, "The Pattern of Leisure in Contemporary American Culture."

15 Rugh, *Are We There Yet? The Golden Age of Family Vacations*.

16 Bossemeyer, "Travel: American Mobility."

17 Katona, *The Mass Consumption Society*, 278.

18 United States Bureau of the Census. *Historical Statistics of the United States, Colonial Times to 1970*, Series G, Table 459. Personal Consumption Expenditures, by Type of Product: 1929 to 1970, Part 1, 317. Dollar deflator from www.measuringworth.com, accessed 8 May 2018.

19 Katona, *The Mass Consumption Society*, 278.

20 My book *1938 Modern Britain* describes the continuities between the late 1930s and the return to prosperity in the 1950s.

21 Thomas, "Will the Real 1950s Please Stand Up?"

22 This was the story of my own family. My grandfathers, a railway fireman and a shop worker, had a child each, who became in the 1950s a teacher and a bank official, lived in a suburban house, and by the end of the decade had their own car.

23 Mort, "The Commercial Domain: Advertising and the Cultural Management of Demand," 56.

24 Dobson, *Anglo-American Relations in the Twentieth Century*, Chapter 6.

25 Bartlett, 'The Special Relationship,' 48; Bartlett, *The Long Retreat*, 147; Dumbrell, *A Special Relationship: Anglo-American Relations in the Cold War and After*, 47; Dobson, *Anglo-American Relations in the Twentieth Century*, 117 et seq.

26 Harper, *British Cinema of the 1950s: The Decline of Deference*.

27 Williams, *The American Invasion*, 37; Porter and Harper, "Throbbing Hearts and Smart Repartee."

28 Pells, *Not Like Us*; McKay, ed. *Yankee Go Home (& Take Me With U)*; Malchow, *Special Relations: The Americanization of Britain?*; Horn, *Juke Box Britain*; Slater and Taylor, eds., *The American Century*; De Grazia, *Irresistible Empire*; Marling, *American Affair: The Americanisation of Britain*; Kroes, "Americanisation: What Are We Talking About?"

29 Kynaston, *Austerity Britain 1945–1951*, 348–51.

30 Middleton, *British Tourism: The Remarkable Story of Growth*, 19.

31 British Travel and Holidays Association, *Annual Report – 1958*, 5.

32 See United States, Bureau of Foreign and Domestic Commerce, *Survey of International Travel, 1959*, Table 11 – Citizens Departing from and Arriving in the United States, annual surveys.

33 www.worldcat.org; beta.worldcat.org/archivegrid; catalog.loc.gov; explore.bl.uk; Briscoe, ed., *American Autobiography, 1945–1980*.

34 Pells, *Not Like Us*, 135. The title of this book echoes Pell's excellent monograph.

35 Sullivan, "Vanity Press Publishing."

36 Dann, "Writing Out the Tourist in Space and Time."

37 Harvey, *The Fifties*.

38 May, *Homeward Bound*, 26.

39 Katherine Fitz-Gerald Ames and Germaine Haney (see Appendix 2).

40 Walton, "Travel as a Force of Historical Change."

Chapter Two

1 Mulvey, *Anglo-American Landscapes*; Mulvey, *Transatlantic Manners*.

2 Watt, *Succeeding John Bull*.

3 Rydell, *Buffalo Bill in Bologna*.

4 Griffith, *Unconventional Europe*, 69.

5 Middleton, *Where Has Last July Gone?*, 187; Bartlett, *The Long Retreat*, 2; Watt, *Succeeding John Bull*.

6 Hendershot, *Family Spats*, 20.

7 Duffus, "Clues to an Understanding of John Bull" (edited for clarity).

8 Louis and Bull, *The Special Relationship*, 57.

9 Kynaston, *Austerity Britain, 1945–1951*, 348–51.

10 Hennessey, *Having It So Good*, 51.

11 Williams and Williams, *The Grass Is Greener*, 40. This popular 1959 British play about Anglo-American relationships referred, unremarkably, to this resentment of a decade earlier.

12 Hendershot, *Family Spats*, 20.

13 Dobson, *Anglo-American Relations in the Twentieth Century*, 113; Dumbrell, *A Special Relationship*, 47; Dobson, *Anglo-American Relations in the Twentieth Century*, 117 et seq.; Bartlett, "*The Special Relationship*," 48.

14 Dumbrell, *A Special Relationship*, 47; Dobson, *Anglo-American Relations in the Twentieth Century*, 117 et seq.; Hennessey, *Having It So Good*, Chapter 9.

15 Dobson, *Anglo-American Relations in the Twentieth Century*, 117 et seq.;
    Bartlett, *The Long Retreat*, 147; Hennessey, *Having It So Good*, 461.
16 Gallup, ed., *The Gallup International Public Opinion Polls, Great Britain,*
    1937–1975. November 1956, 393.
17 Ibid.
18 Hendershot, *Family Spats*, Figure 6.
19 Middleton, *The British*; "Drew Middleton of *The Times* Dies at 76," *New*
    York Times, 12 January 1990.
20 Jones, "Letter to the Editor."
21 Middleton, *The British*, 173.
22 McKay, "Americanization and Popular Culture," 33.
23 Green, "A Mirror for Anglo-Saxons," 31.
24 Ibid., 36.
25 "Out of Hours," *Harper's Magazine*, February 1954.
26 McClune, "Letter to the Editor" (emphasis in the original).
27 Highmore, *Everyday Life and Cultural Theory*, 77.
28 Hubble, *Mass-Observation and Everyday Life*.
29 Mass-Observation, "File Report 2544," 1 (1947).
30 Vanderschmidt, *What the English Think of Us*.
31 Bingham, *Family Newspapers?* 19.
32 Vanderschmidt, *What the English Think of Us*, 141.
33 Ibid., 143.
34 Perry, "The American Cast of Mind."
35 Belson, *The Impact of Television*, 85.
36 Ibid., 90.
37 Lyons, *American in the British Imagination*, 50; Worpole, *Dockers and*
    Detectives.
38 Baron, *People and Americans*, 19.
39 Coughlan, "How We Appear to Others," 150.
40 Ibid.
41 Ibid.
42 Ibid., 154.
43 Dann, "Writing out the Tourist in Time and Space."
44 Mulvey, *Transatlantic Manners*, 71.
45 Haney, *No Reservations*, 35.
46 Beadle, *These Ruins Are Inhabited*, 34.
47 Aldor, *The Good Time Guide to London*, 11.

48 Reynolds, *Rich Relations*.

49 Ovendale, *The English-Speaking Alliance*, 79.

50 Judt, *Postwar: A History of Europe Since 1945*, 247.

51 A useful military history of the USAF in Britain can be found in Jackson, *Strike Force*.

52 Gallup, ed., *The Gallup International Public Opinion Polls, Great Britain, 1937–1975*, May 1954, 325.

53 "Yanks in England," *Picture Post*, 28 June 1952, 24.

54 Morton, *Get Out!*

55 Ibid., 3.

56 Ibid., 7.

57 Law, *1938 Modern Britain*, 83.

58 "Yanks in England," *Picture Post*, 28 June 1952, 24.

59 Ibid., 26.

60 Huntington, *A Bean from Boston*, 38.

61 Hendershot, *Family Spats*, 57.

62 "US Tourists: Good or Ill-will Envoys?" *New York Times*, 1 September 1957.

63 Steinbeck, "The Yank in Europe."

64 Duffus, "Still the Innocents Abroad."

65 Wechsberg, "The American Abroad."

66 Reid, "Amsterdam Is Meaning Eyes."

67 Baron, *People and Americans*, 205.

68 Meyer, *Go It Alone, Lady!* 82.

69 Arwe, *Bring Your Own Soap*, 15.

70 Running, *From Thames to Tigris*, 17; Bossemeyer, "Travel: American Mobility."

71 Baron, *People and Americans*, 205.

72 Jackman Custom Originals advertisement, *Holiday*, July 1947.

73 *Punch*, 31 May 1950. Some excellent 1950s sunglasses can be seen in an advertisement for Willsonite Sunglasses, *Holiday*, July 1951.

74 Baron, *People and Americans*, 92.

75 Johnston, "Eastward Ho!"

76 Kimbrough, *Forty Plus and Fancy Free*, 213. Text has been adjusted to remove Kimbrough's attempt at rendering a cockney accent in a Mary Poppins style.

77 Churchill, "A Million Pair of Eyes Focus on the Palace."

78 Friedlander, "Tourists Take Over Britain."

79 Meyer, *Go It Alone, Lady!* 112.

80 Ibid., 124.

81 "What to Wear in London," *Holiday*, April 1956.

82 *Daily Mirror*, 23 April 1957, 2.

83 Muggeridge, "The American in England."

84 I am grateful for this observation from an anonymous referee for this book.

85 Rydell, *Buffalo Bill in Bologna*.

86 Anonymous cartoon accompanying article by Cooke, "The American Abroad."

87 "A London American: British View," *London American*, 31 March 1960.

88 My thanks to design historian Deborah Sugg Ryan for her advice on these details.

89 Jensen, "Giles, Ronald [Carl] (1916–1995)."

90 *Daily Express*, 5 August 1959.

91 Stone, "Screening the Yank."

92 Rolinson and Cooper, "'Bring Something Back.'"

93 Guest, *The Quatermass X-Periment*, 07″.

94 Humberstone, *Happy Go Lovely*.

95 Parry, *A Yank in Ermine*, based on a 1948 novel, Carstairs, *Solid! Said the Earl*.

96 Ibid., 1′ 06″.

97 Ibid., 1′ 18″.

98 Arkell, *Trumpets Over Merriford*.

99 Pells, "American Culture Abroad," 69.

100 Dumbrell, *A Special Relationship*.

101 Edwards, "'From Here Lincoln Came.'"

102 Otte, "'The Shrine at Sulgrave,'" 120.

103 Moser, *Twisting the Lion's Tail*.

104 Baxendale. "The Construction of the Past," 30.

105 Mulvey, *Transatlantic Manners*, 209.

106 Hendershot, *Family Spats*, 2.

107 Reynolds, *Rich Relations*.

108 Gee, *American England*, 3.

109 Beadle, *These Ruins Are Inhabited*.

110 Wrench, *Transatlantic London*, 28.

111 Kent, *London for Americans*; Kent, "American Associations with London."

112 Mulvey, *Anglo-American Landscapes*; Wrench, *Transatlantic London*; Commager, *Britain through American Eyes*.

113 Commager, *Britain through American Eyes*; Mowat, *Americans in England*; "Biographical Chronology of Henry S. Commager," www.commager.org, accessed 23 April 2018.

114 Even as late as 1943, the term "England" was understood to include the other countries of the United Kingdom.

115 Commager, "English Traits, One Hundred Years Later," 750.

116 Mowat, *Americans in England*, vi.

117 Hendershot, *Family Spats*, 28.

118 A search for views on Americans in British newspapers of the 1950s produces a large number of articles. Searching the other way around, in, for example, the *New York Times*, reveals little.

119 Campbell, "Letter to the Editor."

120 USAF, *In Focus*, 7.

121 Barsness, *Europe Calling*, 44.

122 Kimbrough, *And a Right Good Crew*, 96.

123 Freeman, *You Don't Look Like a Musician*, 56.

124 Duffus, "Clues to an Understanding of John Bull."

125 Matthews, *Come Abroad with Me*, 31.

126 Stock, *Eight Pence a Mile*, 23.

127 USAF, *In Focus: The Americans in Britain*, 10.

128 A survey response from an anonymous subscriber to *Bushy Tales* (see Chapter 8).

129 Fielding, *Fielding's Travel Guide to Europe, 1956–57*, 233.

130 Schweppes commercial, undated, c. 1956, https://youtu.be/qCygHT4V4z4, accessed 2 April 2018; Hazel Hartman Radio Show: WFPG 1450 Atlantic City, 1955, https://youtu.be/ogKFkZ-TBls, accessed 2 April 2018.

131 Muggeridge, "The American in England," 59.

132 "Portrait of a Britisher," *London American*, 24/31 March 1960.

133 Donovan, "Cooke, Alistair."

134 Alistair Cooke, "The Face of England."

135 Ibid.

136 https://www.census.gov/newsroom/cspan/1940census/CSPAN_1940slides.pdf, accessed 2 February 2018.

137 Hendershot, *Family Spats*, 30.

138 Glancy, "'Temporary American Citizens'?"

139 Norman, *Babycham Nights*, 100.

140 Nott, *Music for the People*.

141 Daiches, "Britons Find It Jolly Good Reading," *New York Times*, 5
     September 1954; Worpole, *Dockers and Detectives*.

142 http://news.gallup.com/poll/5299/queen-elizabeth-years-public-opinion,
     accessed 23 March 2018.

Chapter Three

1 Lyons, *America in the British Imagination*, 36. Although Lyons is explaining here how few Britons crossed the Atlantic, he understates the movement in the opposite direction.

2 See Appendices 1 and 6.

3 See Appendix 1.

4 Home Office, *Statistics of Foreigners Entering and Leaving the United
   Kingdom, 1954*, Table 1.

5 Summary statistics from Middleton, *British Tourism*, Table AV.8 – Visits
   and expenditure for all purposes – inbound tourism to the UK, 193. The
   1952 statistics from *Manchester Guardian*, 4 July 1953.

6 United States, Bureau of Foreign and Domestic Commerce, *Survey of
   International Travel*, Appendix, Table II – Aliens Departing from and
   Arriving in the United States; United States, Department of Commerce,
   Participation in International Travel – 1959.

7 Adrian, "A Dollar for the Bell-hop." See Whitehorn, *Selective Memory*,
   120.

8 McKenney and Bransten, *Here's England*, 9.

9 Larsson and Zekria, Pan American World Airlines, "System Time Table,"
   1 August 1953; Anon., *Official Guide to the Railways*, August 1952.

10 United States, Bureau of Foreign and Domestic Commerce, *Survey of
    International Travel*, Table 11 – Citizens Departing from and Arriving in
    the United States, 1953.

11 Ibid., Table 10 – Passports Issued and Renewed, by State of Residence of
    Recipients, 1948–55.

12 By 1954 there was a slight move away from the eastern seaboard towards
    the Midwest. The figures became less reliable over time, as increased
    flying meant that not everyone travelled through New York.

13 United States, Department of Commerce, *Participation in International Travel – 1959*, Table 46 – Passports Issued and Renewed, by Metropolitan Area of Residence of Recipients, 1958.

14 McKenney and Bransten, *Here's England*, 9.

15 Bernat, "Convergence in State Per Capita Personal Income, 1950–1999," June 2001.

16 United States, Department of Commerce, *Participation in International Travel – 1959*, Table 13 – State of Residence of United States Travelers Returning by Air from Trips to Cuba, 1958.

17 United States, Department of Commerce, *Participation in International Travel – 1959*, 34.

18 The *Los Angeles Times* was full of advertisements for European travel in the early 1950s.

19 The summaries shown in Table 3.3 have been prepared by the author. "Professionals" includes: doctors, engineers, teachers, scientists, and lawyers. "Business owners" includes: farmers, merchants, sales. "Creative" includes: actors, artists, musicians. "Skilled" includes: skilled workers, clerks, barbers, nurses, tradesmen, contractors, and technicians. "Unskilled" includes: unskilled workers and servants. The authorities also recorded a further large group, the members of which described themselves as housewives. It is assumed for simplicity that this group was spread evenly across the other categories. Statistics for 1958 were taken from United States, Department of Commerce, *Participation in International Travel – 1959*, Table 42 – Passports Issued and Renewed by Occupation, July through December 1958. Classification of occupation was much cruder and fits easily into the summary categories used for 1950 and 1955.

20 Fish, *Invitation to England*, 21 (author's italics).

21 As the 1958 figures are for the second half of the year only, this might bias the result toward lower-cost travel in September to March.

22 Steinbeck, "The Yank in Europe."

23 Churchill, "Well, What Do You Know! Said the Rubbernecks."

24 Stock, *Eight Pence a Mile*, 9.

25 "Britain as Seen by Visitors," *Times*, 9 August 1958.

26 United States Department of Commerce, "Consumer Income."

27 Halsey, *British Social Trends Since 1900*, Table 7.2.

28 Snyder, *120 Years of American Education*, Table 3.
29 Ibid. About 10 per cent of the US population was black and about four times less likely to go to college, which, if taken into account, would increase the advantage of white American women over white British women.
30 Green, *Sociology*, 202.
31 United States, Department of Commerce, *Participation in International Travel – 1959*, 5.
32 Ibid., Table 32.
33 Weiler, producer, *6½ Magic Hours*.
34 United States, Bureau of Foreign and Domestic Commerce, *Survey of International Travel*, Table XV.
35 British Travel and Holidays Association; Scottish Tourist Board; Social Surveys (Gallup Poll), *A Survey of the Tourist Trade in Scotland, 1956*, 14.
36 Jackson, *Strike Force*, 42.
37 Ferguson, *Eighth Air Force Base Air Depot, Burtonwood*, 88.
38 USAF, *In Focus*.
39 Morton, *Get Out!* 3.
40 Geiger, "US-UK Wedding Bells."
41 USAF Directorate of Statistical Services, *United States Air Force Statistical Digest – Fiscal Year 1955*, Table 143, Departmental Strength of Female Personnel.
42 Quoted in Grandstaff, *Foundation of the Force: Air Force Enlisted Personnel Policy, 1907–1956*, 108.
43 USAF Directorate of Statistical Services, *United States Air Force Statistical Digest – Fiscal Year 1955*, Table 170, Distribution of Departmental Strength Officers by Grade in which Serving, by Age – 30 Sept. 1954 and Table 171, Distribution of Airmen by Grade in which Serving, by Age – 30 Sept. 1954.
44 It has been assumed that forces deployed to Britain were representative of the whole USAF.
45 USAF Directorate of Statistical Services, *United States Air Force Statistical Digest – Fiscal Year 1955*, Table 172 – Distribution of USAF Military Personnel by Grade in which Serving, by Highest Level of Education – 31 May 1955.
46 Green, *Sociology*, 202.

47 USAF Directorate of Statistical Services, *United States Air Force Statistical Digest – Fiscal Year 1955*, Table 169 – Percentage Distribution of Pre-Service Residence of USAF Military Personnel – 28 Feb. 1955.

48 Cooke, "The American Abroad."

49 Jones and Bostock. "US Multinationals in British Manufacturing before 1962"; Pells, *Not Like Us*, 188.

50 Wilson, *My Trip to Europe – February 1954* (and supplementary notes).

51 https://www.rhodeshouse.ox.ac.uk/community/list-of-rhodes-scholars, accessed 26 November 2017.

52 Lyon, Carolyn Bartel, *Diary 1953*.

53 Lyon, interview with author, 19 September 2017.

54 May, *Homeward Bound*, 79.

55 Arwe, *Bring Your Own Soap*, 1.

56 United States, Bureau of Foreign and Domestic Commerce, *Survey of International Travel*, 34, and Table 45.

57 Stock, *Eight Pence a Mile*, 9; *Independent Press-Telegram*, 16 June 1957.

58 "The American Matriarchy," *Times*, 11 February 1957.

59 Hollinger, *The Humanities and the Dynamics of Inclusion since World War II*, 54.

60 Hummel, *Pardon My Thumb*.

61 Burrell, *European Tour, Summer 1958*.

62 Stock, *Eight Pence a Mile*.

63 Urry, *The Tourist Gaze*.

64 Dann, "Writing out the Tourist in Space and Time."

65 Hays, "Emily Kimbrough, 90, Magazine Editor and Popular Author," *New York Times*, 11 February 1989.

66 Ritchie, *Diary of a European Trip*, 3.

67 Payne, *Home Was Never Like This*, 168.

68 Rumble, correspondence with the author, September 2017.

Chapter Four

1 Vanderschmidt, *What the English Think of Us*, provides a good summary of American and English prejudices at the start of the decade.

2 McKenney and Bransten, *Here's England*, 9.

3 Dilley, "Tourist Brochures and Tourist Images," 59–65.

4 British Travel and Holidays Association, *Annual Report – 1951*, 6.

5 "Come to Britain. A Survey by the *Times*, in Co-operation with the British Travel Association," January 1949; British Tourist and Holidays Board, *Second Annual Report, 1948–49*.

6 "Come to Britain in Festival Year," *Life*, 23 October 1950.

7 British Travel and Holidays Association, *Annual Report – 1951*, unpaginated.

8 Jensen, "Emett, (Frederick) Rowland (1906–1990)."

9 British Travel and Holidays Association, *Annual Report – 1951*, 27.

10 Buzard, "Culture for Export," 312.

11 Griffith, *Unconventional Europe*, 115.

12 Middleton, *The British*, 14.

13 Churchill, "A Million Pair of Eyes Focus on the Palace."

14 Prochaska, *The Eagle and the Crown*, 160–5.

15 British Travel and Holidays Association, *Scotland*, 6.

16 This emphasis on landscape and history in British tourist material continued through the rest of the twentieth century. *See* Dilley, "Tourist Brochures and Tourist Images," 59–65.

17 British Travel and Holidays Association, Scottish Tourist Board, and Social Surveys (Gallup Poll), *A Survey of the Tourist Trade in Scotland, 1956*, 20.

18 Ibid., 12.

19 Hummel, *Pardon My Thumb*, 7.

20 Manchester Municipal Information Bureau, *Why Manchester?*

21 "Come Visit Britain in Royal Autumn," *Los Angeles Times*, 7 October 1953.

22 "Devon and Cornwall Fascinating in Fall," *Los Angeles Times*, 24 August 1952; Kellogg, "Down from London in a British Car."

23 "*Holiday* Magazine Sold," *Lakeland Ledger*, 10 July 1977.

24 "Literary Guide to Britain," *Holiday*, April 1956.

25 Hubbard and Lilley, "Selling the Past"; Mulvey, *Anglo-American Landscapes*, 74; "Stratford-upon-Avon," *American and Commonwealth Visitor*, February 1954.

26 Fielding, *Fielding's Travel Guide to Europe, 1956–57*, 86.

27 TWA, TWA *Vacation Guide and World Atlas*, front flap.

28 Ibid., 37.

29 *Clipper Travel*, March 1954.

30 Toogood, director, *Wings to Britain*.

31 Mersfelder, *We Were the Foreigners*, 12.

32 Hummel, *Pardon My Thumb*, 2.

33 Laughlin, *So You're Going to England!* This was a postwar revision of a book originally published in 1926. Fish, *Invitation to England*; McKenney and Bransten, *Here's England*; Thayer, *Holiday in England*.

34 Peel and Sørensen, *Exploring the Use and Impact of Travel Guidebooks*.

35 Koshar, "Guidebooks and National Identities in Germany and Europe," 327.

36 Thayer, at least, uses the term "England" to mean just that.

37 Thayer, *Holiday in England*, vii.

38 McKenney and Bransten, *Here's England*, blurb from inside front cover.

39 Ibid., 195, 205.

40 Ibid., 224.

41 Thayer, *Holiday in England*, 198.

42 McKenney and Bransten, *Here's England*, 21.

43 "American Tourist Optimism," *Times*, 5 June 1959.

44 Fodor, *Woman's Guide to Europe*; Meyer, *Go It Alone, Lady!*

45 Meeker, "The European Male."

46 Mikes, "The American Female."

47 Meyer, *Go It Alone, Lady!* 115.

48 Ibid., 112.

49 Ibid, 115. I like the idea that to describe a lone woman as "single" in 1957 required quote marks.

50 Ibid.

51 The heritage theme could still be found late in the decade, in travelogues such as Price, *Innocents in Britain*.

52 "England Swings," a hit song for Roger Miller in 1965, which in its lyrics encourages American tourists to save up their money and get across the sea to England, www.songmeanings.com/songs/view/3530822107858 506375, accessed 3 December 2017.

53 Mort, *Capital Affairs*.

54 www.allmusic.com/album/songs-for-young-lovers-mw0000851214, accessed 14 June 2018.

55 https://youtu.be/tVCDZaApwV8, accessed 14 June 2018.

56 www.allmusic.com/album/come-fly-with-me-mw0000194130, accessed 14 June 2018.

57 Coates, "London by Night."

58 Endy, *Cold War Holidays*, 7; Levenstein, *We'll Always Have Paris*.

59 Minnelli, director, *An American in Paris*.

60 Minnelli, director, *Gentlemen Prefer Blondes* and *Gigi*.

61 Negulesco, director, *Three Coins in the Fountain*.

62 Minnelli, director, *Brigadoon*.

63 Aldor, *The Good Time Guide to London*.

64 Ibid., 20.

65 Ibid., 13.

66 Ibid., 275.

67 Ibid., 278.

68 Ibid., 210.

69 USAF, *In Focus*.

70 Morgan, "Day of Shortage Is Behind."

71 "Britain as Seen by Visitors," *Times*, 9 August 1958.

72 Wechsberg, "The American Abroad." This sounds like a reference to Aldor's guidebook.

73 Meeker and Meeker, "London's Prim Burlesque."

74 Katona, *The Mass Consumption Society*.

75 Purchase tax on luxury items was at 33.3 per cent. Friedlander, "Tourists Take Over Britain."

76 Churchill, "A Million Pairs of Eyes Focus on the Palace."

77 "Britain as Seen by Visitors," *Times*, 9 August 1958.

78 TWA *Vacation Guide and World Atlas*, 71.

79 "Silver for the Tourist," *Times*, 10 February 1958.

80 Sone, *13 Innocents Abroad*, 41.

81 "Shopper's Guide to Britain," *New York Times*, 5 August 1956.

82 *Clipper Travel*, March 1954.

83 Fielding, *Fielding's Travel Guide to Europe, 1956–57*, 244.

84 Ibid., 280.

85 Ibid., 271.

86 Ibid., 273.

87 Kaledin, *Mothers and More*.

88 Fodor, *Woman's Guide to Europe*, 297.

89 Ibid., 306. The Duchess of Kent and her sister-in-law Princess Alexandra were twenty-three and twenty years old respectively and very fashionable minor royals at the time of the writing of this guidebook. See "Elegant Clothes for Spring," *Times*, 20 January 1956.

90 For a satirical view of this idea, see Norman Mansbridge's cartoon, "An American's Map of England," *Punch*, 6 July 1953.

Chapter Five

1 Bransby, director, *Getting There Is Half the Fun*, 9' 44".

2 Board of Trade, "Response to the Note by the Foreign Secretary on Steps to be Taken to Increase Dollar Earnings from Tourism," 3 November 1949, The National Archives, BT 64/1250.

3 Pan American World Airways, Timetable for "The President" service, June 1954. Sourced from https://jpbtransconsulting.com/category/merchant-marine/, accessed 30 March 2017.

4 Blackburn, "Blue Riband Route," *Flight*, 28 October 1955.

5 Ackerman, *Bushy Tales*.

6 Bransby, director, *Getting There Is Half the Fun*, is a colour film that provides an upbeat survey of travelling across the Atlantic on the *Queen Elizabeth*. Although boosterish, it is full of fascinating detail.

7 *Life*, 27 June 1955.

8 Department of Commerce, *Participation in International Travel – 1959 Supplement to Survey of International Travel with Revised Data through 1958*, Table I – Citizens Departing from and Arriving in the United States by Means of Transportation, 1958. These figures show the preference of some travellers to go to Britain by sea and return at the end of their vacation by air.

9 Miller, *The Last Atlantic Liners*.

10 *Life*, 27 June 1955.

11 www.measuringworth.com/uscompare, accessed 30 March 2017.

12 "Proving Flight for Tourist Services," *Times*, 30 April 1952.

13 Blackburn, "Blue Riband Route."

14 "How Peter Pan Flew to Paris," *Holiday*, January 1956.

15 Fielding, *Fielding's Travel Guide to Europe, 1956–57*, 87.

16 *Holiday*, April 1956.

17 United States Lines, advertisement, *Holiday*, April 1956.

18 Miller, *The Last Atlantic Liners*.

19 "How Peter Pan Flew to Paris."

20 "Biggest Rush in History," *Daily Mail*, 23 May 1956; ABC *World Airlines Guide*.

21 British Travel and Holidays Association, *Annual Report, 1958*, 13.

22 United States, Bureau of Foreign and Domestic Commerce, *Survey of International Travel*, Table 6 – Departure Month for United States Citizens Traveling to Europe and the Mediterranean.

23 Medlik, *The British Hotel and Catering Industry*, 33.

24 "Encouraging the Out-of-season Visitor from U.S.," *Manchester Guardian*, 26 October 1950.

25 Ibid.

26 *Los Angeles Times*, 24 August 1952.

27 "Britons Here to Seek 'Middle Class' Tourists," *Los Angeles Times*, 25 October 1949; Grant, "'Working for the Yankee Dollar.'"

28 "BOAC Makes Your Two Weeks' Vacation a Full 14-Day European Holiday," *Time*, 12 June 1950.

29 Thomas, "When Are You Going Abroad?"

30 Rugh, *Are We There Yet?* 17.

31 Johnston, "Eastward Ho!"

32 "Student Tourists," *Manchester Guardian*, 9 July 1952.

33 Meyer, *Go It Alone, Lady!* 81.

34 Ibid., 83.

35 Baldwin, "The Pan Am Series."

36 Wilson, *My Trip to Europe*.

37 Matthews, *Come Abroad with Me*, 12.

38 Ibid., 13

39 Price, *Innocents in Britain*, Chapter 1.

40 Butler, *My Trip to Europe*.

41 Baldwin, "The Pan Am Series," PAA, October 1957 timetable.

42 Ibid., Pan American, October 1958 timetable.

43 "Atticus Meets the Americans in Britain," *Sunday Times*, 31 January 1960. Presumably Cowles was talking about the late 1950s, after the introduction of jet planes. But perhaps not.

44 Gordon, *Naked Airport*.

45 Gross, director, *Jet Terminal*.

46 A good picture of the state of play in 1949 can be seen in Crown Productions, *London Airport*.

47 Crown Productions, *London Airport*.

48 Arwe, *Bring Your Own Soap*, 26.

49 Miller, *The Last Atlantic Liners*.

50 Glick, *It's Too Late to Wait*, 100.

51 Bransby, director, *Getting There Is Half the Fun*.

52 Mersfelder, *We Were the Foreigners*, 13.

53 "Atlantic Riband for America," *Times*, 8 July 1952.

54 *Los Angeles Times*, 24 August 1952.

55 Miller, *The Last Atlantic Liners*.

56 Hummel, *Pardon My Thumb*.

57 Stott, *Our European Tour*.

58 Goossens, "ss *Constitution* and ss *Independence*."

59 Butler, *My Trip to Europe*.

60 Burrell, *European Tour, Summer 1958*, 1959.

61 Butler, *My Trip to Europe*.

62 Hummel, *Pardon My Thumb*.

63 Lyon, interview with author, 19 September 2017.

64 Hummel, *Pardon My Thumb*.

65 Burrell, *European Tour, Summer 1958*.

66 Branham, *Good Morning, American Ladies*, 5.

67 Stott, *Our European Tour, April–May 1954*.

68 Ibid.

69 Branham, *Good Morning, American Ladies*, 5.

70 Butler, *My Trip to Europe*.

71 Hummel, *Pardon My Thumb*, 2.

72 McCarey, *An Affair to Remember*.

73 Lyon, *Diary, 1953*.

74 Hummel, *Pardon My Thumb*, 2.

75 Branham, *Good Morning, American Ladies*, 5.

76 "Atlantic Collision: The Sinking Italian Liner," *Times*, 27 July 1956.

77 Burrell, *European Tour, Summer 1958*.

78 Stott, *Our European Tour, April–May 1954*.

79 Butler, *My Trip to Europe*.

80 Lyon, *Diary, 1953*.

81 "An Ocean Terminal without Rival in the World," *Illustrated London News*, 5 August 1950.

82 *Premier Opens New Ocean Terminal*, director unknown, 1950; British Pathé, United Kingdom.

83 Geoffrey Wakeford, "Is Britain's Gateway a Shabby Back Door?" *Daily Mail*, 22 October 1952.

84 Hummel, *Pardon My Thumb*; Lyon, *Diary, 1953*.

Chapter Six

1   Dann, "Writing Out the Tourist in Space and Time."

2   Law, "Charabancs and Social Class in 1930s Britain."

3   Matless, *Landscape and Englishness*.

4   Laughlin, *So You're Going to England!* 563, converted from Laughlin's attempt at a local dialect into standard English for clarity.

5   Mersfelder, *We Were the Foreigners*, 12.

6   Advertisement in *Los Angeles Times*, 11 May 1952.

7   McKenney and Bransten, *Here's England*, 155.

8   "Britain as Seen by Visitors," *Times*, 9 August 1958.

9   Ibid.

10 Duffus, "Still 'The Innocents Abroad.'"

11 Stott's *Our European Tour* and Running's *36 Days and a Dream* provide good examples.

12 Price, *Innocents in Britain*, 209.

13 Dobie, "Shakespeare's Home Town."

14 British Travel Association, *Shakespeare's Country*. This 1960 promotional colour film shows American tourists enjoying the region.

15 Hoyer, *Shakespeare's Country*; Fox, *Shakespeare's Country*.

16 Mersfelder, *We Were the Foreigners*, 53.

17 Royal Shakespeare Company, www.rsc.org.uk, accessed 17 January 2018.

18 Dundas, *So We Went to Europe*, 38.

19 Price, *Innocents in Britain*, 211.

20 Bloom, *Broadway: An Encyclopaedia*, 398; Hilliard, "Broadway Time Capsule."

21 Stott, *Our European Tour*, 60.

22 Baxendale, "The Construction of the Past."

23 Lyon, *Diary, 1953*, 25 June 1953.

24 Roberts, *And the Children Came Too*, 20.

25 Matthews, *Come Abroad with Me*, 19.

26 Ibid., 27.

27 Ibid., 28.

28 Ibid., 29.

29 Stott, *Our European Tour*, 69.

30 "See Europe from as Little as $6.45 a Day," advertisement in *New York Times*, 11 January 1953.

31 Matthews, "The Very Model of a Modern Travel Agency?"

32 Stott, *Our European Tour*, 57.

33 Lyon, *Diary, 1953*, 17 July 1953.

34 Lyon interview.

35 Russell Brockbank, untitled cartoon, *Punch*, 31 May 1950.

36 Cynthia Kellogg, "Down from London in a British Car." The BTHA magazine *Coming Events in Britain*'s advertising was dominated by car-rental companies from as early as November 1952.

37 McKenney and Bransten, *Here's England*, 157.

38 *Coming Events in Britain*, March 1954.

39 *Holiday*, April 1958.

40 Friedlander, "Tourists Take Over Britain."

41 Victor Britain Rent-a-Car System, "Dine and Drive Through Britain," brochure 1959.

42 "English Motor Tour," *Holiday*, April 1958.

43 "American Tourist Optimism," *Times*, 5 June 1959.

44 Price, *Innocents in Britain*, 130.

45 Baron, *People and Americans*, 116.

46 "Complaints of Dirty Trains," *Times*, 3 August 1955.

47 "… But Bad Service, and Manners, Send Our Visitors on – to Paris," *Picture Post*, 10 April 1954.

48 Iddon, "Diary."

49 "Complaints of Dirty Trains," *Times*, 3 August 1955.

50 British Travel and Holidays Association, *Britain*, introduction.

51 *Holiday*, April 1956.

52 Davis, "The Rain Isn't as Bad as the B.R. Trains."

53 Hahn, *Hitchhiking through Europe*.

54 Hummel, *Pardon My Thumb*, 8.

55 Pauley, *Pioneering History on Two Continents*, 118.

56 Roberts, *And the Children Came Too*, 40.

57 Borah, "Landmarks of Literary England."

58 Hutchison, "Poets' Voices Linger in Scottish Shrines."

59 "Guide to Tourist London," *Holiday*, April 1956.

60 Stock, *Eight Pence a Mile*, 11.

61 Ibid., 19.

62 Roberts, *And the Children Came Too*, 43.

63 Beadle, *These Ruins Are Inhabited*, 137.

64 Borah, "Landmarks of Literary England."

65 Dobie, "Shakespeare's Home Town."

66 Law, *The Experience of Suburban Modernity*, Chapter 6.

67 Urry, *The Tourist Gaze*, 8.

68 "A Cruise on Canals: Noted Americans See Fresh-water England," *Life*, 2 September 1957.

69 Kimbrough, *And a Right Good Crew*, 67.

70 MacCannell, *The Tourist*, 92.

71 Dann, "Writing out the Tourist in Time and Space."

72 Haney, *No Reservations*, 26.

73 Kimbrough, *And a Right Good Crew*, 11.

74 Griffith, *Unconventional Europe*, 193.

75 Wyler, director, *Dodsworth*.

Chapter Seven

1 Mrs Walt H. Bradley, quoted in Davis, "The Rain Isn't as Bad as the B.R. Trains!"

2 Rugh, *Are We There Yet?*

3 Brough, "American Hotels, Well –."

4 Medlik, *The British Hotel and Catering Industry*, 33.

5 Board of Trade, "Brief for Sir Leslie Rowan on North American Tourism," 21 November 1949, The National Archives, BT 64/1259.

6 "Happy Landings," *Hotel Management*, June 1948.

7 Ferry, *The Nation's Host*.

8 Law, "Turning Night into Day."

9 Pocock, "Roadhouse, 1949."

10 Golders Green was a suburb with many Jewish residents; "merchants" is also a coded reference to Jewishness.

11 Letter from W.J. Hughes, Department of Trade, to F.J. Root, Ministry of Works, 26 September 1949, The National Archives, WORK 17/266.

12 Ibid.

13 British Tourist and Holidays Board, *Report on an Inquiry Carried Out by the Hotels Committee into Hotel Services in Great Britain from the User's Point of View*.

14 "Will BHRA Condemn BTHB Hotels Report?" *Hotel Management*, May 1950.

15 British Tourist and Holidays Board, *Report on an Inquiry Carried Out by the Hotels Committee into Hotel Services in Great Britain from the User's Point of View*, 3.

16 Ibid., 8.

17 Kimbrough, *And a Right Good Crew*, 156.

18 Adrian, "A Dollar for the Bell-hop."

19 Friedlander, "Tourists Take Over Britain."

20 Wakeford, "Is Britain's Gateway a Shabby Back Door?"

21 Board of Trade, "Hotel Grants Scheme," The National Archives, BT 177/290; Board of Trade, "Financial Assistance for New Building and Re-equipment of Hotels Catering for the North American Market," The National Archives, BT 15/344, 1950.

22 "Hotels: Function and Organization," *Architectural Review*, September 1960.

23 "Will BHRA Condemn BTHB Hotels Report?" *Hotel Management*, May 1950.

24 Astor, "Catering for Americans," letter to the editor of the *Times*, 8 February 1950, in response to a letter from Evelyn Wrench, 2 February 1950, which proposed that Britain should adopt the standards of modern American hotels.

25 Baron, *People and Americans*, 47.

26 Arwe, *Bring Your Own Soap*, 19–20.

27 Stock, *Eight Pence a Mile*, 20.

28 Ritchie, *Diary of a European Trip*, 1.

29 Maudin, "Europe on Less than $28,411."

30 Adrian, "A Dollar for the Bell-hop."

31 Beadle, *These Ruins Are Inhabited*, 42.

32 Ibid., 47–9, edited for clarity.

33 Wilson, *My Trip to Europe* and supplementary notes.

34 Wilson, supplementary notes.

35 Fielding, *Fielding's Travel Guide to Europe, 1956–57*, 246.

36 Ibid., 245–7.

37 Adrian, "A Dollar for the Bell-hop."

38 "The First American Hotel Ever Built in London: Views of the Westbury, in Bond Street, The West-end's First New Hotel for Twenty Years," *Illustrated London News*, 5 March 1955.

39 "Britain's First American Hotel Opens in London," *Caterer and Hotel-Keeper*, 19 March 1955.

40 Ibid.

41 "Our London Correspondence," *Manchester Guardian*, 2 March 1955.

42 Atticus, "People and Things," *Sunday Times*, 6 March 1955.

43 Fielding, *Fielding's Travel Guide to Europe, 1956–57*, 247.

44 "Our London Correspondence," *Manchester Guardian*, 2 March 1955.

45 Adrian, "A Dollar for the Bell-hop."

46 "Man about Town about to Go West," *Sunday Times*, 27 December 1959.

47 "Westbury Hotel, Bond Street, London; Architect: Michael Rosenauer," *Architectural Review*, May 1955, 336–7.

48 "Hotels: Function and Organization," *Architectural Review*, September 1960.

49 Bailey, "Jazz at the Spirella: Coming of Age in Coventry in the 1950s," 23.

50 "Coventry's New Hotel Opens," *Caterer and Hotel-Keeper*, 7 May 1955.

51 Williams, *The American Invasion*, 32.

52 "Hotels: Function and Organization," *Architectural Review*, September 1960.

53 Aslet, *All That Life Can Afford*.

54 "Hotels: Function and Organization," *Architectural Review*, September 1960.

55 The launch brochure is reproduced in full in Aslet, *All That Life Can Afford*.

56 Malchow, *Special Relations*, 34.

57 Wilson, *My Trip to Europe – February* 1954 and supplementary notes.

58 Sutherland, *Portrait of a Decade*, 70.

59 "… But Bad Service, and Manners, Send Our Visitors on – to Paris," *Picture Post*, 10 April 1954.

60 "News from Scotland," *Hotel Management*, June 1950.

61 Raymond Postgate, quoted in Driver, *The British at Table, 1940–1980*, 49, emphasis in the original.

62 Wilson, "So Completely Unspoiled," *Punch*, 6 July 1953, 14.

63 British Tourist and Holidays Board, *Report on an Inquiry Carried Out by the Hotels Committee into Hotel Services in Great Britain from the User's Point of View*, 5.

64 Raymond Postgate, quoted in Driver, *The British at Table, 1940–1980*, 52.

65 Kimbrough, *Forty Plus and Fancy Free*, 212.

66 Kimbrough, *Water, Water Everywhere*, 268.

67 Griffith, *Unconventional Europe*, 137.

68 Stott, *Our European Tour*, 62.

69 Ibid., 3.

70 Arwe, *Bring Your Own Soap*, 24.

71 Hummel, *Pardon My Thumb*, 8.

72 Running, *From Thames to Tigris*, 19.

73 Driver, *The British at Table, 1940–1980*.

74 Chamberlain, *Etched in Sunlight*, 181–2.

75 Arwe, *Bring Your Own Soap*, 24.

76 Stock, *Eight Pence a Mile*, 20.

77 Griffith, *Unconventional Europe*, 33.

78 Mackenzie, "How to Make the Best Coffee," *Hotel Management*, June 1950.

79 Advertisement in *Hotel Management*, June 1950.

80 Gutzke and Law, *The Roadhouse Comes to Britain*, 85.

81 Kimbrough, *And a Right Good Crew*, 157.

82 Reynolds, *Rich Relations*, 252.

83 Parry, director, *A Yank in Ermine*.

Chapter Eight

1 USAF, *In Focus – The Americans in Britain*, 7.

2 "What the Americans Think of Us," *Picture Post*, 28 June 1952.

3 Stott, *Our European Tour, April–May 1954*, 61.

4 Hummel, *Pardon My Thumb*, 6.

5 "4-year Sentence on US Airman," *Manchester Guardian*, 19 July 1952.

6 "Testing Ground for Anglo-American Relations: Problem of Peripatetic Teen-agers," *Manchester Guardian*, 27 November 1952.

7 "Stronger Patrols of US Police," *Manchester Guardian*, 28 October 1952.

8 Raymond, "The Yanks in England."

9 David Lampe, "The 'GI problem': An American Airman's View," *Manchester Guardian*, 20 September 1952.

10 "Community Relations," *Brize Breeze*, 3 February 1956.

11 Pereira, *Brize Norton – Gateway to the World*.

12 "Community Relations," *Brize Breeze*, 3 February 1956.

13 "Bee Bozeman Wins Flower Best at Witney Show," *Brize Breeze*, 12 October 1956.

14 *Brize Breeze*, subsequent issues, 1956.

15 Gropman, *The Air Force Integrates, 1945–1964*, 145.

16 "What the Americans Think of Us," *Picture Post*, 28 June 1952.

17 "American Families in English Communities," *Times*, 19 September 1956. Kathryn Dugdale, thirty-one years old in 1955, was a member of two important aristocratic families, with the Marquess of Londonderry and Lord Derby as grandparents.

18 "Lady Dugdale," Obituary, *Telegraph*, 26 April 2004.

19 USAFE Senior High Schools, *1958 Vapor Trails*.

20 Ender, *Military Brats and Other Global Nomads*. This term dates from the 1980s and summarizes the longer-term consequences of children living with military-disciplined fathers who moved frequently from base to base. See Oxford Dictionaries, www.oxforddictionaries.com

21 Bugge, "'Selling Youth in the Age of Affluence'" and Savage, *Teenage*, identify earlier antecedents.

22 Quite a good pun.

23 www.bushypark.org/Start_News.htm, accessed 24 October 2017.

24 www.bushypark.org, homepage, accessed 24 October 2017.

25 Rumble, Correspondence, 16 August 2017. Bill Rumble, the editor of *Bushy Tales*, was extremely helpful in the research for this book by reaching out to the surviving alumni of Central High to get their thoughts and memories about living in Britain as teenage Americans.

26 Of the 600 elderly subscribers, 37 people responded to the survey. Men responded more than women, even though they were outnumbered in the population. Younger readers were also more likely to respond. Where it has been possible, the survey has been triangulated with primary sources that address the experiences of the USAF in Britain.

27 Rumble, Correspondence, 7 November 2017.

28 www.bushypark.org, class rosters, accessed 24 October 2017.

29 USAF Bushy Park Dependents School, *The Londoner*.

30 USAF Bushy Park Dependents School, *The Londoner*, "Editorial," 4.

31 A review of Central High yearbooks shows that about 90 per cent of the pupils were white.

32 USAFE Senior High Schools, *1958 Vapor Trails*.

33 Ibid., 142.

34 Ibid., 205.

35 Ibid., 198.

36 *Bushy Tales*, September 2017.

37 Alm, *Bushy Tales*, April 2004.

38 Correspondence with "V.," September 2017. To maintain the anonymity of the survey, private correspondence with respondents is designated with their initials. Historical quotations from *Bushy Tales* usually provide the contributors' full names, so they are identified in that manner in this book.

39 "J." survey response, September 2017.

40 Reynolds, *Rich Relations*.

41 McQuillan, *Bushy Tales*.

42 See for example, Walters, "How Can a Carrion Crow Serve a Good Breakfast?"

43 "H." survey response, September 2017.

44 Correspondence with "B.," September 2017.

45 Correspondence with "K.," September 2017.

46 Correspondence with "G.," March 2018.

47 Correspondence with "W.," March 2018.

48 Correspondence with "K.," March 2018.

49 Correspondence with "E.," March 2018.

50 Bules, *Bushy Tales*, October 2017.

51 For British teenagers, see Bugge, "'Selling Youth in the Age of Affluence'"; Todd and Young, "Baby-Boomers"; Savage, *Teenage*.

52 Todd and Young, "Baby-Boomers."

53 Hennessy, *Having It So Good*, 125; May, *Homeward Bound*, 28.

54 Correspondence with "V.," September 2017.

55 Muggeridge, "The American in England."

56 Correspondence with "V.," September 2017.

57 Slepetz, *Bushy Tales*, April 2001.

58 Pat, Bushy *Tales*, January 2007.

59 Horn, *Juke Box Britain*, 98.

60 Reed, "Upholding Reputations." This excerpt has been converted into the past tense for consistency with the rest of this chapter.

61 Correspondence with "B.," September 2017.

62 Correspondence with "V.," September 2017.

63 Waldo, Bushy *Tales*, June 2001.

64 Ritt, director, *Blackboard Jungle*.

65 Mark Abrams quoted in Bugge, "'Selling Youth in the Age of Affluence,'" 188.

66 Hoggart, *The Uses of Literacy*.

67 Hopkins, *The New Look*.

68 Cohen, *Folk Devils and Moral Panics*, 154.

69 Horn, *Juke Box Britain*.

70 Correspondence with "G.," September 2017.

71 Shelton, *Bushy Tales*, April 2009.

72 Sandry, *Bushy Tales*, January 2008; Shroeder, *Bushy Tales*, undated 2000.

73 Shelton, *Bushy Tales*, May 2005; Mitchell, *Bushy Tales*, February 2015.

74 Pollock, *Third Culture Kids*; Ender, *Military Brats and Other Global Nomads*.

75 Bules, *Bushy Tales*, October 2017.

76 Driver, *The British at Table, 1940–1980*.

Chapter Nine

1 Baron, *People and Americans*, 90.

2 Barsness, *Europe Calling*, 44.

3 Walters, "How Can a Carrion Crow Serve a Good Breakfast?"

4 Haessler, "US Students Report on Study Tours Abroad."

5 Kimbrough, *And a Right Good Crew*, 96.

6 Roberts, *And the Children Came Too*, 33.

7 Sharp, *Happy Landings in Europe*, 49.

8 Pemberton, "Affluence, Relative Decline and the Treasury." Statistics from measuringworth.com and usgovernmentspending.com, accessed 2 July 2018.

9 Federal Reserve Bank of St Louis, "State per Capita Personal Income."

10 Griffith, *Unconventional Europe*, 35.

11 Ibid., 61.

12   Sutherland, *Portrait of a Decade*, 49.

13   Matthews, *Come Abroad with Me*, 31.

14   Hummel, *Pardon My Thumb*.

15   McKenney and Bransten, *Here's England*, 13.

16   Arwe, *Bring Your Own Soap*, 25.

17   Ritchie, *Diary of a European Trip*, 6.

18   Stock, *Eight Pence a Mile*, 20.

19   Arwe, *Bring Your Own Soap*, 17.

20   Beadle, *These Ruins Are Inhabited*, 11.

21   Tiratsoo and Tomlimon, "Exporting the 'Gospel of Productivity.'"

22   Raymond, "The Yanks in England."

23   Wilson, *My Trip to Europe – February 1954*.

24   Arwe, *Bring Your Own Soap*, 23, emphasis in the original.

25   Ibid., 24.

26   *Independent Press-Telegram*, 16 June 1957.

27   Stock, *Eight Pence a Mile*, 23.

28   Glick, *It's Too Late to Wait*, 99.

29   Kalfatovic, "Knowles, John (1926–2001)," in Garraty and Carnes, *American National Biography*.

30   Knowles, *Double Vision*, 5.

31   Matthews, *Come Abroad with Me*, 30.

32   Halsey, *British Social Trends Since 1900*, Tables 5.3 and 5.4.

33   Green, *Sociology*.

34   Hummel, *Pardon My Thumb*, 7.

35   Beadle, *These Ruins Are Inhabited*, 144.

36   Ibid.

37   Arwe, *Bring Your Own Soap*, 23.

38   Lyon, interview with author, 19 September 2017, edited for clarity.

39   "College Prexy, Family Will Sail for Europe," *Los Angeles Times*, 14 June 1953.

40   Lyon, interview with author, 19 September 2017,

41   McKibbin, *Classes and Cultures*, 98.

42   United States Bureau of the Census, *Historical Statistics of the United States, Colonial Times to 1970*, Chapter D, Labor Force, Tables D29-41; United States, Bureau of Foreign and Domestic Commerce, *Participation in International Travel – 1959*, Table 42 – Passports Issued and Renewed by Occupation of Applicant, July through December, 1958.

43   Corer, *The American People*, Chapter 2, "Mother-Land."

44 Leland Stowe, quoted in Connolly, "The Tragedy of Mom," *Sunday Times*, 16 September 1956.

45 Dingwall, *The American Woman*, 125 and 171.

46 Mulvey, *Transatlantic Manners*, 70.

47 Stock, *Eight Pence a Mile*, 23.

48 Ibid., 37.

49 Haney, *No Reservations*, 25. Actor Terry-Thomas epitomized this type of British "gent" on film. See https://youtu.be/-418SbXncFA, accessed 4 October 2017.

50 Haney, *No Reservations*, 52.

51 Ibid., 35.

52 Sutherland, *Portrait of a Decade*.

53 Knowles, *Double Vision*, 5.

54 Middleton, *Where Has Last July Gone?* 186.

55 Pearson, "John Crosby Dies at 79."

56 Crosby, "Traveling, You Might Meet People with a Lot of Money."

57 Ames, *Adventures Abroad*, 25.

58 Ibid., 26.

59 Davis, "The Rain Isn't as Bad as the B.R. Trains!"

60 "Dearer London Taxi Fares," *Times*, 1 June 1951. The article shows the previous fare scheme operating at the time of Ritchie's visit.

61 Ames, *Adventures Abroad*, 26.

62 Freeman, *You Don't Look Like a Musician*, 53.

63 Ibid., 56.

64 Matthews, *Come Abroad with Me*, 27.

65 Roberts, *And the Children Came Too*, 32.

66 Haney, *No Reservations*, 52. "Pig Latin" is a secret language. This experience works the same in the opposite direction. On my first trip to New York in the 1980s, I went into an old-style Manhattan sandwich bar (now all replaced by artisan coffee shops), and despite years of watching American television, I couldn't understand a word.

67 Hummel, *Pardon My Thumb*, 5.

68 Ibid., 3.

69 Griffith, *Unconventional Europe*, 7.

70 Payne, *Home Was Never Like This*, 168.

Bibliography

Archival Sources

Adam Matthew Archive – Leisure, Travel, and Mass Culture
Claremont Colleges Library – Special Collections, Claremont, CA
David M. Rubenstein Rare Book and Manuscript Library, Duke University, Raleigh, NC
Harold B. Lee Library, Brigham Young University, Provo, UT
Library of Congress, Washington, DC
London School of Economics Library, London, UK
Mason Library, University of North Carolina, Chapel Hill, NC
Mass-Observation Archive, University of Sussex, Falmer, UK
Oxfordshire History Centre, Cowley, UK
The National Archives, Kew, UK
Vanderbilt Peabody College, Nashville, TN

Sources

Ackerman, Dick. *Bushy Tales*, August 2002.
Adrian, Leslie. "A Dollar for the Bell-hop." *Spectator*, 11 January 1957.
Aldor, Francis. *The Good Time Guide to London*. Boston: Houghton Mifflin Company, 1951.
Alm, Norman. *Bushy Tales*, April 2004.
Ames, Katherine Fitz-Gerald. *Adventures Abroad*. New York: Vantage, 1955.
Anderson, Carolyn. "Cold War Consumer Diplomacy and Movie-induced Roman Holidays." *Journal of Tourism History* 3, no. 1 (2011): 1–19.
Anon. *ABC World Airlines Guide*. London: T. Skinner, 1955.
Anon. *Official Guide to the Railways*. New York: National Railway Publication Co., 1952.

Arkell, Reginald. *Trumpets Over Merriford*. London: Michael Joseph, 1955.

Arwe, Ethel Moller. *Bring Your Own Soap*. New York: Vantage Press, 1955.

Aslet, Clive. *All That Life Can Afford: A Celebration of the Carlton Tower Hotel on Its 50th Anniversary*. London: Hoberman, 2011.

Astor, Nancy. "Catering for Americans," letter to the editor of the *Times*, 8 February 1950.

Bailey, Peter. "Jazz at the Spirella: Coming of Age in Coventry in the 1950s." In Conekin, Mort, and Waters, *Moments of Modernity: Reconstructing Britain, 1945–1964*, 22–40.

Baldwin, James Patrick. "The Pan Am Series." jpbtransconsulting.com/category/merchant-marine (accessed 17 September 2017).

Baranowski, Shelley, and Ellen Furlough. "Introduction." In *Being Elsewhere: Tourism, Consumer Culture, and Identity in Modern Europe and North America*, edited by Shelley Baranowski and Ellen Furlough, 1–21. Ann Arbor: The University of Michigan Press, 2001.

Baron, Stanley Wade. *People and Americans*. London: Rupert Hart-Davis, 1953.

Barsness, Edward. *Europe Calling: A Minnesota Newspaperman's New Adventures in the Old World*. New York: Exposition, 1959.

Bartlett, Christopher J. *The Long Retreat: A Short History of British Defence Policy, 1945–70*. London: Macmillan / St Martin's Press, 1972.

Bartlett, Christopher J. *"The Special Relationship": A Political History of Anglo-American Relations since 1945*. London: Longman, 1995.

Baxendale, John. "The Construction of the Past and the Origins of Royal Tourism in 19th-Century Britain." In *Royal Tourism: Excursions around Monarchy*, edited by Philip Long and Nicola J. Palmer, 26–50. Clevedon: Channel View Publications, 2007.

Beadle, Muriel. *These Ruins Are Inhabited*. Garden City: Doubleday, 1961.

Behrman, Samuel. *The Suspended Drawing Room*. London: Hamish Hamilton, 1966.

Belson, William A. *The Impact of Television: Methods and Findings in Program Research*. London: Crosby Lockwood & Son Ltd, 1967.

Bernat, G. Andrew Jr. "Convergence in State per Capita Personal Income, 1950–1999." *Survey of Current Business*, June 2001.

Bingham, Adrian. F*amily Newspapers? Sex, Private Life, and the British Popular Press, 1918–1978*. Oxford: Oxford University Press, 2009.

Blackburn, Robert J. "Blue Riband Route." *Flight*, 28 October 1955.

Bloom, Ken. *Broadway: An Encyclopaedia*. New York: Routledge, 2004.

Borah, Leo. A. "Landmarks of Literary England: The Reverently Guarded Haunts and Homes of Britain's Great Writers Provide Modern Pilgrims with a Rewarding Glimpse of the Past." *National Geographic Magazine*, September 1955.

Bossemeyer, James L. "Travel: American Mobility." *The Annals of the American Academy of Political and Social Science* 313 (1957): 113–16.

Branham, Mary. *Good Morning, American Ladies*. New York: Pageant Press Inc., 1956.

Bransby, John, director. *Getting There Is Half the Fun*, c.1952. Cunard, New York City.

Briscoe, Mary Louise, ed. *American Autobiography, 1945–1980: A Bibliography*. London: University of Wisconsin Press, 1982.

British Tourist and Holidays Board. *Second Annual Report, 1948–49*. London: British Tourist and Holidays Board, 1949.

– *Report on an Inquiry Carried Out by the Hotels Committee into Hotel Services in Great Britain from the User's Point of View*. London: British Tourist and Holidays Board, 1950.

British Tourist Authority. *The British Travel Association, 1929–1969*. London: British Tourist Authority, 1970.

British Travel Association. *Shakespeare's Country* (promotional film), director unknown, 1960, United Kingdom, Associated British Pathé.

British Travel and Holidays Association. *Annual Report – 1951*. London: British Travel and Holidays Association, 1952.

– *Annual Report – 1958*. London: British Travel and Holidays Association, 1958.

– *Britain: A Book Which Attempts to Do More Than Its Size Permits*. London: British Travel and Holidays Association, 1952.

– *Scotland*. London: British Travel and Holidays Association, 1957.

British Travel and Holidays Association; Scottish Tourist Board; Social Surveys (Gallup Poll). *A Survey of the Tourist Trade in Scotland, 1956*. London: British Travel and Holidays Association, 1956.

Brough, James. "American Hotels, Well –." *Men Only*, July 1954.

Bugge, Christian. "'Selling Youth in the Age of Affluence': Marketing to Youth in Britain since 1959." In *An Affluent Society? Britain's Post-war "Golden Age" Revisited*, edited by Lawrence Black and Hugh Pemberton, 185–202. Aldershot: Ashgate, 2004.

Bules, Billie Culp (Mrs). *Bushy Tales*, October 2017.

Burrell, Julia. *European Tour, 1958*. Manuscript Vanderbilt Library, Vanderbilt Peabody College, Nashville, TN, 1959.

Burrows, Abram. *Honest, Abe: Is There Really No Business Like Show Business?* Boston, MA: Little, Brown, 1980.

Butler, Susie. *My Trip to Europe*. Tom Perry Special Collections, Harold B. Lee Library, Brigham Young University, Provo, Utah, 1953.

Buzard, James. "Culture for Export: Tourism and Autoethnography in Post-war Britain." In *Being Elsewhere: Tourism, Consumer Culture, and Identity in Modern Europe and North America*, edited by Shelley Baranowski and Ellen Furlough, 299–317. Ann Arbor: The University of Michigan Press, 2001.

Campbell, F.E. "Letter to the Editor," *Los Angeles Times*, 22 April 1952.

Campbell, Neil, Jude Davies, and George McKay. *Issues in Americanisation and Culture*. Edinburgh, 2004.

Carstairs, John Paddy. *Solid! Said the Earl*. London: Hurst & Blackett, 1948.

Chamberlain, Samuel. *Etched in Sunlight*. Boston: Boston Public Library, 1968.

Churchill, Rhona. "A Million Pair of Eyes Focus on the Palace." *Daily Mail*, 14 May 1956.

– "Well, What Do You Know! Said the Rubbernecks." *Daily Mail*, 15 May 1956.

Clark, Sydney. *All the Best in England*. New York: Dodd Mead, 1957.

Coates, Carroll. "London by Night." www.azlyrics.com/lyrics/franksinatra/londonbynight.html (accessed 9 September 2017).

Cohen, Erik. "Authenticity and Commoditization in Tourism." *Annals of Tourism Research* 15, (1988): 371–86.

Cohen, Lizbeth. *A Consumers' Republic*. New York: Vintage Books, 2004.

Cohen, Stanley. *Folk Devils and Moral Panics: The Creation of the Mods and Rockers*. Oxford: Routledge, 2002.

Commager, Henry Steele, ed. *Britain through American Eyes*. London: The Bodley Head, 1971.

– "English Traits, One Hundred Years Later." In *Britain through American Eyes*, edited by Henry Steele Commager, 749–60. London: The Bodley Head, 1971.

Conekin, Becky, Frank Mort, and Chris Waters. *Moments of Modernity: Reconstructing Britain, 1945–1964*. London: Rivers Oram Press, 1999.

Connolly, Cyril. "The Tragedy of Mom." *Sunday Times*, 16 September 1956.

Cooke, Alistair. "The American Abroad." *Listener*, 22 May 1958.

– "The Face of England – American Stereotypes." *Manchester Guardian*, 27 June 1959.

Corer, Geoffrey. *The American People: A Study in National Character*. New York: W.W. Norton & Company Inc., 1948.

Coughlan, Robert. "How We Appear to Others." *Life*, 23 December 1957.

Crosby, John. "Traveling, You Might Meet People with a Lot of Money." *Washington Post*, 6 June 1954.

Crown Productions. *London Airport*, director unknown, 1949, United Kingdom.

Daiches, David. "Britons Find It Jolly Good Reading: They Like American Fiction." *New York Times*, 5 September 1954.

Dann, Graham. "Writing Out the Tourist in Space and Time." *Annals of Tourism Research*, 26 (1999): 159–87.

David, Elizabeth. *French Country Cooking*. London: John Lehmann, 1956.

Davis, Rosemary. "The Rain Isn't as Bad as the B.R. Trains." *Daily Mail*, 10 September 1958.

De Angeli, Marguerite. *Butter at the Old Price*. Garden City: Doubleday, 1971.

De Grazia, Victoria. *Irresistible Empire: America's Advance through Twentieth-Century Europe*. London: Belknap, 2005.

Defense Manpower Data Center. *Worldwide Manpower Distribution by Geographical Area, Historical Statistics, 1950–1959*. Washington, DC: Department of Defense, 1950–1959.

Department of the Air Force. *United States Air Force Statistical Digest – Fiscal Years, 1950–1959*. Washington, DC: United States Air Force, 1950–1959.

Dilley, Robert S. "Tourist Brochures and Tourist Images." *The Canadian Geographer* 30, no. 1, (1986): 59–65.

Dingwall, Eric John. *The American Woman*. London: Gerald Duckworth & Co Ltd, 1956.

Dobie, J. Frank. "Shakespeare's Home Town." *Holiday*, July 1951.

Dobson, Alan P. *Anglo-American Relations in the Twentieth Century*. London: Routledge, 1992.

Donovan, Paul. "Cooke, Alistair." *Oxford Dictionary of National Biography*, https://doi-org.ref:ondb/93542.

Driver, Christopher. *The British at Table, 1940–1980*. London: Chatto and Windus, 1983.

Duffus, Robert Luther. "Clues to an Understanding of John Bull." *New York Times*, 20 August 1950.

– "Still 'The Innocents Abroad.'" *New York Times*, 2 August 1959.

Dulles, Foster Rhea. *Americans Abroad: Two Centuries of European Travel*. Ann Arbor: University of Michigan Press, 1964.

Dumbrell, John. *A Special Relationship. Anglo-American Relations in the Cold War and After*. Basingstoke: Palgrave Macmillan, 2001.

Dunbar, Mary. "Easily Answered." *Sunday Times*, 8 March 1953.

Dundas, Esther Hilton. *So We Went to Europe: An Ancestral History*. Chicago: L. Mariano, 1959.

Dunning, Brian. "American Tourists in Victorian Britain." *Country Life*, 3 April 1969.

Edwards, Sam. "'From Here Lincoln Came': Anglo-Saxonism, the Special Relationship, and the Anglicisation of Abraham Lincoln, c. 1860–1970." *Journal of Transatlantic Studies*, 11 (2013): 22–46.

Ender, Morten G., ed. *Military Brats and Other Global Nomads: Growing Up in Organization Families*. Westport: Praeger, 2002.

Endy, Christopher. *Cold War Holidays*. Chapel Hill: University of North Carolina Press, 2004.

Federal Reserve Bank of St Louis. "State Per Capita Personal Income," https://fred.stlouisfed.org. (accessed 3 December 2017).

Ferguson Aldon P. *Eighth Air Force Base Air Depot, Burtonwood*. Reading: Airfield Publications, 1986.

Ferry, Kathryn. *The Nation's Host: Butlin's and the Story of the British Seaside: The Official History*. UK: Viking, 2016.

Fielding, Temple. *Fielding's Travel Guide to Europe, 1956–57*. New York: William Sloane Associates, 1956.

Fish, Helen D. *Invitation to England*. New York: Washburn, 1950.

Fodor, Eugene, ed. *Woman's Guide to Europe*. London: Newman Neame, 1956.

Fox, Levi. *Shakespeare's Country*. Norwich: Jarrold and Sons, 1953.

Freeman, Bud. *You Don't Look Like a Musician*. Detroit: Balamp Publishing, 1974.

Friedlander, Paul J.C. "Tourists Take Over Britain: A Visiting American Finds His Compatriots." *New York Times*, 15 July 1956.

Gallup, George H., ed. *The Gallup International Public Opinion Polls, Great Britain, 1937–1975*. New York: Random House, 1976.

Garraty, John Arthur, and Mark C. Carnes, *American National Biography*. New York: Oxford University Press, 1998–99.

Gee, Herbert Leslie. *American England: An Epitome of a Common Heritage*. London: Methuen & Co., 1943.

Geiger, Jack. "US-UK Wedding Bells." *London American*, 7 January 1960.

Glancy, Mark. "'Temporary American Citizens'? British Audiences, Hollywood Films, and the Threat of Americanisation in the 1920s." *Historical Journal of Film, Radio and Television* 26, no. 4 (2006): 461–84.

Glick, Loele. *It's Too Late to Wait.* Los Angeles: Wetzel Publishing Co., 1950.

Goossens, Reuben. "ss *Constitution* and ss *Independence*," http://www.ssmaritime.com/ss-independence-constitution.htm (accessed 15 October 2017).

Gordon, Alastair. *Naked Airport: A Cultural History of the World's Most Revolutionary Structure.* New York: Holt, 2004.

Grandstaff, Mark R. *Foundation of the Force: Air Force Enlisted Personnel Policy, 1907–1956.* Washington, DC: Air Force History Support Office, 1997.

Grant, Mariel. "'Working for the Yankee Dollar': Tourism and the Festival of Britain as Stimuli for Recovery." *Journal of British Studies* 45 (2006): 581–601.

Green, Arnold Wilfred. *Sociology.* New York: McGraw Hill, 1956

Green, Martin. "A Mirror for Anglo-Saxons." *Harper's Magazine*, August 1959.

Greene, Graham. *The Quiet American.* London: William Heinemann, 1955.

Griffith, Margaret D. *Unconventional Europe.* Washington, DC: Peabody Press, 1952.

Gropman, Alan L. *The Air Force Integrates, 1945–1964.* Washington DC: Smithsonian Press, 1977.

Gross, Harvey Yale, director. *Jet Terminal*, 1959. New York: Coleman Productions for Pan American Airlines.

Guest, Val, director. *The Quatermass Xperiment*, 1955. United Kingdom: Hammer Films.

Gutzke, David W., and Michael John Law. *The Roadhouse Comes to Britain: Drinking, Driving, and Dancing, 1925–1955.* London: Bloomsbury, 2017.

Haessler, Herb. "US Students Report on Study Tours Abroad." *New York Times*, 24 September 1950.

Hahn, Joseph. *Hitchhiking through Europe during the Summer of 1956.* New York: Page Publishing, 2016.

Halsey, A.H., ed. *British Social Trends since 1900.* Basingstoke: Macmillan, 1988.

Haney, Germaine. *No Reservations: A Personal Narrative by a Woman Who Traveled Alone in European Countries without Reservations.* Minneapolis, MN: T.S. Denison & Company, 1958.

Harper, Sue. *British Cinema of the 1950s: The Decline of Deference.* Oxford: Oxford University Press, 2003.

Harvey, Brett. *The Fifties: A Women's Oral History*. New York: Harper Perennial, 1995.

Hays, Constance L. "Emily Kimbrough, 90, Magazine Editor and Popular Author." *New York Times*, 11 February 1989.

Hendershot, Robert M. *Family Spats: Perception, Illusion, and Sentimentality in the Anglo-American Special Relationship, 1950–1976*. Germany: VDM Verlag Dr Müller, 2008.

Hennessy, Peter. *Having It So Good: Britain in the Fifties*. London, Penguin Books, 2007.

Highmore, Ben. *Everyday Life and Cultural Theory: An Introduction*. New York: Routledge, 2001.

Hilliard, Peter. "Broadway Time Capsule." https://peterhilliard.wordpress.com/2011/09/17/broadway-time-capsule-1955-1956-season (accessed 22 December 2017).

Hoggart, Richard. *The Uses of Literacy: Aspects of Working-Class Life, with Special Reference to Publications and Entertainments*. London: Chatto & Windus, 1957.

Hollinger David A., ed. *The Humanities and the Dynamics of Inclusion since World War II*. Baltimore: Johns Hopkins University Press, 2006.

Home Office. *Statistics of Foreigners Entering and Leaving the United Kingdom 1954*. London: HMSO, 1955.

Hopkins, Harry. *The New Look: A Social History of the Forties and Fifties in Britain*. London: Secker and Warburg, 1963.

Horn, Adrian. *Juke Box Britain: Americanisation and Youth Culture, 1945–60*. Manchester: Manchester University Press, 2009.

Hoyer, Maria A. *Shakespeare's Country*. London: E. Nister, 1894.

Hubbard, Phil, and Lilley, Keith. "Selling the Past: Heritage-tourism and Place Identity in Stratford-upon-Avon." *Geography* 85, no. 3 (2000): 221–32.

Hubble, Nick. *Mass-Observation and Everyday Life: An Introduction*. London: Palgrave Macmillan, 2010.

Humberstone, Bruce, director. *Happy Go Lovely*, 1951. United Kingdom: Associated British Pictures Corporation.

Hummel, Carol. *Pardon My Thumb: The Author's Account of Her Hitchhiking Experiences*. Davis Library, University of North Carolina at Chapel Hill, Chapel Hill, 1957.

Huntington, John. *A Bean from Boston: Memoirs of an American in London, 1946–1987*. London: Bacon, Weightman, and Pickens, 1991.

Hutchison, Isobel Wylie. "Poets' Voices Linger in Scottish Shrines." *National Geographic Magazine*, October 1957.

Iddon, Don. "Diary." *Daily Mail*, 16 July 1952.

Jackson, Robert. *Strike Force: The USAF in Britain since 1948*. London: Robson Books, 1986.

Jennings, Charles. *Them and Us: The American Invasion of High Society*. Stroud: Sutton Publishing, 2007.

Jensen, John. "Emett, (Frederick) Rowland (1906–1990)," in *Oxford Dictionary of National Biography*, https://doi-org./ref:odnb/39957.

– "Giles, Ronald [Carl] (1916–1995) in *Oxford Dictionary of National Biography*, https://doi-org./ref:odnb/60110.

Johnston, Denis. "Eastward Ho!" *Listener*, 20 August 1953.

Jones, Betty. "Letter to the Editor." *Manchester Guardian,* 28 December 1950.

Jones, Geoffrey, and Frances Bostock. "U.S. Multinationals in British Manufacturing before 1962." *The Business History Review* 70, no. 2 (1996): 207–56.

Joseph, Richard, ed. *Esquire's Europe in Style*. London: Frederick Muller, 1961.

Judt, Tony. *Postwar: A History of Europe since 1945*. London: William Heinemann, 2005.

Kaledin, Eugenia. *Mothers and More: American Women in the 1950s*. Boston: Twayne Publishers, 1984.

Kalfatovic, Mary C. "Knowles, John (1926–2001)." *American National Biography*, https://doi-org. /anb/9780198606697.article.1603498.

Kane, Tim. "Global U.S. Troop Deployment, 1950–2005," http://www.heritage.org/defense/report/global-us-troop-deployment-1950-2005 (accessed 15 December 2017).

Katona, George. *The Mass Consumption Society*. New York: McGraw-Hill Inc., 1964.

Kellogg, Cynthia. "Down from London in a British Car." *New York Times*, 30 July 1950.

Kent, William. "American Associations with London." Travel Association pamphlet, undated late 1940s.

– *London for Americans*. London: Staples Press, 1950.

Kimbrough, Emily. *And a Right Good Crew*. New York: Harper & Bros., 1958.

– *Forty Plus and Fancy Free*. New York: Harper, 1954.

– *Water, Water Everywhere*. London: William Heinemann, 1957.

Knowles, John. *Double Vision: American Thoughts Abroad*. London: Secker & Warburg, 1964.

Koshar, Rudy. "'What Ought to Be Seen': Tourist' Guidebooks and National Identities in Modern Germany and Europe." *Journal of Contemporary History*, 33 (1998): 323–40.

Kroes, Rob. "Americanisation: What Are We Talking About?" In Kroes, Rydell, and Bosscher, *Cultural Transmissions and Receptions*, 302–20.

Kroes, Rob, R.W. Rydell, and D.F.J. Bosscher, eds. *Cultural Transmissions and Receptions: American Mass Culture in Europe*. Amsterdam: VU University Press, 1993.

Kynaston, David. *Austerity Britain, 1945–1951*. London: Bloomsbury, 2007.

– *Family Britain, 1951–1957*. London: Bloomsbury, 2009.

– *Modernity Britain, 1957–1962*. London: Bloomsbury, 2015.

Lampe, David. "The 'GI Problem': An American Airman's View." *Manchester Guardian*, 20 September 1952.

Langhamer, Claire. "'Who the Hell Are Ordinary People?' Ordinariness as a Category of Historical Analysis." Transactions of the Royal Historical Society 28 (2018): 175–95.

Larsson, Björn, and David Zekria. "Pan Am." www.timetableimages.com (accessed 3 December 2017).

Laughlin, Clara E. *So You're Going to England!* Boston: Houghton Mifflin Company, 1948.

Law, Michael John. "Charabancs and Social Class in 1930s Britain." *Journal of Transport History*, 36 (2015): 41–57.

– *The Experience of Suburban Modernity*. Manchester: Manchester University Press, 2014.

– *1938 Modern Britain*. London: Bloomsbury Academic, 2018.

– "Turning Night into Day: Transgression and Americanization at the English Interwar Roadhouse." *Journal of Historical Geography* 35, no. 3 (2009): 473–94.

Levenstein, Harvey. *We'll Always Have Paris: American Tourists in France since 1930*. Chicago: University of Chicago Press, 2004.

Lyon, Carolyn Bartel. *Diary 1953*. E. Wilson and Carolyn Bartel Lyon papers, Box 22, Honnold/Mudd Library, Claremont Colleges, Claremont, CA.

Lyon, John Wilson. Interview with author, 19 September 2017.

Lyons, John F. *America in the British Imagination: 1945 to the Present*. London: Palgrave Macmillan, 2013.

MacCannell, Dean. *The Tourist: A New Theory of the Leisure Class*. Berkeley: University of California Press, [1976] 2013.

Mackenzie, K.B. "How to Make the Best Coffee." *Hotel Management*, June 1950.

Malchow, H.L. *Special Relations: The Americanization of Britain?* Stanford: Stanford University Press, 2011.

Manchester Municipal Information Bureau. *Why Manchester?* Manchester: MMIB, undated c. late 1950s.

Marling, Susan. *American Affair: The Americanisation of Britain*. London: Boxtree, in association with Carlton Television, 1993.

Matless, David. *Landscape and Englishness*. London: Reaktion, 1998.

Matthews, Neil. "The Very Model of a Modern Travel Agency? The Polytechnic Touring Association, 1888–1962." Unpublished doctoral thesis, University of Westminster, 2013.

Matthews, Ruth Lois. *Come Abroad with Me: On Vacation Tour through Europe*. New York: Exposition, 1955.

Maudin, Bill. "Europe on Less than $28,411." *Life*, 17 August 1953.

Maxtone-Graham, John. *Atlantic Run – "The Only Way to Cross."* London: Cassell, 1972.

May, Elaine Tyler. *Homeward Bound: American Families in the Cold War Era*. New York: Basic Books, 2017.

McCarey, Leo, director. *An Affair to Remember*, 1957. Los Angeles, CA: Jerry Wald Productions.

McClune, A. "Letter to the Editor." *Picture Post*, 26 July 1952.

McKay, George. "Americanization and Popular Culture." In *Yankee Go Home*, edited by George McKay, 11–52.

– ed. *Yankee Go Home (& Take Me with U)*. Sheffield: Sheffield Academic Press, 1997.

McKenney, Ruth, and Richard Bransten. *Here's England: A Highly Informal Guide*. London: Rupert Hart-Davis, 1955.

McKibbin, Ross. *Classes and Cultures: England, 1918–1951*. Oxford: Oxford University Press, 1998.

McQuillan Deanna. *Bushy Tales*, October 2012.

Mead, Margaret. "The Pattern of Leisure in Contemporary American Culture." *The Annals of the American Academy of Political and Social Science* 313 (1957): 11–15.

Medlik, Slavoj. *The British Hotel and Catering Industry. An Economic and Statistical Study*. London: Sir Isaac Pitman & Sons, 1961.

Meeker, Oden, and Olivia Meeker. "London's Prim Burlesque." *Los Angeles Times*, 29 June 1952.

Meeker, Olivia. "The European Male: Different Approach, Same Old Object." In *Woman's Guide to Europe*, edited by Eugene Fodor, 60–9. London: Newman Neame, 1956.

Mersfelder, Larry. *We Were the Foreigners*. New York: Vantage Press, 1957.

Meyer, Edith Patterson. *Go It Alone, Lady! The Woman's Guide to European Travel*. New York: Harper & Bros., 1957.

Middleton, Drew. *The British*. London: Pan Books, 1958.

– *Where Has Last July Gone?* New York: Quadrangle/The New York Times Book Co., 1973.

Middleton, Victor T.C. *British Tourism: The Remarkable Story of Growth*. London: Butterworth-Heinemann, 2007.

Mikes, George. "The American Female: Too Timid, or Too Bold?" In *Woman's Guide to Europe*, edited by Eugene Fodor, 70–80. London: Newman Neame, 1956.

Miller, William H. *The Last Atlantic Liners*. London: Conway Maritime Press, 1985.

Minnelli, Vincente, director. *An American in Paris*, 1951. Culver City, CA: Metro-Goldwyn-Mayer.

– director. *Brigadoon*, 1954. Culver City, CA: Metro-Goldwyn-Mayer.

– director. *Gentlemen Prefer Blondes*, 1953. Culver City, CA: Metro-Goldwyn-Mayer.

– director. *Gigi*, 1958. Culver City, CA: Metro-Goldwyn-Mayer.

Mitchell, Carol. *Bushy Tales*, February 2015.

Mitchell, Gillian A.M. "Reassessing 'the Generation Gap': Bill Haley's 1957 Tour of Britain, Inter-Generational Relations, and Attitudes to Rock 'n' Roll in the Late 1950s." *Twentieth Century British History* 24, no. 4 (2013): 573–605.

Morgan, Gwen. "Day of Shortage Is Behind." *Los Angeles Times*, 23 May 1954.

Mort, Frank. *Capital Affairs: London and the Making of the Permissive Society*. London: Yale University Press, 2010.

– "The Commercial Domain: Advertising and the Cultural Management of Demand." In Conekin, Mort, and Waters. *Moments of Modernity: Reconstructing Britain, 1945–1964*, 55–75.

Morton, A.L. *Get Out!* Colchester: The Communist Party, East Anglia District Committee, 1953.

Moser, John E. *Twisting the Lion's Tail: Anglophobia in the United States, 1921–48*. Basingstoke: Macmillan Press, 1999.

Mowat, R.B. *Americans in England.* London: George G. Harrap & Co. Ltd, 1935.

Muggeridge, Malcolm. "The American in England." In *Esquire's Europe in Style*, edited by Richard Joseph, 59–63. London: Frederick Muller, 1961.

Mulvey, Christopher. *Anglo-American Landscapes: A Study of Anglo-American Travel Literature.* Cambridge: Cambridge University Press, 1983.

– *Transatlantic Manners: Social Patterns in Nineteenth-century Anglo-American Travel Literature.* Cambridge: Cambridge University Press, 1990.

Negulesco, Jean, director, *Three Coins in the Fountain*, 1955. Los Angeles, CA: Twentieth-Century Fox.

Nixon, Sean. *Hard Sell.* Manchester: Manchester University Press, 2013.

Norman, Philip. *Babycham Nights.* London: Macmillan, 2003.

Nott, James. *Music for the People: Popular Music in Britain between the Wars.* Oxford: Oxford University Press, 2002.

Otte, T.G. "'The Shrine at Sulgrave': The Preservation of the Washington Ancestral Home as an 'English Mount Vernon' and Transatlantic Relations." In *Towards World Heritage: International Origins of the Preservation Movement, 1870–1930*, edited by Melanie Hall, 109–38. Farnham: Ashgate, 2011.

Ovendale, Richie. *The English-Speaking Alliance: Britain, the United States, the Dominions, and the Cold War, 1945–1951.* London: George Allen and Unwin, 1985.

Packard, Vance. *The Status Seekers.* New York: Pocket Books, 1960.

Parry, Gordon, director. *A Yank in Ermine*, 1955. United Kingdom, Monarch Productions.

Pauley, Bruce F. *Pioneering History on Two Continents: An Autobiography.* Lincoln: Potomac Books, 2014.

Payne, Etta. *Home Was Never Like This: A Trailer's-eye View of Europe Today.* New York: Greenwich, 1957.

Pearson, Richard. "John Crosby Dies at 79." *Washington Post*, 9 September 1991.

Peel, Victoria, and Anders Sørensen. *Exploring the Use and Impact of Travel Guidebooks.* Bristol: Channel View Publications, 2016.

Pells, Richard H. "American Culture Abroad: The European Experience since 1945." In Kroes, Rydell, and Bosscher, *Cultural Transmissions and Receptions.*

– *Not Like Us: How Europeans Loved, Hated, and Transformed American Culture since World War II.* New York: Basic Books, 1997.

Pemberton, Hugh. "Affluence, Relative Decline, and the Treasury." In *An Affluent Society? Britain's Post-war "Golden Age" Revisited*, edited by Lawrence Black and Hugh Pemberton, 107–28. Aldershot: Ashgate, 2004.

Pereira, Wilf. *Brize Norton – Gateway to the World*. Yeovil, 1993.

Perry, R.B. "The American Cast of Mind." *Listener*, 11 December 1947, broadcast on the Third Programme on 7 December 1947.

Pocock, Tom. "Roadhouse, 1949." *Daily Mail*, 9 July 1949.

Pollock, David C. *Third Culture Kids: The Experience of Growing Up among Worlds*. London: Nicholas Brealey Publishing, 2001.

Porter, Vincent, and Sue Harper. "Throbbing Hearts and Smart Repartee: The Reception of American Film in 1950s Britain." *Media History* 4, no. 2 (1998): 175–93.

Postgate, Raymond. *The Good Food Guide, 1951–1952*. London: Cassell & Co., 1951.

Powell, Michael, and Emeric Pressburger, directors, *The Red Shoes*, 1948. United Kingdom: The Archers.

Price, Willard. *Innocents in Britain*. London: Heinemann, 1958. Published in the United States as *Roaming Britain: 8,000 Miles through England, Scotland, and Wales*. New York: J. Day Co.,1958.

Prochaska, Frank. *The Eagle and the Crown: Americans and the British Monarchy*. New Haven: Yale University Press, 2008.

Raymond, Robert. "The Yanks in England." *Picture Post*, 28 June 1952.

Reed, Elizabeth Leah. "Upholding Reputations: American Kids in London, England, September 1954–August 1955." Unpublished essay.

Reid, Charles. "Amsterdam Is Meaning Eyes." *Punch*, 13 July 1955.

Reynolds, David. *Rich Relations: The American Occupation of Britain, 1942–1945*. London: HarperCollins, 1995.

Ritchie, William A. *Diary of a European Trip: July-August 1950*. Omaha: privately published, 1950.

Ritt, Martin, director. *Blackboard Jungle*, 1955. Culver City, CA: Metro-Goldwyn-Mayer.

Roberts, Paul M. *And the Children Came Too*. London: Elek Books, 1959.

Rolinson, Dave, and Nick Cooper. "'Bring Something Back': The Strange Career of Professor Bernard Quatermass." *Journal of Popular Film and Television* 30, no. 3 (2002): 158–65.

Ronay, Egon. *Egon Ronay Recommends 175 Eating Places in and around London*. London: Egon Ronay, 1959.

Rugh, Susan Sessions. *Are We There Yet? The Golden Age of Family Vacations*. Lawrence: University Press of Kansas, 2008.

Rumble, William (Bill), correspondence with the author, August to November 2017.

Running, Leona Glidden. *From Thames to Tigris*. Washington, DC: Washington College Press, 1958.

– *36 Days and a Dream*. Washington, DC: Review and Herald Publishing Association, 1952.

Rydell, Robert W. *Buffalo Bill in Bologna: The Americanization of the World, 1869–1922*. Chicago: University of Chicago Press, 2005.

Sandry, Terry. *Bushy Tales*, January 2008.

Savage, Jon. *Teenage: The Creation of Youth Culture*. London: Chatto & Windus, 2007.

Schroeder, Gary. *Bushy Tales,* undated 2000.

Sharp, Nathan. *Happy Landings in Europe*. New York: Vantage Press, 1959.

Shelton, Lillian. *Bushy Tales*, April 2009.

Slater, David, and Peter J. Taylor, eds. *The American Century: Consensus and Coercion in the Projection of American Power*. Oxford: Blackwell, 1999.

Slepetz, Betsy. *Bushy Tales*, April 2001.

Snyder, Thomas D., ed. *120 Years of American Education: A Statistical Portrait*. Washington: National Center for Education Statistics, 1993.

Sone, Violet West. *13 Innocents Abroad*. San Antonio: The Naylor Company, 1959.

Steinbeck, John. "The Yank in Europe." *Holiday*, January 1956.

Stock, Phyllis Swale. *Eight Pence a Mile*. Boston: Bruce Humphries, 1958.

Stone, James D. "Screening the Yank: The Cinematic Americanization of British National Identity, 1930–1960." Unpublished doctoral thesis, University of New Mexico, 2003.

Stott, Juanita. *Our European Tour, April–May 1954*. David M. Rubenstein Rare Book & Manuscript Library, Duke University, Raleigh, NC. 1954.

Sullivan, H.A. "Vanity Press Publishing." *Library Trends* 7, no. 1 (1958): 105–15.

Sutherland, Douglas. *Portrait of a Decade: London Life, 1945–1955*. London: Harrap, 1988.

Taylor, Peter J. "Locating the American Century: World Systems." In Slater and Taylor, eds., *The American Century*, 3–16.

Thayer, Anna G.C. *Holiday in England*. New York: Dodd, Mead, 1952.

Thomas, Lowell. "When Are You Going Abroad?" *Los Angeles Times*, 27 April 1952.

Thomas, Nick. "Will the Real 1950s Please Stand Up? Views of a Contradictory Decade." *Cultural and Social History* 5, no. 2 (2008): 227–35.

Tindall, George B., and David E. Shi. *America: A Narrative History*. New York: W.W. Norton & Company, 1989.

Tiratsoo, Nick, and Jim Tomlimon. "Exporting the 'Gospel of Productivity': United States Technical Assistance and British Industry, 1945–1960." *Business History Review* 71, no. 1 (1997): 41–81.

Todd, Selina, and Hilary Young. "Baby-Boomers to 'Beanstalkers': Making the Modern Teenager in Post-War Britain." *Cultural and Social History* 9, no. 3 (2012): 451–67.

Toogood, Stanley, director. *Wings to Britain*, 1957. United Kingdom: International Film Productions Ltd for Braniff International Airways and Pan American.

TWA. *TWA Vacation Guide and World Atlas*. Maplewood: C.S. Hammond and Company, 1956.

United States Bureau of the Census. *Historical Statistics of the United States, Colonial Times to 1970*. Washington: Bureau of the Census, 1975.

United States, Bureau of Foreign and Domestic Commerce. *Survey of International Travel*. Washington: Bureau of Foreign and Domestic Commerce, 1956.

United States, Department of Commerce. "Consumer Income." *Current Population Reports*, 9 June 1961.

– *Participation in International Travel – 1959: Supplement to Survey of International Travel with Revised Data through 1958*. Washington: Department of Commerce, 1959.

Urry, John. *The Tourist Gaze*. London: Sage, 1990.

USAF Bushy Park Dependents School. *The Londoner*, private circulation, 1953.

USAF Directorate of Statistical Services. *United States Air Force Statistical Digest – Fiscal Year 1955*. Washington: USAF, 1955.

USAF. *In Focus – The Americans in Britain*, pamphlet, private circulation, 1953.

USAFE Senior High Schools. *1958 Vapor Trails*, private circulation, 1958.

Vanderschmidt, Fred. *What the English Think of Us*. London: Quality Press, 1951.

Victor Britain Rent-a-Car System. "Dine and Drive through Britain." Brochure, 1959.

Wakeford, Geoffrey. "Is Britain's Gateway a Shabby Back Door?" *Daily Mail*, 22 October 1952.

Walters, John. "How Can a Carrion Crow Serve a Good Breakfast?" *Daily Mirror*, 14 March 1951.

Walton, John K. "Travel as a Force of Historical Change." *Journal of Tourism History* 3, no. 2 (2011): 85–9.

Watt, D. Cameron. *Succeeding John Bull. America in Britain's Place, 1900–1975*. Cambridge: Cambridge University Press, 1984.

Wechsberg, Joseph. "The American Abroad." *Atlantic*, November 1957.

Weiler, G.E., producer. *6½ Magic Hours*, 1958. United States: Pan American Airlines.

Whitehorn, Katharine. *Selective Memory*. London: Virago, 2007.

Williams, Francis. *The American Invasion*. London: Anthony Blond, 1962.

Williams, Hugh, and Margaret Williams. *The Grass Is Greener*. In *Plays of the Year: Volume 19*, edited by J.C. Trewin, 13–105. London: Elek Books, 1960.

Williams, Raymond. *Keywords: A Vocabulary of Culture and Society*. London: Fontana, 1976.

Wilson, Angus. "So Completely Unspoiled." *Punch*, 6 July 1953, 14.

Wilson, Edward G. *My Trip to Europe – February 1954* (and supplementary notes), J. Walter Thompson Archive, Boxes 19 and 89. David M. Rubenstein Rare Book & Manuscript Library, Duke University, Raleigh, NC, 1954.

Worpole, Ken. *Dockers and Detectives: Popular Reading, Popular Writing*. London: Verso, 1983.

Wrench, Evelyn. *Transatlantic London: Three Centuries of Association between England and America*. London: Hutchinson & Co., 1949.

Young, Estelle. *Gone to Europe*. New York: R.R. Smith, 1952.

Zuelow, Eric. *A History of Modern Tourism*. Basingstoke: Palgrave Macmillan, 2015.

Index